First World War
and Army of Occupation
War Diary
France, Belgium and Germany

63 (ROYAL NAVAL) DIVISION
Divisional Troops
63 Sanitary Section,
53 Mobile Veterinary Section and
Divisional Train (761, 762, 763, 764 Companies A.S.C.)
18 May 1916 - 1 April 1919

WO95/3107

The Naval & Military Press Ltd
www.nmarchive.com
Published in association with The National Archives

Published by

The Naval & Military Press Ltd

Unit 10 Ridgewood Industrial Park,

Uckfield, East Sussex,

TN22 5QE England

Tel: +44 (0) 1825 749494

www.naval-military-press.com

www.nmarchive.com

This diary has been reprinted in facsimile from the original. Any imperfections are inevitably reproduced and the quality may fall short of modern type and cartographic standards.

© **Crown Copyright**
Images reproduced by permission of The National Archives, London, England, 2015.

Contents

Document type	Place/Title	Date From	Date To
Heading	63rd Division Sanitary Section R.N.D. 1916 May 1917 Mar to 1 Army		
Miscellaneous	63rd Div Sanitary Section R.N.D.		
War Diary		31/05/1916	31/05/1916
Heading	War Diary of Sanitary Section, Royal Naval Division From 1st June 1916 To 30th June 1916.		
War Diary	Hallencourt	01/06/1916	04/06/1916
War Diary	Abbeville	04/06/1916	26/06/1916
War Diary	Ourton	29/06/1916	30/06/1916
Miscellaneous	War Diary of Sanitary Section 63rd (R.N.) Division From 1st July To 31st July 1916 Volume 2		
War Diary	Ourton	01/07/1916	17/07/1916
War Diary	Boyeffles	17/07/1916	31/07/1916
Map	Sanitary Areas		
War Diary	Boyeffles		
Heading	War Diary of Sanitary Section 63rd (R.N.) Division From 1st August To 31st August 1916		
War Diary	Boyeffles	01/08/1916	31/08/1916
Heading	War Diary of Sanitary Section From 1st September 1916 To 30th September 1916		
War Diary	Boyeffles	01/09/1916	19/09/1916
War Diary	Bruay	19/09/1916	21/09/1916
War Diary	Ourton	21/09/1916	30/09/1916
Heading	War Diary of Sanitary Section 63rd (R.N.) Division From October 1st To 31st 1916		
War Diary	Ourton	01/10/1916	04/10/1916
War Diary	Forceville	05/10/1916	17/10/1916
War Diary	Verannes	18/10/1916	18/10/1916
War Diary	Hedauville	19/10/1916	31/10/1916
Heading	War Diary of Sanitary Section 63rd (RN) Division From 1st November To 30th November 1916		
War Diary	Hedauville	01/11/1916	17/11/1916
War Diary	Sarton	17/11/1916	18/11/1916
War Diary	Doullens	19/11/1916	19/11/1916
War Diary	Yvrench	20/11/1916	22/11/1916
War Diary	Rue	23/11/1916	30/11/1916
Heading	War Diary of Sanitary Section 63rd (R.N.) Division From December 1st To 31st 1916		
War Diary	Rue	01/12/1916	31/12/1916
Heading	War Diary of Sanitary Section 63rd (R.N.) Division From January 1st To 31st 1917		
War Diary	Rue	01/01/1917	12/01/1917
War Diary	Nouvion	13/01/1917	31/01/1917
Heading	War Diary of Sanitary Section 63rd (R.N.) Division From Feby 1st To 28 1917		
Miscellaneous	Messages And Signals.		
Miscellaneous	D.A.G Base Forwarded	05/03/1917	05/03/1917
War Diary	Nouvion	01/02/1917	28/02/1917
Heading	War Diary of Sanitary Section 63rd (R.N.) Division From March 1st To 31st 1917		

War Diary	Nouvion	01/03/1917	01/03/1917
War Diary	Domvast	02/03/1917	31/03/1917
Heading	63rd Division 53rd Mobile Vety Section May 1918 Apr 1919		
Heading	War Diary of 53rd Mobile Veterinary Section From 30th May To 30th June 1916		
War Diary	Woolwich	30/05/1916	30/05/1916
War Diary	Southampton	30/05/1916	30/05/1916
War Diary	La Havre	31/05/1916	31/05/1916
War Diary	Pont Remy	02/06/1916	02/06/1916
War Diary	Hallencourt	02/06/1916	17/06/1916
War Diary	Abbeville	17/06/1916	17/06/1916
War Diary	Bruay	18/06/1916	18/06/1916
War Diary	Magnicourt	18/06/1916	30/06/1916
Heading	War Diary 53rd Mobile Rely Section From To July 1916		
War Diary	Magnicourt	01/07/1916	18/07/1916
War Diary	Barlin	18/07/1916	31/07/1916
Heading	War Diary of 53rd Mobile Veterinary Section. (63rd (R.M) Division). Volume No.3 From 1st August, 1916 To 31st August, 1916		
War Diary	Barlin	01/08/1916	31/08/1916
Heading	War Diary of 53rd Mobile Veterinary Section. From 1st September, 1916 To 30th September, 1916 Volume 4.		
War Diary	Barlin	01/09/1916	19/09/1916
War Diary	Ourton	20/09/1916	30/09/1916
Heading	War Diary of 53rd Mobile Veterinary Section. 63rd (R.N.) Division. From 1st October, 1916 To 31st October, 1916 Volume 5		
War Diary	Ourton	01/10/1916	03/10/1916
War Diary	Frevent	04/10/1916	04/10/1916
War Diary	Lealvillers	04/10/1916	07/10/1916
War Diary	Hedauville	07/10/1916	31/10/1916
Heading	War Diary of 53rd Mobile Veterinary Section 63rd (R.N.) Division. From 1st November 1916 To 30th November 1916 Volume 5		
War Diary	Hedauville	01/11/1916	17/11/1916
War Diary	Arqueves	18/11/1916	18/11/1916
War Diary	Geyincourt	18/11/1916	19/11/1916
War Diary	Feinvillers	20/11/1916	21/11/1916
War Diary	Masnil Gomquer	22/11/1916	22/11/1916
War Diary	Buigny St Maclou	23/11/1916	24/11/1916
War Diary	Larrouville	25/11/1916	30/11/1916
Heading	War Diary of 53rd Mobile Veterinary Section. From December 1st 1916 To December 31st 1916		
War Diary	Larrouville (Rue)	01/12/1916	16/12/1916
War Diary	Favieres	17/12/1916	31/12/1916
Heading	War Diary of 53rd Mobile Veterinary Sect. From January 1st 17 To January 31st 17		
War Diary	Favieres	01/01/1917	13/01/1917
War Diary	Binging St Maclon	14/01/1917	14/01/1917
War Diary	Noyelles on Chausses	15/01/1917	15/01/1917
War Diary	Bernaville	16/01/1917	16/01/1917
War Diary	Marieux	17/01/1917	19/01/1917
War Diary	Forceville	20/01/1917	31/01/1917

Heading	War Diary of 53rd Mobile Veterinary Section. 63rd (R.N.) D From February 1st 1917 To February 28th 1917		
War Diary	Forceville	01/02/1917	23/02/1917
War Diary	Hedauville	23/02/1917	28/02/1917
Heading	War Diary (Volume 10) Of 53rd Mobile Vety Section. 63rd (R.N.) Div. From 1st March 1917 To 31st March 1917		
War Diary	Hedauville	01/03/1917	19/03/1917
War Diary	Harponville	19/03/1917	20/03/1917
War Diary	Beauval	20/03/1917	21/03/1917
War Diary	Bonnieres	21/03/1917	22/03/1917
War Diary	Herlin-Le-Sec	22/03/1917	24/03/1917
War Diary	Pernes	25/03/1917	25/03/1917
War Diary	Estree Blanche	25/03/1917	26/03/1917
War Diary	Robecq	27/03/1917	31/03/1917
Heading	War Diary of 53rd Mobile Veterinary Section. From 1st April 1917 To 30th April 1917 Volume-XI		
War Diary	C4 Robecq	01/04/1917	10/04/1917
War Diary	Bruay	11/04/1917	11/04/1917
War Diary	La Comte	12/04/1917	14/04/1917
War Diary	Aguieres	15/04/1917	17/04/1917
War Diary	Maroeuil	18/04/1917	30/04/1917
Heading	War Diary of 53rd Mobile Veterinary Section. From 1st May 1917 To 31st May 1917 Volume XII		
War Diary	Mingoval	01/05/1917	20/05/1917
War Diary	Anzin	21/05/1917	31/05/1917
Heading	War Diary of 53rd Mobile Veterinary Section. From 1st June 1917 To 30th June 1917 Volume 13		
War Diary	Auzin	01/06/1917	30/06/1917
Heading	War Diary of 53rd Mobile Veterinary Section. From 1st July 1917 To 31st July 1917 Volume No 14		
War Diary	Auzin	01/07/1917	31/07/1917
Heading	War Diary of 53rd Mobile Vety Section. From 1st August 1917 To 31st August 1917 Volume No.15		
War Diary	Auzin	01/08/1917	31/08/1917
Heading	War Diary From 53rd Mobile Veterinary Section From 1st September 1917 To 30th September 1917 Volume 16		
War Diary	Auzin	01/09/1917	25/09/1917
War Diary	Bethencourt	26/09/1917	30/09/1917
Heading	War Diary of 53rd Mobile Veterinary Section From 1st October 1917 To 31st October 1917 Volume 16		
War Diary	Bethencourt	01/10/1917	03/10/1917
War Diary	Ham Hoek	04/10/1917	31/10/1917
Heading	War Diary of 53rd Mobile Veterinary Section From 1 November 1917 To 30th November 1917 Volume 16		
War Diary	Ham Hoek	01/11/1917	13/11/1917
War Diary	Arneke Area	14/11/1917	14/11/1917
War Diary	Earesbluvgge	16/11/1917	28/11/1917
War Diary	Houtkerque	29/11/1917	30/11/1917
Heading	War Diary of 53rd Mobile Veterinary Section From 1st December 1917 To 31st December 1917 Volume No 19		
War Diary	Houtkerque	01/12/1917	07/12/1917
War Diary	Godewaersvelde	08/12/1917	15/12/1917
War Diary	Manancourt	16/12/1917	17/12/1917

War Diary	Le Mesnil	18/12/1917	31/12/1917
Heading	War Diary of 53rd Mobile Veterinary Section From January 1st 1918 To January 31st 1918 Volume 20		
War Diary	Le Mesnil	01/01/1918	31/01/1918
Heading	War Diary of 53rd Mobile Veterinary Section From February 1st 1918 To February 28 1918 Volume 21		
War Diary	Le Mesnil	01/02/1918	14/02/1918
War Diary	Neuville	15/02/1918	21/02/1918
War Diary	Neuvi	21/02/1918	26/02/1918
War Diary	Neuville	27/02/1918	22/03/1918
War Diary	Lechelle	23/03/1918	23/03/1918
War Diary	Bazentin Le Petit	24/03/1918	24/03/1918
War Diary	Dernancourt	25/03/1918	25/03/1918
War Diary	Lealvillers	26/03/1918	27/03/1918
War Diary	Puchevillers	28/03/1918	29/03/1918
War Diary	Pernois	30/03/1918	31/03/1918
Heading	War Diary of 53rd Mobile Veterinary Section From April 1st 1918 To April 30 1918 Volume 23		
War Diary	Pernois	01/04/1918	03/04/1918
War Diary	Puchevillers	04/04/1918	07/04/1918
War Diary	Toutencourt	08/04/1918	30/04/1918
Heading	War Diary of O.C.53. Mob Vety Section From 1 May 1918 To 31 May 1918		
War Diary	Toutencourt	01/05/1918	31/05/1918
Heading	War Diary of 53rd Mobile Veterinary Section From June 1st 1918 To June 30th 1918 Volume 25		
War Diary	Toutencourt	01/06/1918	31/07/07/1
Heading	War Diary of 53rd Mobile Veterinary Section From August 1st 1918 To August 31st 1918 Volume 27		
War Diary	Sarton	01/08/1918	04/08/1918
War Diary	Raincheval	05/08/1918	08/08/1918
War Diary	Arqueves	09/08/1918	09/08/1918
War Diary	Contay	10/08/1918	14/08/1918
War Diary	Esbarts	15/08/1918	15/08/1918
War Diary	Sarton	16/08/1918	16/08/1918
War Diary	Famechon	17/08/1918	19/08/1918
War Diary	Couin	20/08/1918	25/08/1918
War Diary	Hannescamps	26/08/1918	31/08/1918
War Diary	Sarton	01/08/1918	04/08/1918
War Diary	Raincheval	05/08/1918	08/08/1918
War Diary	Arqueves	09/08/1918	09/08/1918
War Diary	Contay	10/08/1918	14/08/1918
War Diary	Esbarts	15/08/1918	15/08/1918
War Diary	Sarton	16/08/1918	16/08/1918
War Diary	Famechon	17/08/1918	19/08/1918
War Diary	Couin	20/08/1918	25/08/1918
War Diary	Hannescamps	26/08/1918	31/08/1918
Heading	War Diary of O.C. 53rd Mobile Veterinary Section From 1st Sept. 1918 To 30th Sept 1918.		
War Diary	Hannescamps	01/09/1918	01/09/1918
War Diary	Blaireville	02/09/1918	04/09/1918
War Diary	Henin	05/09/1918	05/09/1918
War Diary	Fontaine Les Croiselles	06/09/1918	08/09/1918
War Diary	Bellacourt	09/09/1918	15/09/1918
War Diary	Boyelles	17/09/1918	20/09/1918
War Diary	Boyelles-St Leger Rd	21/09/1918	27/09/1918

War Diary	Longatte	28/09/1918	28/09/1918
War Diary	Moeuvres	29/09/1918	29/09/1918
War Diary	Sugar Factory	30/09/1918	30/09/1918
War Diary	Sugar Factory (Near Graincourt)	01/10/1918	09/10/1918
War Diary	Morchies	10/10/1918	10/10/1918
War Diary	Bailleulmont	11/10/1918	12/10/1918
War Diary	Roellecourt	13/10/1918	22/10/1918
War Diary	Berlencourt	22/10/1918	31/10/1918
Heading	War Diary of 53rd Mobile Veterinary Section From Nov. 1st 1918 To Nov 30th 1918 Volume 30		
War Diary	Berlencourt	01/11/1918	01/11/1918
War Diary	Carrency	02/11/1918	02/11/1918
War Diary	Courcelles	03/11/1918	05/11/1918
War Diary	Thiant	06/11/1918	09/11/1918
War Diary	Saultain	10/11/1918	10/11/1918
War Diary	Angre	11/11/1918	11/11/1918
War Diary	Blaugies	12/11/1918	12/11/1918
War Diary	Harvengt	13/11/1918	28/11/1918
War Diary	Angre	29/11/1918	30/11/1918
Heading	War Diary of 53rd Mobile Veterinary Section From Dec. 1st 1918 To Dec. 31st 1918 Volume 31		
War Diary	Angre	01/12/1918	31/12/1918
Heading	War Diary of 53rd Mobile Veterinary Section From January 1st 1918 To January 31st 1919 Volume 32		
War Diary	Angre	01/01/1919	31/01/1919
Heading	War Diary of 53rd Mobile Veterinary Section From February 1st 1919 To February 28th 1919 Volume 33		
War Diary	Angre	01/02/1919	28/02/1919
Heading	War Diary of 53rd Mobile Veterinary Section From March 1st 1919 To March 31st 1919 Volume 34		
War Diary	Angre	01/03/1919	15/03/1919
War Diary	St. Ghislain	16/03/1919	31/03/1919
Miscellaneous	Egyptian Expeditionary Force. War Diary		
War Diary	Chalby	01/04/1919	01/04/1919
War Diary	Alexandria	02/04/1919	10/04/1919
War Diary	Chalby	11/04/1919	21/04/1919
War Diary	Alexandria	22/04/1919	30/04/1919
Heading	63rd Division 63rd (RN) Divl Train May 1916-Apr 1919		
Heading	War Diary of Royal Naval Divisional Train		
War Diary	Abbeville	18/05/1916	29/05/1916
War Diary	Hallencourt	30/05/1916	30/05/1916
Heading	War Diary of R.N Divisional Train From 1st June 1916 To 30th June 1916		
War Diary	Hallencourt	01/06/1916	11/06/1916
War Diary	Abbeville	12/06/1916	12/06/1916
War Diary	Houvelin	13/06/1916	16/06/1916
War Diary	Magnicourt	18/06/1916	30/06/1916
Heading	War Diary of 63rd (R.N.) Divisional Train From 1st July 1916 To 31st July 1916 Volume 2		
War Diary	Magnicourt	01/07/1916	17/07/1916
War Diary	Barlin	18/07/1916	25/07/1916
Heading	War Diary of 63rd (R.N.) Divisional Train. Volume 3. From 1st August, 1916 To 31st August, 1916.		
War Diary	Barlin	01/08/1916	31/08/1916

Heading	War Diary of 63rd (R.N.) Divisional Train. From 1st September, 1916 To 30th September, 1916 (Volume 4)		
War Diary	Barlin	19/09/1916	20/09/1916
War Diary	Bruay	21/09/1916	21/09/1916
War Diary	Ourton	27/09/1916	30/09/1916
War Diary	Barlin	04/09/1916	19/09/1916
Heading	War Diary of 63rd (R.N.) Divisional Train. Volume 5 From 1st October, 1916 To 31st October, 1916		
War Diary	Ourton	01/10/1916	03/10/1916
War Diary	Rebreuviette	04/10/1916	04/10/1916
War Diary	O.1.Central	16/10/1916	27/10/1916
Heading	War Diary 63rd (R.N.) Div Train Volume VI		
War Diary	O.1. Central	02/11/1916	18/11/1916
War Diary	Doullens	19/11/1916	21/11/1916
War Diary	Bernaville	21/11/1916	27/11/1916
War Diary	Mesnil-Domqueur	28/11/1916	28/11/1916
War Diary	St. Riquier	23/11/1916	23/11/1916
War Diary	Buigny	24/11/1916	24/11/1916
War Diary	Rue	25/11/1916	30/11/1916
Heading	War Diary of 63rd (RN) Divisional Train Volume 7 From 1-12-16 To 31-12-16		
War Diary	Rue	04/12/1916	31/12/1916
Heading	War Diary of 63rd (RN) Divisional Train Volume 2. From 1st January, 1917 To 31st January, 1917		
War Diary	Rue	01/01/1917	13/01/1917
War Diary	Buigny St Maclou	14/01/1917	14/01/1917
War Diary	Noyelle En Chaussee	15/01/1917	15/01/1917
War Diary	Feinvillers	15/01/1917	17/01/1917
War Diary	Val De Maison	18/01/1917	30/01/1917
Heading	War Diary of 63rd (RN) Divisional Train Volume 9 From 1st Feb 1917 To 28th Feb 1917		
War Diary	Englebelmer	01/02/1917	27/02/1917
Heading	War Diary March 1917 Volume 10		
War Diary	Englebelmer	01/03/1917	02/03/1917
War Diary	Bouzincourt	06/03/1917	18/03/1917
War Diary	Harponville	19/03/1917	19/03/1917
War Diary	Beauval	20/03/1917	25/03/1917
War Diary	Pernes	25/03/1917	25/03/1917
War Diary	Busnes	28/03/1917	30/03/1917
Miscellaneous	Moves & RE-Filling Points.		
Heading	War Diary April 1917 Volume 11		
War Diary	Busnes	01/04/1917	07/04/1917
War Diary	Bruay	08/04/1917	14/04/1917
War Diary	E 29	15/04/1917	15/04/1917
War Diary	E 29 B Sheet 51 C	16/04/1917	19/04/1917
War Diary	Maroeuil	20/04/1917	30/04/1917
Heading	War Diary May 1917 Volume 12		
War Diary	Mingoval	01/05/1917	20/05/1917
War Diary	Maroeuil	21/05/1917	25/05/1917
War Diary	Near Ecurie	26/05/1917	31/05/1917
Heading	War Diary Volume 13. June 1917		
War Diary	Near St Catherine	02/06/1917	12/06/1917
War Diary	Near Ecourie	14/06/1917	29/06/1917
Heading	War Diary Volume 14 July 1917		
War Diary	Near Ecurie	02/07/1917	28/07/1917
Heading	63 Div Train Vol 16 War Diary Volume No.15		

War Diary	Near Ecurie	01/08/1917	31/08/1917
Heading	63 D Train Vol 17 Volume 16 Sept 30-1917		
War Diary	Near Ecurie	02/09/1917	27/09/1917
War Diary	Savy	29/09/1917	30/09/1917
Heading	63 D Train War Diary Volume No. 17 October 1917		
War Diary	Savy	01/10/1917	01/10/1917
War Diary	Wormhoudt	02/10/1917	25/10/1917
War Diary	Near Vlamertinghe	27/10/1917	31/10/1917
Heading	63 D train War Diary Volume 18		
War Diary	Near Vlamertinghe	02/11/1917	05/11/1917
War Diary	L 4 b 5.5 Sheet 27 Near Poperinghe	06/11/1917	09/11/1917
War Diary	Near Poperinghe Near Lederzeele	18/11/1917	18/11/1917
War Diary	Lederzeele	18/11/1917	25/11/1917
War Diary	Near Poperinghe	29/11/1917	30/11/1917
Heading	63 D Train December War Diary Volume No.19		
War Diary	Near Poperinghe	01/12/1917	11/12/1917
War Diary	Achiet Le Petit	11/12/1917	13/12/1917
War Diary	Le Mesnil 0.35 D Sheet 57 C	14/12/1917	14/12/1917
War Diary	Le Mesnil	16/12/1917	22/01/1918
War Diary	Bancourt	23/01/1918	31/01/1918
Heading	War Diary 63rd (R.N.) Divisional Train February Volume 21		
War Diary	Bancourt	01/02/1918	13/02/1918
War Diary	Neuville	14/02/1918	27/02/1918
Heading	War Diary 63rd (RN) Divisional Train March 1918 Volume 22		
War Diary	Neuville	04/03/1918	22/03/1918
War Diary	Le Transloy	23/03/1918	23/03/1918
War Diary	Bazentin Grand	24/03/1918	24/03/1918
War Diary	Dernancourt	25/03/1918	25/03/1918
War Diary	Lealvillers	26/03/1918	27/03/1918
War Diary	Puchvillers	28/03/1918	30/03/1918
Heading	War Diary 63rd (R.N.) Divisional Train April 1918 Volume 23		
War Diary	Near Puchevillers	01/04/1918	03/04/1918
War Diary	Puchevillers	04/04/1918	05/04/1918
War Diary	Near Toutencourt	06/04/1918	30/04/1918
Heading	War Diary May 1918 Volume No 24		
War Diary	Near Toutencourt	02/05/1918	31/05/1918
Heading	War Diary 63rd (R.N.) Divisional Train June 1918 Volume 25. July 2/1918		
War Diary	Near Toutencourt	02/06/1918	04/06/1918
War Diary	Herissart	05/06/1918	22/06/1918
War Diary	Near Raincheval	23/06/1918	29/06/1918
Heading	War Diary 63rd (R.N.) Divisional Train July 1918 Volume No.26		
War Diary	Raincheval	06/07/1918	29/07/1918
War Diary	Pas	31/07/1918	31/07/1918
Heading	War Diary 63rd (RN) Divisional Train Aug 1918 Volume 27		
War Diary	Pas	02/08/1918	02/08/1918
War Diary	Near Rain Cheval	04/08/1918	08/08/1918
War Diary	Ebart Farm	08/08/1918	15/08/1918
War Diary	Pas	15/08/1918	24/08/1918
War Diary	Nr. Bucquoy	25/08/1918	27/08/1918
War Diary	Miraumont	29/08/1918	30/08/1918

War Diary	Douchy	30/08/1918	31/08/1918
War Diary	Blaireville	31/08/1918	31/08/1918
Heading	63rd (RN) Divisional train War Diary September 1918 Volume No 28		
War Diary	Blairville	01/09/1918	03/09/1918
War Diary	Croisilles	04/09/1918	04/09/1918
War Diary	Bavincourt	08/09/1918	16/09/1918
War Diary	Nr St Leger	17/09/1918	26/09/1918
War Diary	Near Ecoust	26/09/1918	27/09/1918
War Diary	Near Moeuvres	28/09/1918	30/09/1918
Heading	War Diary 63rd (R.N.) Divisional Train October 1918 Volume 29		
War Diary	Near Moeuvres	01/10/1918	09/10/1918
War Diary	Ecoust	11/10/1918	11/10/1918
War Diary	St Michel	12/10/1918	15/10/1918
War Diary	Berlincourt	22/10/1918	28/10/1918
War Diary	Carency	31/10/1918	31/10/1918
Heading	War Diary 63rd (R.N.) Divn Train Volume XXX		
War Diary	Le Forest	01/11/1918	01/11/1918
War Diary	Cuincy	02/11/1918	04/11/1918
War Diary	Monchaux	05/11/1918	06/11/1918
War Diary	Saultain	07/11/1918	07/11/1918
War Diary	Angre	09/11/1918	09/11/1918
War Diary	Blaugies	10/11/1918	11/11/1918
War Diary	Harvengt	19/11/1918	27/11/1918
War Diary	Fayt Le Franc	28/11/1918	28/11/1918
Heading	War Diary 63rd (R.N.) Divisional Train December 1918 Volume No.31		
War Diary	Audregnies	01/12/1918	31/12/1918
Heading	War Diary January 1919 Volume 32 63rd (RN) Divisional Train		
War Diary	Audregnies	01/01/1919	31/01/1919
Heading	War Diary 63rd (RN) Divisional Train February 1919. Volume No. 33		
War Diary	Audregnies	17/02/1919	17/02/1919
Heading	War Diary 63rd (RN) Divisional Train March 1919 Volume No 34		
War Diary	Hornu	12/03/1919	31/03/1919
Heading	War Diary 63rd (R.N.) Divisional Train April 1919 Volume 35		
War Diary	Hornu	01/04/1919	01/04/1919

63RD DIVISION

SANITARY SECTION R.N.D.

~~MAY - DEC 1916~~

1916 MAY — 1917 MAR

To 1 ARMY

63rd Div.

Sanitary Section R.N.D.

May 1915

COMMITTEE FOR THE
MEDICAL HISTORY OF THE WAR
Date 26 JUN 1915

Sanitary Section, Royal Naval Division

WAR DIARY
or
INTELLIGENCE SUMMARY

Army Form C. 2118.

(Erase heading not required.)

Hour, Date, Place	Summary of Events and Information	Remarks and references to Appendices
31.5.16	The Sanitary Section has been formed to-day by the appointment provisionally of an officer & by drawing personnel (3 Corporals & 22 men) from the 3rd Field Ambulance. The necessary gear has been indented for, as well as the huts lent by the A.D.M.S. of the Division. E. Gallop Surgeon RN	

CONFIDENTIAL.

Sanitary Section,
Royal Naval Division.
......July 3rd..'16.

WAR DIARY

of

Sanitary Section, Royal Naval Division.

from

1st   June   1916

to

30th   June   1916.

R H Krumbs.

O. C., Sanitary Section.
R. N. Division.

To,

The A. G's Office,

3rd Echelon.

COMMITTEE FOR THE
MEDICAL HISTORY OF THE WAR

Date   31 AUG. 1916

Sanitary Section, Royal Naval Division

Army Form C. 2118.

WAR DIARY
or
INTELLIGENCE SUMMARY.
(Erase heading not required.)

Instructions regarding War Diaries and Intelligence Summaries are contained in F. S. Regs., Part II. and the Staff Manual respectively. Title pages will be prepared in manuscript.

(1)

Place	Date	Hour	Summary of Events and Information	Remarks and references to Appendices
HALLENCOURT	1st June 1916		Sanitary Section formed. 1 Officer and 21 men, including 3 Corporals. Informed last night 2 cases of Diphtheria from Anson Batt: at ARRAINES had been sent to 1st Field Ambulance at PONT REMY. Visited ARRAINES first thing this morning and found Anson Batt: on march to Rathved, and the pre immediate contacts were isolated in 1st Field Amb: and then Isolates re-isolated. A party went to ARRAINE and disinfected the building.	
	2nd June		All billets used by R.N.D. were reported on after visits by men/Sanitary Section and except in a few unimportant details were found to be satisfactory. Part of advance stores arrived.	
	3rd June		Received telegram informing me that Pte H. Yoxhull 5/4155, previously attached to Sanitary Section, who had admitted sick on May 26th, was found by 2nd Stationary Hospital to be suffering from TYPHUS FEVER. Sanitary section was required to quarters and in inspection found to be clean and free from lice and spits.	
	4th June		Remaining advance stores arrived. Billet occupied by Sanitary Section thoroughly washed and disinfected. The whole party were then by lorry to ABBEVILLE, segregated and isolated.	

Army Form C. 2118.

WAR DIARY
or
INTELLIGENCE SUMMARY.
(Erase heading not required.)

Instructions regarding War Diaries and Intelligence Summaries are contained in F. S. Regs., Part II. and the Staff Manual respectively. Title pages will be prepared in manuscript.

(2)

Place	Date	Hour	Summary of Events and Information.	Remarks and references to Appendices
ABBEVILLE	14th June (cont.)		Nk:- Pte H. Yoxhall 5/4135, was a member of a Temporary Sanitary Section at MUDROS, being attached from the Rifle Depot men. Just before leaving MUDROS, the Sanitary party was attached to the 3rd Field Ambulance which was in the process of formation. Then left MUDROS on May 19th on H.M.T. FRANCONIA, arrived at MARSEILLES on May 23rd, left MARSEILLES May 23rd, arriving at PONT REMY (RAILHEAD) in HALLERCOURT on May 25th. Pte H. Yoxhall/4135 was ascertained to have a rise talk daily. The O.C. Sanitary Section ✱ Temp. Surg. E.S. CALTHROP, R.N.	✱Diagnosis:-
"	15th June		refused sick and was admitted to Hospital (24th Stationary). Sanitary Section left ABBEVILLE on June 21st arriving at OURTON on	
"	26th June		June 29th.	
OURTON	29th June		Temp. Surgeon R.H. KNOWLES. R.N. arrived command of Sanitary Section vice Temp Surg E.S. CALTHROP. R.N. — evacuated to ENGLAND – sick ✱	✱ Progressive Muscular atrophy.
"	30th June		Stores checked. First inspection of mens clothing - deficiencies indented for.	

R.H. Knowles Surg RN
Temp Surgeon RN
O.C.

"Confidential"

69 / 6 July
Sample 3
63 D 3 Vol. 3

"Head Quarters"
Sanitary Section
63rd (R.N.) Division

War Diary
of
Sanitary Section
63rd (R.N.) Division
From 1st July to 31st July 1916.

Volume 2

To. D.H.Q.
63rd (R.N.) Division

R.A.Kn————
Temp. Surgeon R.N.
O.C.
Sanitary Section
63rd (R.N.) Division

Despatched. August 1st/1916.

COMMITTEE FOR THE
MEDICAL HISTORY OF THE WAR
Date   5-SEP 1916

Army Form C. 2118.

WAR DIARY
or
INTELLIGENCE SUMMARY.
(Erase heading not required.)

Instructions regarding War Diaries and Intelligence Summaries are contained in F. S. Regs., Part II. and the Staff Manual respectively. Title pages will be prepared in manuscript.

Place	Date	Hour	Summary of Events and Information	Remarks and references to Appendices
OURTON	July 1st		Arranged for men of Sanitary Section to be returned by 1st Field Ambulance. Mapels and Batman returned by D.H.Q. Batman went to 3rd Field Ambulance at LA THIEULOYE and obtained horse which had been drawn by him for C.E. Sanitary Section. Men of Sanitary Section employed as to (1) Scales, (2) Disinfectors, (3) Gas helmets (emptying) (4) Gas goggles. Held wring sort for day to A.D.M.S. Men working on Sanitary arrangements round their billets, fitting up offices etc. I rode over to FRESNICOURT to see Sani. Office of 2nd DIVISION at CAMBLAIN L'ABBÉ — Capt CLAYTON R.A.M.C. He showed me his office and men and gave me a general idea of his methods and the work in his area.	
	July 2nd		Dealt with routine etc. Drew money from Field Cashier and payed men. Two men went to CAMBLAIN CHATELAIN on temp. guard for stores laundry. Will of men obtained from pay books and sent to Record Office London. Party from Sector supervised renovation of two wrecked parties which had arrived in billets at OURTON.	
	July 3rd		Paid in went to Major HAWKE Batt. at DIEVAL, 2 Bn H.Q. + Trench Motor group at BEUGIN, Machine Gun Coy at CATUS, 7th H.Q. etc at OURTON also Bomb school	

Place	Date	Hour	Summary of Events and Information	Remarks and references to Appendices
OURTON (cont.)	July 4th (cont)		and Mounted Police at OURTON. Refils to the where satisfactory - improvements suggested and commenced.	
	July 5th		Parties sent to inspect Animal Lines at HAGNICOURT. Two detailed to go daily to D.H.Q. for sanitary duties to work with R.A.P. sanitary staff. A boy in village of OURTON found suffering from virulent SCABIES, steps taken to get him transferred to French Hospital at BETHUNE. Suspected member of Animal Bath acted for SCABIES - 5 cases found and sent to no 5 Field Ambulance. Visited A.S.C. ad went round sanitary arrangements with camp sergt: except for Hay there was no incidents - good. Treated their incinerator which is built. Three men working in yard of A.D.M.S. office at Dejection driven.	
	July 6th		Three men inspected 316th Artillery Brigade at CAMBLAIN CHATELAIN. Ranfurly and one other man helped Mantel Julia to fund ten latrines, open one manure heap. I visited quarters etc. of Mounted & Foot Police Gun Drill for members of Sanitary Section. Arrangements made for 4 men to be attached to 3rd Bde H.Q. for Sanitary duties to brigade area.	
	July 7th		Two men made washing place. Three men go to EALONNE RICOUART and	

Army Form C. 2118.

WAR DIARY
or
~~INTELLIGENCE SUMMARY.~~
(Erase heading not required.)

Place	Date	Hour	Summary of Events and Information	Remarks and references to Appendices
OUTROV (cont)	July 7th (cont)		inspect 315th Artillery Brigade. One man to superintend sanitation of B and C sectors of 315th, 316th & 317th Brigades R.F.A., attached to this division. I saw the Medical Officers of Sanitary Section. Shrapnel N.C.O's and more men has to work with Tent Officer (in gas evening). Two men who had been detached for duty at Laundry returned.	
	July 8th		Men to STAPS & Coul actual or wounded. Carpenter working in latrines etc. Party of three men to BOURS to inspect 317th Brigade R.F.A. I saw Staff Sergt of 2nd Bde at DIEVAL and arranged to send him for new men in Brigade area. Went to see 3rd F.A. at LA THIEULOYE 30 cwt Lorry detached for use of Divisional Laundry at CAMBLAIN CHATELAINE.	
	July 9th		Pte Load S/4022 made Acting Lance Corporal (without pay), and three more sent to 1st Brigade (one late 3rd Brigade) at FRESNICOURT. Went to CAMBLAIN CHATELAINE and saw Laundry. Medical Officers of 316th Brigade R.F.A. and Nelson Batt Headquarters. (only about 150 men and headquarters of Nelson Batt there). 1 Sergeant & 1 cook sent to 315th Brigade R.F.A. at town.	
	July 10th		Corporal Platt and three men sent to 2nd Brigade at DIEVAL. 3 inspected	

Army Form C. 2118.

WAR DIARY
or
INTELLIGENCE SUMMARY.
(Erase heading not required.)

Instructions regarding War Diaries and Intelligence Summaries are contained in F. S. Regs., Part II. and the Staff Manual respectively. Title pages will be prepared in manuscript.

Place	Date	Hour	Summary of Events and Information	Remarks and references to Appendices
OURTON (cont.)	July 10 (cont.)		Office quarters at OURTON. Found a suitable place for the Officers' latrine for Eclair B. Inspected and available man for it to find lime as near latrines as officers. One for A.D.M.S. Office staff. Visited with A.D.M.S. in afternoon. The billets etc. and new Medical Officers. Demanded train at MAGNICOURT, M.O. R.M. Batt.: W FREVILLERS, 2nd R.M. Batt. at MAGNICOURT, HOWE Batt. at HERMIN and RAWSON Batt. at ESTRÉE CAUCHIE; also saw staff. Eo/r of the Brigade with reference to sanitary matters. Large Expand Land mown seen as reported wanting 2nd Regt. a previous day and Bde H.Q. - ventilation except for few details satisfactory.	
	July 11		Latrines for Officers and A.D.M.S. Office staff at OURTON fixed up - Visited DIEVAL - fixed to attend 2nd Brigade - sanitation not - Visited BRYAS and men and latrines of 3/1st Royal (now called 225 R. Brig.) with Medical Officer. Latrines seemed very bad but will help ground latrines in course of construction.	
	July 12		Visited D.H.Q. and attended H.Q. 4 of 2nd Company, 1st H.A.C. 1/1 Batt. at La Bruste - officer latrines - promised to have them erected. Inspected B water schemes.	

Army Form C. 2118.

WAR DIARY
or
INTELLIGENCE SUMMARY.
(Erase heading not required.)

Place	Date	Hour	Summary of Events and Information	Remarks and references to Appendices
OURTON (cont)	July 12th (cont)		at OURTON — no cases found	
	July 13th		Party went to BEUGIN to inspect 2nd Brigade Horse Lines. Went to RIOCOURT and saw water supply — good. Few openings in side of well — no evidence of contamination; also visited farm at MAGNICOURT and saw and with Medical Officer. Box latrine fly proof, open & foul site — good. No incinerator, all food stuff is buried — he has ordered protection and sited the incinerator as not allowed. New latrines made for Brunts school at OURTON.	
	July 14th		Inspected billets for troops actually at OURTON. Visited FRESNICOURT and inspected sanitary arrangements of 2nd Field Ambulance — all in very good condition. 6th London Regiment now occupy huts at FRESNICOURT — my sanitary men now attached for returning to 2nd F.A. — To report to M.O. of 6th London — any depts. in construction. Attended lecture by Colonel Wallace — Consulting Surgeon — 1st Army — at OURTON.	
	July 15th		In morning went on to BARLIN with ADMS. ++ADMS — saw ADMS 2 DADMS. Went to BOYEFFLES with ADMS in reviewing and and 47th DIVISION. R.A.M.C. o/c sanitary section of 47th Division, Col. Sir J. C. & B.	

Army Form C. 2118.

WAR DIARY
or
INTELLIGENCE SUMMARY.
(Erase heading not required.)

Instructions regarding War Diaries and Intelligence Summaries are contained in F. S. Regs, Part II. and the Staff Manual respectively. Title pages will be prepared in manuscript.

Place	Date	Hour	Summary of Events and Information	Remarks and references to Appendices
OURTON (cont)	July 14th (cont)		his officers, N.C.O.s and men's billets and arrangements were made for taking over more quarters from him.	
			Adopted R.N.D. Medical Unit Operation Order No. 1 (in so far as refers to Sanitary Sect).	
			" On the R.N.Division taking over the sector of the line now occupied by the 47th Division the following reliefs and moves will take place.	
			5/ On the morning of the 17th July the Sanitary Section will take over the present position of the Sanitary Section 47th Division at BOUYEFFLES.	
			The detail for relief of Units should be arranged between the Officers Commanding units concerned. All moves to be completed by 3.0.P.M. on Monday 17th. Completion of moves to be reported to A.D.M.S. or V 27 & C.1. BARLIN."	
	July 16th		Went on with advanced party of men, mess ahead and arranged to complete relief at BOUYEFFLES about 12 noon on following day. Gave some information from R.S.M. Galpin regarding the area and work to be done. Rode on from BURTON with S.M. & C.1. to CAMBLAIN CHATELAINE. NELSON Hut had already moved. Saw laundry. Remainder of Men packed and collected ready for moving.	

T2134. Wt. W708—776. 500000. 4/16. Str J. C. & S.

Army Form C. 2118.

WAR DIARY
or
INTELLIGENCE SUMMARY.
(Erase heading not required.)

Instructions regarding War Diaries and Intelligence Summaries are contained in F. S. Regs., Part II. and the Staff Manual respectively. Title pages will be prepared in manuscript.

Place	Date	Hour	Summary of Events and Information	Remarks and references to Appendices
GURTON	July 17th		Billets cleared up. Latrine filled in etc. Bu actual latrine fillers in Mule Lines left remainder of platoon and men left behind on to BOYEFFLES.	
BOYEFFLES			Sanitary Section of 47th Division left at about 2.30 P.M. Relief reported complete to A.D.M.S. I called at Town Major's offices at BARLIN and HERSIN and arranged to send parties of men for cleaning up in those areas.	
BOYEFFLES	July 18th		Men employed in opening up of others, making new washing places etc etc. Pte PRICE made Acting Sergeant (without pay) and sent into to HERSIN with ten men to report to Town Major at BARLIN, to be billeted and rationed by him and to supervise work in his area. Corpl Platt and 3 men were sent up to HERSIN with 2nd Brigade to work with Town Major of HERSIN in similar way. Arranged for a billet for them and for them to draw rations from 1st Field Ambulance. 3 new Town Major at FOSSE 10 was arranged their billets. Alterman + one man sent into to FOSSE 10 arranging for rations with the W.W. L. Enft Ld. + 3 men who had come from FRESNICOURT with 2nd Field Ambulance returned to me to-day. I saw D.A.D.O.S. and found my bicycle of the two bicycles we are entitled to have not	

WAR DIARY
or
INTELLIGENCE SUMMARY
(Erase heading not required.)

Place	Date	Hour	Summary of Events and Information	Remarks and references to Appendices
BOYEFFLES	July 18th (cont)		Yet arrived. Obtained permission from A.D.M.S. of our division for my men to wear M.P. Badges on left arm, when actually inspecting.	
	July 19th		Drew money from Field Cashier. Arrangements made to visit 2nd Field Ambulance that that motor car also brings up our supplies. Visited BARLIN and saw ADMS. Visited 2nd Field Ambulance at BARLIN and inspected their sanitary arrangements; suggested the monitors of the active filled drain in transport lines or prisoner enough pit for one or two mules and have urine not category. Case of Measles reported Herein in French child — by Lieut. Major.	
	July 20		Party went to inspect villets etc. at BOUVIGNY. Went to HERSIN and saw child (MEASLES) — no rash for 14 days — discharging ears — Two NG young children in the house — not had measles. Two men R.E. Bridging train billeted in out-house. There is a French doctor in attendance. Horses put out of bounds and men warned not to enter. (Men have since been moved to another villet). Went into BARLIN and saw ADMS. & DADMS. In afternoon ADMS. & DADMS. came to BOYEFFLES and visited	see Appendix 1 & 2

WAR DIARY
or
INTELLIGENCE SUMMARY.
(Erase heading not required.)

Army Form C. 2118.

Instructions regarding War Diaries and Intelligence Summaries are contained in F. S. Regs., Part II. and the Staff Manual respectively. Title pages will be prepared in manuscript.

Place	Date	Hour	Summary of Events and Information	Remarks and references to Appendices
BOYEFFLES	July 20th (cont)		Men's Mess and Officers: which was enriched attendances. Case of Enteric Fever reported by Sergt Price at BARLIN - no trace in name - local doctor in attendance. Have put "out of bounds" for troops. Parties sent to BOUVIGNY to repair incinerator: also visits S.A.E.W's in -B- FOSSELLE. I visited AIX NOULETTE and trenches of right sect. of defence inc. A.D.M.S. & A.D.H.S. Latrine matters & incinerator E/ff. Mens fly proof Beef trenches - Also the new model.	
	July 21st		Work (1) Rifle line up to Headquarters Trench for a range in BOIS de BOUVIGNY - this water is not chlorinated - attaching area-springs and crewed that - tested mine all round and permanent guard on. (2) Bomarck at FRENCH DUMP which are filled by mob cart with chlorinated water at night and carried up trenches by hand. Went to HERSIN and BARLIN and saw my men in - all examined for SCABIES. No cases found.	
	July 22nd		I inspected at BOUVIGNY completed. Manure dump at FOSSE 10 sprayed, also small dumps at BOYEFFLES. I visited SAENs in BOHELLE and saw	

Army Form C. 2118.

WAR DIARY
or
INTELLIGENCE SUMMARY.
(Erase heading not required.)

Instructions regarding War Diaries and Intelligence Summaries are contained in F. S. Regs., Part II. and the Staff Manual respectively. Title pages will be prepared in manuscript.

Place	Date	Hour	Summary of Events and Information	Remarks and references to Appendices
BOYEFFLES	July 22. (cont)		Public Latrine lunge, refuse and transport lines of H.Q. RFA. 2nd Field Co: Engineers. Visited A.D.S. at AIX NOULETTE, inspected Kitchen arrangements, and Bois de NOULETTE where NELSON Batt: was. Sanitation satisfactory.	
	July 23rd		Inspected Bath at Brewery near FOSSE 10. Drainage etc not in bad condition to be reported to Engineers. Inspected latrines to west of FOSSE 10 — with the exception of a bit running to one of the cess, in good condition. General work in village of BOYEFFLES by men of Sanitary Section. ? ran A.D.M.S. & D.A.D.M.S. in BARLIN.	
	July 24		Party sent to AIX NOULETTE. A man sent to mend urinal at FOSSE 10. Was in bed unwell. Went to BARLIN and met D.D.M.S. 1st Corps; former at entrance A.D.M.S., D.A.D.M.S. O.C's 1st, 2nd & 3rd Field Ambulances D.A.D.M.S. IV Corps & myself. D.A.D.M.S. complained of latrines at FOSSE 10 & need (Army Rly): also condition of huts at employer; In afternoon 3 visited 2/4 London Regt. at Fosse 10 — and after latrines found. Supplied them with some wood and Key joined to remedy this much. Went to Hut at employer — H.A.C. and	

Army Form C. 2118.

WAR DIARY
or
INTELLIGENCE SUMMARY.
(Erase heading not required.)

Instructions regarding War Diaries and Intelligence Summaries are contained in F. S. Regs., Part II. and the Staff Manual respectively. Title pages will be prepared in manuscript.

Place	Date	Hour	Summary of Events and Information	Remarks and references to Appendices
BOYEFFLES	July 24th (cont)		and Military POLICE hutted in some of the huts. Others used as stores. Wood behind huts in dirty condition – have evidently been many old latrines etc. Large working party from H.Q.C. were cleaning up and also cleaning cesspool round huts which to some can were choked. Spoken of huts not good. I inspected the sites of affairs to Town Major and suggested that when the troops vacated the huts a party should be sent to rout down the troubles etc. in huts. When in BARLIN saw in inadequate Report from Air NOULETTE and noticed lines on the situation.	
	July 25th		Report from Air NOULETTE my good. Paths near again and in the rations noted that the conditions were greatly improved. Loved latrines were being made and in good dispord of. Also old kinds had been filled in. I visited BULLY GRENAY and inspected advanced dressing station – good condition. Saw several latrines in bad condition belonging to different units. Saw Staff Captain and arranged to ceny these men up – to be hutted and rationed by 23 Fld Ambulance for general improvement of sanit with in the area. Staff Capt. said that he would provide necessary working parties.	
			Regt. TATE visited FOSSE 10 and reported that there were several latrines which needed repair.	
	July 26th		Paths near to BOIS de NOULETTE, BOUVIGNY HUTS, + BOUVIGNY – Report in consequence	

T2134. Wt. W708—776. 500000. 4/15. Sir J. C. & S.

WAR DIARY or INTELLIGENCE SUMMARY

Army Form C. 2118.

Place	Date	Hour	Summary of Events and Information	Remarks and references to Appendices
NOYELLES	July 26th		Conditions good. Walk for funds in NOULETTE WOOD is piped to about 1/2 from a spring, enclosed and guarded in small wood about 500 yards from huts. Bath here no good in good condition. I visited baths at FOSSE 10 into 2 after MARSHALL of an Div Engineers, and he said that he would have a pipe drain made to take away dirty water. I saw Town Major and arranged for him to send working party to huts. I saw E.R.E. at SAENS-EN-GOHELLE, and arranged to put up new cupboards of right rooms as afternoon of July 28th. Town Major at FOSSE 10 has been unable to get transport for disposal of refuse — 3 units at huts to see rifuse is incinerated or the ash — or to refuse is accumulating daily. a, A.Q.M.G. providing him with incinerators as he required.	
	July 27th		Park visited and reported on. Bowl School Wires — to East of railway in HERSIN-COUPIGNY, and now under inspection. I visited HERSIN + COUPIGNY, and new unit Engineer School latrines, under construction, 176 Tunnelling Co; 190th Brigade Signals, B Battery, 316th Brig R.F.A, Horse Transport; also staff public incinerators and manure dumps. Saw the French estaminets in an extremely dirty condition, and recommended Town Major should take steps to have them closed or emptied. Reports on 4 & M.	

PLATT.

WAR DIARY or INTELLIGENCE SUMMARY

Army Form C. 2118.

Place	Date	Hour	Summary of Events and Information	Remarks and references to Appendices
BUYEFFLES	July 2nd (cont. July 3rd)		Heavy Artillery H.Q. and R.E. Bridging Company good. Went round billets and other details of Indian Regiment at BOYEFFLES. Not a very dirty condition. Men soon to have movements of H.A.E. & M.late oldm. reports letter. Met C.R.E. at 2 P.M. and went with him and D.A.D.M.S. via AIX NOULETTE to BOIS de NOULETTE. Saw spring there (? Source du SURFEON) – well protected – no signs of any contamination – it is piped to standpipes near HUTS. Also near terminus BOIS de BOUVIGNY. Found LORETTE SPUR all over marks of men going to be entered. Water is piped up to Headquarters trench. Water is collected from springs in retentive a covered tent and thence can either go direct to trenches or pass through two very large galvanized iron tanks; there are no signs of any contamination – at present the water is not chlorinated – an examination will be made at an early date. – Sergt Tate visited AIX NOULETTE, and saw Bde H.Q. (157) 1½ Companies of HOOD Batt. 2nd Field Company Engineers. Three men sent to BULLY GRENAY for sanitary duties, to be billeted & rationed by 2nd Field Ambulance.	
	July 3rd		Inspected H.A.C. at BOYEFFLES, employed. New latrines etc. built to begin time. 22nd Brig. R.E.A. Marines help approved. A visit to COURTENAY and saw	

Army Form C. 2118.

WAR DIARY
or
INTELLIGENCE SUMMARY.
(Erase heading not required.)

Instructions regarding War Diaries and Intelligence Summaries are contained in F. S. Regs., Part II. and the Staff Manual respectively. Title pages will be prepared in manuscript.

Place	Date	Hour	Summary of Events and Information	Remarks and references to Appendices
BOYEFFLES	July 29th (cont)		A.P.M. regarding a horse. Visited 3. W. Field Ambulance – It again recommended for this transport lines almost completed and enough pits seen at present have had been filled in. Saw Sergt Price who has been at BARLIN Cell centre examining for Scabies, Helmets (Gas), & feet. Borrowed plans of HERSIN & BOUVIGNY and made tracings. Emniences map. I am a to show Wallis Marne dumps etc. Sergt Price is preparing a map of BARLIN.	
	July 30th		Continued with map in the morning. Men in local work in villages. New refuge pits dug behind Jam Villa. I went to VERDREL saw Medical Officer of 9th Royal Fusiliers. The men were changing billets when I was there. About half of them were in huts & remainder mostly will. Latrines & urinals were in disgraceful state as in hut inspected & also of netting – from which went to Coupigny. Told the M.O. to inform the medical officer of this – especially in local garrisons. The last two days have been very hot but all the covers of flies is very marked. Disinfection of 22nd Inf. Brigade (R.F.) nos. 223–3 Brig. (Auc) 911.9 o.B. 1622 1/24[?]/16.)	
	July 31st		Party went to inspect AIX NOULETTE, noticed grassily improved. I visited BOUVIGNY & IVY-BOYEFFLES and saw billets, site of pits of 75 H.O.D. mens. They had just arrived and the officer in charge promised to remedy defective latrines.	

Army Form C. 2118.

WAR DIARY
or
INTELLIGENCE SUMMARY.
(Erase heading not required.)

Instructions regarding War Diaries and Intelligence Summaries are contained in F. S. Regs., Part II. and the Staff Manual respectively. Title pages will be prepared in manuscript.

Place	Date	Hour	Summary of Events and Information	Remarks and references to Appendices
BOYEFFLES	July 3rd (cont)		Visited H.A.C. Batt. in huts BOUVIGNY WOODS, inspected the arrangements with Medical Officer. Camp clean, incinerators working well, latrines clean. M.O. is going to inspect for fire risk, for men's coffee. Latrines a few yards, majority deep pit covered in. All with screens from roads, Inspected in camp. Smelt BULLY & GRAVY in afternoon. Went round Latrines etc of 1st R.M. with R.M. M.O. also inspected baths. General conditions much better than a German mine – all old latrines have been filled in. Also saw latrines of two companies of HONKE Batt. Lieut. TATE talked with of 4 wells in village of BOYEFFLES, generally from one of the wells or rather ends of villages appears fit for drinking, and taken only after chlorination: the four other sources of supply are in Brewery and will be written up.	night.

R. H. Knowles.
Temp. Surgeon R.N.
O/c Sanitary Section
63rd (R.N.) Division.

SANITARY SECTION,
ROYAL NAVAL
DIVISION.
3/7/16

Army Form C. 2118.

WAR DIARY
or
INTELLIGENCE SUMMARY.
(Erase heading not required.)

Instructions regarding War Diaries and Intelligence Summaries are contained in F. S. Regs., Part II. and the Staff Manual respectively. Title pages will be prepared in manuscript.

Place	Date	Hour	Summary of Events and Information	Remarks and references to Appendices
Boyeffles	July 31st		Appendix 'A' The present distribution of the Sanitary Section is as follows:—	
			BOYEFFLES. Headquarters. Store, Office, motor lorry and huts of men.	
			Sergt TATE in charge.	
			Corporal BILSBOROUGH acting as Q.M. Sergt	
			1 Cook, 1 Storeman, 1 Carpenter, 1 Clerk, 1 Postman (on wiring militia), 5 men for inspecting and general duties, and 2 M/T Transport men.	
			BARLIN Acting Sergt Price and 3 men (Two Myn)	
			HERSIN Corporal Pluitt and 3 men (Two Myn)	
			FOSSE 10 Corporal Willson and 1 man (Two Myn)	
			BULLY GRENAY Three men (Sergt/Corpl 13 5th Bn).	
			With the men detached as above, and by sending out men inspecting to huts to have the units are occupied by the Division under inspection.	
			See rough diagrammatic sketch Appendix B.	R.W.Wrington

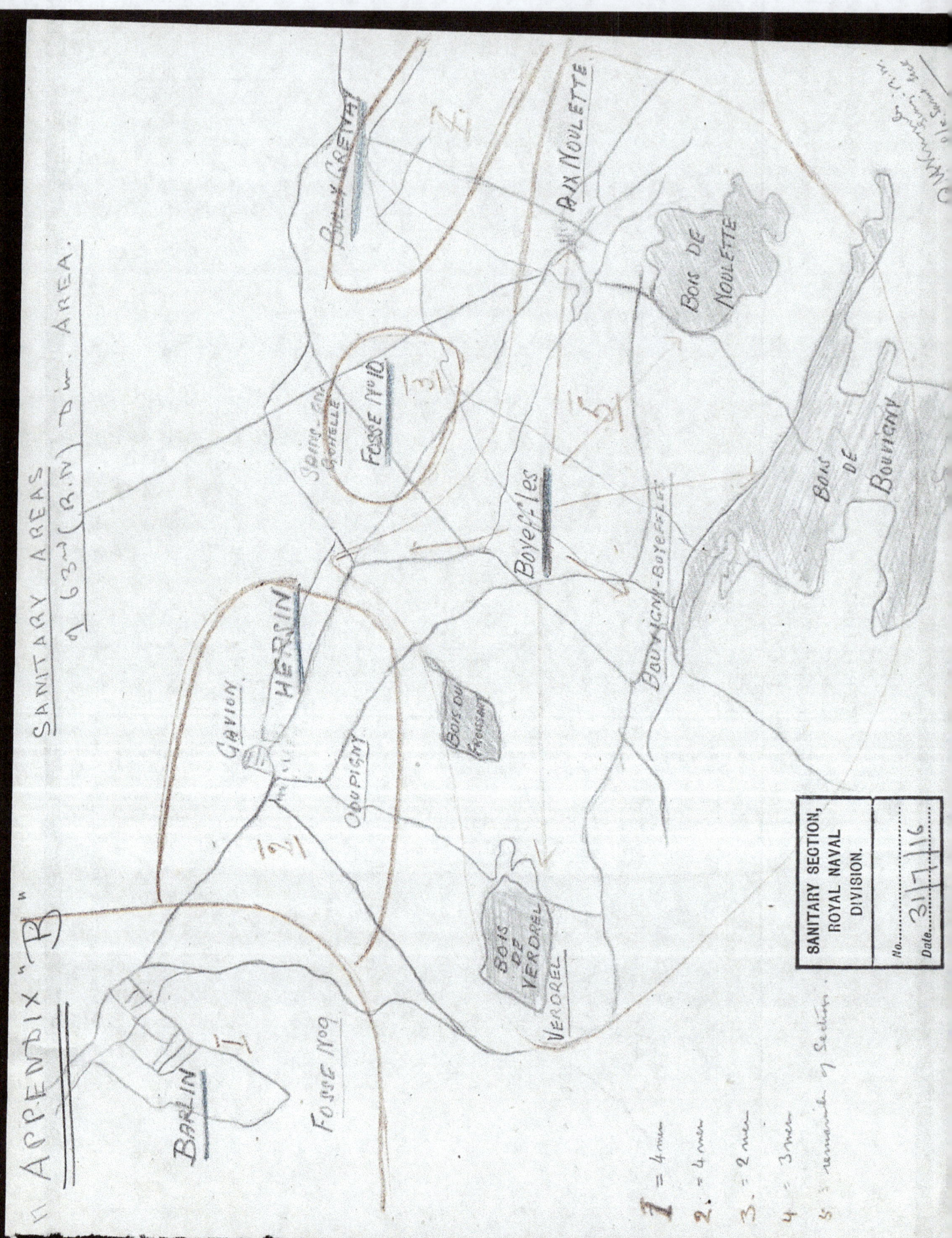

Army Form C. 2118.

WAR DIARY
or
INTELLIGENCE SUMMARY.
(Erase heading not required.)

Place	Date	Hour	Summary of Events and Information	Remarks and references to Appendices
BOYEFFLES			Appendix "C"	
			Copy of ROUTINE ORDER 318 - 1 July 20th. 16.	
			318. DESIGNATION.	
			The ROYAL NAVAL DIVISION will in future be known as the 63rd (ROYAL NAVAL) division.	
			The 1st NAVAL BRIGADE becomes the 188th BRIGADE.	
			The 2nd NAVAL BRIGADE " " 189th BRIGADE	
			The 3rd NAVAL BRIGADE " " 190th BRIGADE	
			The word NAVAL will be omitted from the designation of the Brigades	

63

"Confidential"

Sanitary Section
63rd (R.N) Division
1st September 1916.

VK

COMMITTEE FOR THE
MEDICAL HISTORY OF THE WAR
Date -9 OCT. 1916

War Diary
of
Sanitary Section
63rd (R.N) Division
From 1st August to 31st August 1916.

J. C. Blackwell Surgeon R.N.
for Surgeon Knowles R.N. O.C.
Sanitary Section
63rd (R.N) Division.

To D.H.Q.
63rd (R.N) Division.

August

Despatched 8.30p.m. Sept 2nd/1916.

Army Form C. 2118.

WAR DIARY
or
INTELLIGENCE SUMMARY.
(Erase heading not required.)

Sanitary Section. 63rd (R.N.) Divl

Place	Date	Hour	Summary of Events and Information	Remarks and references to Appendices
BOYEFFLES.	Aug 1st		Men sent to BOUVIGNY to repair latrines and build incinerators. Mean spray maintained in outlays of BOYEFFLES. Sergt Tate visited 223rd (Wt 225th) Brigade R.F.A. 'B' Battery H.A.C. transport lines. & visited Head quarters 315th Bgy. R.F.A., H.A.C. Quartermaster Stores. Visited BARLIN and saw money for payment of men from Field Cashier. The son of ENTERIC (civilian) at BARLIN died; have been disinfected and compulsory and drained by Sanitary Section.	
	Aug 2nd		Men sent to SAENS-EN-GOHELLE and BETHER SCHOOL near HERSIN. Sergt TATE filled with 9 several local wells. Visited BULLY GRENAY and trenches R.A.P. and Bever Pots. Latrines at Bever Pots [Sifffees]. Bait Latrines chiefly buckets type - keep pits have been dug and Syphent pipes will be placed in same in course of next few days. The water supply which is piped up to Bully Alley + Bowit trenches has been cut off by recent shrage. I new Staff Cap. at Brigade (188th) H.Q. and he said that there had been arranged through B.H.Q. to the Division as an on left which is responsible for the water supply in the Magazine that water is carried up in tins from BULLY GRENAY filling. I saw new scheme of R.R.E. for new work system for this section. Men paraded	
	Aug 3rd		Men to HERSIN-COUPIGNY - who inspected and reported in a longer manner	

Army Form C. 2118.

WAR DIARY
or
INTELLIGENCE SUMMARY.
(Erase heading not required.)

SANITARY SECTION.
63rd (R.N.) DIVISION

Instructions regarding War Diaries and Intelligence Summaries are contained in F. S. Regs., Part II. and the Staff Manual respectively. Title pages will be prepared in manuscript.

Place	Date	Hour	Summary of Events and Information	Remarks and references to Appendices
BOYEFFLES	August 3rd (cont)		of units which they visited. Men to BOUVIGNY. 2 men filled in dump in H.A.C. Q.M. area, billet area. H.A.C. have tins & gallon tanks which are not for drinking water after chlorination - for van transport lines and Q.M. store men. I visited BOUCLIVY and inspected huts occupied by 1st Bedfordshire Regt. and H.M.G. - general conditions greatly improved. I also visited IV. Corps R.F.A. Headquarters - sanitation good - all water boiled.	
	Aug 4th		Party to NOULETTE HUTS - report good. I visited BARLIN and saw A.D.M.S. and D.A.D.M.S. Letter received from Town Major HERSIN ref: two nuisances, reported to him by MAIRE of HERSIN. I visited them. (1) On old Manure (?) heap found. (2) Manure dump in a yard - with accumulated stagnant water round. Directed that they should be daily sprayed with CRESOL during the hot weather. Neither of the above could be attributed to the four other troops occupy the town. Cases of DIPTHERIA? reported by MO Field Ambulance - attached from NELSON BATT.	
	Aug 5th		Men to SKENS and GOHELLE + FOSSE 10 (to visit 188th Coy. Machine Gun Corps) visited	

Army Form C. 2118.

WAR DIARY
or
INTELLIGENCE SUMMARY.
(Erase heading not required.)

Army Form C. 2118.

SANITARY SECTION 63rd (R.N.) Division

Place	Date	Hour	Summary of Events and Information	Remarks and references to Appendices
BUEFFLES	Aug 5th (cont)		has just arrived. I visited AIX-NOULETTE mn BATHS, and inspected Well in yard of R.E. Dump. Also new latrine Superintendent. Also visited NELSON Batt: in NOULETTE Hut, saw their M.O. in ref: to ? DIPHTHERIA case reported. He is inoculating remainder of the man's company & examining sore throats etc.	
	Aug 6th		Men sent to repair damaged latrine at FOSSE 10. Men sent to AIX MOULETTE to clean surroundings of well in R.E. Dump also fix up latrine screening in well behind Signal Well. I visited AIX NOULETTE and found work had been done, also visited 3rd Field Company Engineer Works etc. Latrines in good condition, although water in use in these places was not flowing - incinerator for each section Well. Well in R.E. H.Q. yard in clean condition - notice up to the effect that all water must be boiled before drinking. Men sent to Nardet (7th Royal Fusiliers) - latrines not yet erected - Wells from pipe line firm reservoir in gully wood. I visited the transport lines and Quakenekin stores of 1st R.M. Batt at GAVION, ANSON, DRAKE, HAWKE, and HOOD, at HERSIN COUPIGNY. General conditions were satisfactory - meat safe is carried by Batt: cooks and sent up at night to Batt: when in the line. Also visited NELSON Batt at BRACQUENCOURT.	
	Aug 7th		I visited BULLY GRENAY - latrines behind ADS. belonging to ? A company Howe in a bad	

Army Form C. 2118.

WAR DIARY
or
INTELLIGENCE SUMMARY.
(Erase heading not required.)

Sanitary section 63 (RN) Div.

Instructions regarding War Diaries and Intelligence Summaries are contained in F.S. Regs., Part II. and the Staff Manual respectively. Title pages will be prepared in manuscript.

Place	Date	Hour	Summary of Events and Information	Remarks and references to Appendices
BOYEFFLES	Aug 7th		Condition — not fly proof and dirty. Men visited and reported on latrines at FOSSE 10 also in huts at FOSSE 10 — condition good.	
	Aug 8		Two cases of DIPTHERIA in civil inhabitants reported from BARLIN — 1 adult and 9, 4 men killed in home in CITE no 9 — these have been infected a certain time. 3rd Field Ambulance — no latrines in the home. B/R have been put over 9 trench — the nurse doctor is in attendance. I visited 3rd F.A. during the day. Men sent to NOULETTE WOOD, BOMB SCHOOL and HERSIN, and BOUVIGNY. I visited Headquarters Signal Company near BARLIN. I instructed that no of men latrines should be made as it was two men to the earth home.	
	Aug 9th		Men engaged in local work. H.A.C. transport lines inspected. I visited motor Sergt TATE AIR NOULETTE and trenches of M. section. Saw M.O.'s of MELSON and DRAKE Battns. DRAKE Batt: latrines majority of them fly proof. MELSON Batt: still mainly incinerator type. Received memo: from A.D.S. BULLY & RENAY stating new latrines (? HOWE) had not been put right. Sent W.O. to my assistant man at BULLY.	
	Aug 10		Men to BOUVIGNY WOOD — H.A.C. inspected. I visited ABLAIN ST NAZARRE and	

T2134. Wt. W708—776. 500000. 4/15. Sir J. C. & S.

Army Form C. 2118.

WAR DIARY
or
INTELLIGENCE SUMMARY.
(Erase heading not required.)

Sauchaury Section

Place	Date	Hour	Summary of Events and Information	Remarks and references to Appendices
BOYEFFLES	Aug 10th (cont.)		Saw M.O. of 103rd Batt: Itw not yet got word for all latrines - chiefly incinerator system. Water obtained from pump in village - same as used by A.D.S. of Field Ambulance. ½ Man / section not back at FOSSE 10.	
	Aug 11th		Men went to AIX NOULETTE and SAENS en GOHELLE. I went to BERLIN and COUPIGNY. Inspected men for Scabies, inspected gas helmets. Went to BULLY GRENAY. Men had manifestation. All latrines behind A.D.S. has been filled in. Saw well ground which walk to Brigade when Given orders to our Offr. Specimen to be sent down for examination. I am of number reported to have occurred at 323 FOSSE 10. of Sam. officer of 40th Div. Visited the huts - the men have been sent to Field Ambulance. Alcm occupants (5 men Ward Vic) all well - to be kept under observation. Men in attached to 251 Tunnelling Company.	
	Aug 12th		Men to AIX NOULETTE, also men from local sauntany went to the village. 4 wrote 4th Bedfords at COUPIGNY. Camp greatly improved, all latrine inclusive have been Disinfected. Dryryol. Grease for Gas. Saw at pot of Will (hour) to be dried out on a grill. Also to be put down some lime troughs. Carpets + men sent to FOSSE 10 to Make latrines.	

Army Form C. 2118.

Sanitary Section

WAR DIARY
or
INTELLIGENCE SUMMARY.
(Erase heading not required.)

Instructions regarding War Diaries and Intelligence Summaries are contained in F. S. Regs., Part II. and the Staff Manual respectively. Title pages will be prepared in manuscript.

Place	Date	Hour	Summary of Events and Information	Remarks and references to Appendices
BOYEFFLES	Aug 13th		Men to FOSSE 10 to finish repair of latrines: also went with to BOYEFFLES. 9 visited BOUVIGNY and set two which was to pumped to BOUVIGNY WOODS. Well supplied in good condition. Visited as now A Battery 317 RFA — latrines etc good. Wet stores fair seem in use — where water east of 7th Royal Fusiliers & Trench Mortars filled; seen by field officers. The Battery to Verdrel has a 52 gall. tank — in which was stored for drinking water is chlorinated for drinking. Signal H.Q. new latrine put up as suggested. Visited HQRS & B ARMS.	
	Aug 14		Men to FOSSE 10. 9 visited with H.Q. Wagon lines 1 22½st. Bay WFA, A Pty. 316. 11th B wagon line q 31st. also HAC Quadrants Ishmaelite. In afternoon & main D'AIX — A'Ro Howe les — latrines etc good — the light lieu on duty with let men cleaning them up.	
	August		Men to NOULETTE WOOD and BOIS SCHOOL HUTS at HERSIN. I drew hay for the men from CASHIER at BARLIN. Visited BULLY GRENAY and saw M.O. & left group of Artillery. Latrines and Urinals and Waysnets good. General sanitary condition of BULLY GRENAY improving.	
	August 15		Men to AIX NOULETTE and HERSIN to inspect ANSON transport as ordered. Went through NOULETTE WOOD and told i result good. I inspected from no gate. Visited GAVION and Wrecks transport lines, also A.S.C. bins the latrine conditions	

Army Form C. 2118.

SANITARY SECTION.

WAR DIARY
or
INTELLIGENCE SUMMARY.
(Erase heading not required.)

Instructions regarding War Diaries and Intelligence Summaries are contained in F. S. Regs., Part II. and the Staff Manual respectively. Title pages will be prepared in manuscript.

Place	Date	Hour	Summary of Events and Information	Remarks and references to Appendices
BOYEFFLES.	Aug 16th (cont)		good. Also visited latrines at FOSSE 10 and SAENS and BOHELLE, and HAWKE Batt: just hitchens near the transport line. Went to BULLY GRENAY and saw M.O. HOWE Batt: Men paid.	
	Aug 17th		Pte Fernand sent to AIX NOULETTE to report to Staff Captain 189th Brigade (acting on Town Major). He is to go daily for sanitary inspection work. Then to report latrines at FOSSE 10. Sergt TATE visited several units at HERSIN + COUPIGNY, now incinerator built for WORCESTER transport lines. I visited BOUVIGNY BOYEFFLES saw HOOD working party. BOUVIGNY WOODS and saw HAC; one company of HOOD Battal, + one KEH. who are living in huts in woods, VERDREL and saw 7th Royal Fusiliers; their latrines (7th R.F.) are not yet dry properly H.Q. says that he has had men slightly cases of diarrhoea.	
	Aug 18th		Went to SAENS en BOHELLE and ABLAIN ST. NAZAIRE (NELSON Bn). Sergt TATE, who went to ABLAIN reported more increased latrines. He also visited BOUVIGNY and 3 huts of Mil. Foot Police men. I visited NOULETTE - one company of HAWKE Batt: here in dug-outs. Well in village in good condition - water case stands by it to use for all drinking water. Sanitary condition good - billets which are well kept	

Army Form C. 2118.

WAR DIARY
or
INTELLIGENCE SUMMARY.
(Erase heading not required.)

SANITARY SECTION

Place	Date	Hour	Summary of Events and Information	Remarks and references to Appendices
BOYEFFLES	Aug 18th (cont)		and emptied three times a day. M.O. of 31st Bry RFA visited me with reference to obtaining another gathering urn tent for use of wash line in-lieu of home one not on cart — I agreed as it is the advisability of obtaining same recommended this & shall apply to the RE's for one.	
	Aug 19th		Motored part up to latrines + a well in BOYEFFLES + FUSSE 10. Water drawn from pump at BOUVIGNY (opp to ROUVITNY WOOD) — test + good. Latrine made of a police type, not bad. Cleanliness and arrangements for dressings I noticed all well. Latrines and urinals in BOYEFFLES.	
	Aug 20th		3. August S/3335 discharged to 2nd Field Ambulance "? Observation Appendicitis." I visited BARLIN in morning. Saw Serj Price and men of Sanitary section. Men to HERSIN went about and BRENS in GOUELLE. I visited Howe Bns & Trenches, all are with M.O. — all French units was very clean and in good condition — Latrines &c/proof. I who now well in A.T.S., and well in littler in air — Bully GRENAY next week & Notry RE.A. (all with 1dw).	
	Aug 21st		I visited BARLIN and saw ATMs. + TATMs. re leave (vague family matters). Visited line of A.C. wk to TMS. — latrines trot, Incorporations and no attempt number	

Army Form C. 2118.

WAR DIARY
or
INTELLIGENCE SUMMARY.
(Erase heading not required.)

SANITARY SECTION

Place	Date	Hour	Summary of Events and Information	Remarks and references to Appendices
BOYEFFLES	August		to make them fly-proof. Saw new latrine in COUPIGNY - good condition - men also bathing in stream. Sump. 9 visited C.R.E. at SAENS in GOUELLE re new supplies from trench. Then went to VERDREL & NOULETTE WOOD also at work locally. Repaired the latrine at VERDREL my hot cross - letter written to F.I.O. of the R.F.A. to explain this important work.	
	Aug 22nd		Then to SAENS in GOUELLE. Re divn of Defence, BOUVIGNY at BOUVIGNY WOODS. Report as work supplies received from C.R.E. - journeyed on with additions to its report to F.A.R.M.S. 9 visited COUPIGNY. saw M.O. - R.F.A. - consultation good. saw H.P.S. MAGAZINE. Emptied new latrine also HORSE TRANSPORT incinerator and too few required. There is a refuse dump by side of road at SAENS - steps taken to have it removed by nearest unit.	
	Aug 23rd		Went from well at A.D.S. at AIX NOULETTE toilet & refuse sent to A.D.S. Went Marched from engineers for new latrine & FOSSE 10. 9 visited 10th Dublin Fusiliers at FOSSE 7 at HAISNIL. Sergt Price arranging about latrines & incinerators &c. Water Supply (1) Town (2) Well, which have been tested. 9 visited AIX NOULETTE and saw stuff & explain about sanitary matters.	

Army Form C. 2118.

WAR DIARY
or
INTELLIGENCE SUMMARY.
(Erase heading not required.)

Instructions regarding War Diaries and Intelligence Summaries are contained in F. S. Regs., Part II. and the Staff Manual respectively. Title pages will be prepared in manuscript.

Place	Date	Hour	Summary of Events and Information	Remarks and references to Appendices
BOYEFFLES	August 24		Men began routine duties of Fosse 10. Local work. I handed over Sanitary duties to Surgeon T.C. BLACKWELL RN, who is taking charge during the period that I am absent on leave. [Special leave has been granted me to proceed to England.] R.W.Knowles RN Surgeon Lieutenant (sgd) I/c Sanitary	SANITARY SECTION
"	24/8/16	12 noon	I am now the sole of the Sanitary Staff. At 9 am today I visited BARLIN ST NAZAIRE and Sanitary Sugar W.R.O. of the HAWKE Battalion. The Sanitary arrangements of the men were clear & in excellent health. I was another clean latrine pit. In the evening I visited the Sanitary Baths at BULLY GRENAY in company of the Sanitary NCO	Knowles
"	25/8/16	12 noon	I visited BARLIN and HERSIN COUPIGNY during the morning and inspected the Sanitary Staff and their latrines	

WAR DIARY
or
INTELLIGENCE SUMMARY.
(Erase heading not required.)

Army Form C. 2118.

SANITARY SECTION

Place	Date	Hour	Summary of Events and Information	Remarks and references to Appendices
BOYEFFLES	25/8/16	12 noon	I found all in order. Denied the afferer I visited the 7th ROYAL FUSILIERS at VERDREL - all appeared to be in order.	J.C.B.
"	26/8/16	6 a.m.	I visited the 4th K. BEDFORD'S at COUPIGNY and arranged with the M.O. that the manure dumps were to be lit up & stunk. In hurer fiskken over the lines. In the evening I visited FOSSE 10 and SHENS and found everything in order.	J.C.B.
"	27/8/16	10 am	During the morning I sent to AIX NOULETTE on a various errands & met the Colonel there. In the afternoon the C.O. and I went down with him to inspect the position where Dunny & C enquiry took the for preparing other BOYEFFLES with all the Sanitary Staff. Referred on to the field ambu. I found the lines in order, then went to VERDREL and inspected the billets to be taken.	J.C.B.

Army Form C. 2118.

WAR DIARY
or
INTELLIGENCE SUMMARY.
(Erase heading not required.)

SANITARY SECTION
(3RD ARMY DIVISION)

Instructions regarding War Diaries and Intelligence Summaries are contained in F. S. Regs., Part II. and the Staff Manual respectively. Title pages will be prepared in manuscript.

Place	Date	Hour	Summary of Events and Information	Remarks and references to Appendices
GOUY EN LES	28/8/16	10 am	During the morning I visited the 25th A.T. Coy & R.E. at BOUVIGNY. On 4 this men 6th Rent. sick with Rashes the skin & lice. 7 other men. Than the had chilblains. I saw the M.O. who had attended to the men. During the evening I visited NŒUX LETTE. Wood & M 4Co in dells. Men sent to BOUVIGNY and to BOUVIGNY WOOD.	
	29/8/16	10 am	Visited BOUVIGNY and inspected well. Water to be for Clerk. Then sent to AR to be a hotel. The Rev Man there has been removed. An older put on to BOUVIGNY WOOD Trench. H.P.C. running. Two tons to possibly 4 latrine pits kept. Lat left to clean the camp. Sewn man to VERREL TWB	
	30/8/16	6 am	Visited Bains to Barmin 4 men Pour 4 men spot. Clerk a 6.12n. H.P. Bacchus one lin 26th A.T. R.E. The cmcties (things) two to Cork-town The own to BOUVIGNY clear BOUVIGNY WOOD cm to JAPHS3 TWB	

Army Form C. 2118.

SANITARY SECTION
63RD (R.N.) DIVISION

WAR DIARY
or
INTELLIGENCE SUMMARY.
(Erase heading not required.)

Place	Date	Hour	Summary of Events and Information	Remarks and references to Appendices
BOVELLES	31/8/16	10 a.m.	Visited the 2C trenches - SOUCHEZ. Found the heavy rains had caused some of the deep dug-outs to fall into sumps. Saw Surgeon PARKER of the Nelson Battalion who was superintending the HOOD Battalion trenches. Re-crossed by the CRACKEN of the HOOD Battalion and visited HERSIN and COUPIGNY. Greatly improved. SAILLY-LABOURSE 10. Then went to SABLIS and POSSE for Survey work for Blot section. J.C.B.	

WAR DIARY
INTELLIGENCE SUMMARY

Army Form C. 2118.

(Erase heading not required.)

Instructions regarding War Diaries and Intelligence Summaries are contained in F. S. Regs., Part II. and the Staff Manual respectively. Title pages will be prepared in manuscript.

Place	Date	Hour	Summary of Events and Information	Remarks and references to Appendices
COREFFES	31/2/17	6 am	Appendix	
			Marine Rocket Police Returns	
			4t Sanitary Squadron	
			From 2nd Platp. 4 14 · 14 I.P.	
			" 3rd " 4	
			" 11th " 7	
			" 12th " 3	
			Total Rations 18	
			Sanitary Staff 14 By arrangement with I.P.M.	
				In force known on
			Grand Total 32	1 Platoon per...

Volume N° 4

Sanitary Section,
63rd (R.N.) Division
1st October 1916

War Diary
of
Sanitary Section

from
1st September 1916
to
30th September 1916

COMMITTEE FOR THE
MEDICAL HISTORY OF THE WAR
Date 30 OCT. 1916

R.M.Knowles.
Surgeon R.N. &
O.C. Sanitary Section

Army Form C. 2118.

WAR DIARY
or
INTELLIGENCE SUMMARY.
(Erase heading not required.)

Sanitary Section 63rd (R.N.D)

Place	Date	Hour	Summary of Events and Information	Remarks and references to Appendices
BOUVIGNY	1/9/16	11 a.m.	Visited the sanitary staff at BERLIN - HERSIN - COUPIGNY - FOSSE 10 and BULLY. Men were inspected - inspection of latrine accom. L.G. Kennels and gun teams. Visited MDS of 6th Bde. Seen sick at HERSIN & NAPHIRE. T.W.B.	
"	2/9/16	11 a.m.	Visited the off. Pers. C.R.O. and W. Lt. 190 Brigade. I have to the R.F.R.'s and Divl Pion. to M.O.'s & Lt. 1st Rifle Bde R.M.C. 7th R.F. and 13th K.R.R. Nearly an the corps an fly Rood. The 2nd and Rifle Cup. Pass a case Paris CHRONIC Lar bone the off. Commd. Men sent to SIENS - BUBBLE BOUVIGNY and BOUVIGNY Troops - VERDREL. T.W.B.	
"	3/9/16	5 p.m.	Visited the HQ Reliefs at Camigny. Mr Sar. Officer (Rumps) a good lunch - also visited the 2/8 A.T. R.E. Then saw six cases in civil lunch. The and 6 CHLONNE	
			h left Roemper et troth he te level Hammers offer with to henderd. Sanitary Sean. Def. G. Sir J.C.&.S. T.W.B	

Army Form C. 2118.

WAR DIARY
or
INTELLIGENCE SUMMARY.
(Erase heading not required.)

Souchez Sector

Place	Date	Hour	Summary of Events and Information	Remarks and references to Appendices
BOYEFFLES	4/6/16		Local work in BOYEFFLES by men of section – cement cracks filled, cleaned up. Report received from Survey Coy of nuisance near A.D.S. PONT BRENAY. Sgt Tate visited it in afternoon and found open latrines in bad condition used by general staff. Is being rectified. He also went up by motor to CALONNE. I visited BARLIN drew money and paid men of section. Visited A.D.Ms. and D.A.D.M.S. I visited Fosse 10, BULLY GRENAY and AIX NOULETTE.	RWC
	5/6		Men sent to SAENS in POHELLE. Work from CALONNE. Leaves given made for wells in BARLIN. I visited HERSIN-COUPIGNY and inspected transport lines of 16th D. WORCESTERS, and 2nd R.M. Batt. Motor Machine Gun section and wagon lines of Battery of 122nd RFA (they returned from BOYEFFLES). On afternoon I went to BULLY GRENAY. Garrison of B. Letts had been repaired. Visited A.D.S. Pont GRENAY a company of WORCESTERS – new latrines under construction, and 120 Machine gun corps. Men visit BOUVIGNY and WOODS. 1st K.R.R., K.E.H, and company of 10th Durham.	RWC RWC
	6/6		Manlette and also visited. I visited Verdrel 13/17 Fusiliers, 5 Men's Jouelle, reg: eighteen fires and left seven of trenches CALONNE. Was from well in Artillery H.Q. or AIX NOULETTE to G.A.	RWC

Army Form C. 2118.

Instructions regarding War Diaries and Intelligence
Summaries are contained in F.S. Regs., Part II.
and the Staff Manual respectively. Title pages
will be prepared in manuscript.

WAR DIARY
or
INTELLIGENCE SUMMARY.
(Erase heading not required.)

Lourdiay Battn

Place	Date	Hour	Summary of Events and Information	Remarks and references to Appendices
BOYEFFLES	7/9/16		Pk Fennel off duty - one four months notice now to Aix NOULETTE in his place.	
			Pk Flinders went to FOSSE 10 in new Latrine - was drawn for Engineer duty and work situated. Local work in drainage at back of billet. Transport base?	
			10th A Fuid inspected. 3 visited areas of sanitary section in BARLIN + HERSIN COURT & NY, also HAWKE transport, W H.Q. maps line of 188th Brigade. 3 visited DANGE Rat. at ABLAIN SY NAZAIRE. Sanitate render SAENS a TOWELL a public latrine - PANS	
			Two men utilizing in new latrine. Pk MOSS 5/4024 withdrawn from HERSIN	
	8/9/16		Pk JACKSON 9/4013 sent to Aix his place. MOSS (asst.) Lewis Sniper (instructor P.K.) and went up to BULLY & RENAY to the dummy 9 Sanitation.	
			Pt Fennel to Aix NOULETTE Lost unit in BOYEFFLES. 3 went up right section 9 line to HAWKE Bat. in afternoon, inspected then latrine also	

WAR DIARY
or
INTELLIGENCE SUMMARY

Army Form C. 2118.

Sanitary Section

Place	Date	Hour	Summary of Events and Information	Remarks and references to Appendices
AVESNES	9/9/16		by 10th Dublin Fus. for a day or two and before that the area was not under our control. None of the dugouts I inspected had been there for weeks.	
	10/9/16		I visited SAENS-en-GOHELLE and inspected Butler 317th Brig. R.F.A. also transport lines of the same Field Companies & Engineers. Public latrine in a bad state and arrangements made to have it cleared. Notice sent for burning [?] up a latrine well in yard of 1 Battery 217th. In afternoon I went to BARLIN and saw ASST. D.A.D.M.S. of Mines received "Supplementary return for sanitary work."	Bush
	11/9/16		Local work by section in BOYEFFLES — further latrines bored with section in SAENS-en-GOHELLE. further latrine had been cleaned. In afternoon went with ASST.D.D.M.S. IVth Corps to IVth Corps H.Q at REBREUVE. Conference with D.D.M.S. IVth Corps of sanitary apts etc.	
	12/9/16		I visited CALONNE with ST.D.D.M.S. & work myth Jelly
			(1) From Form 11
			(2) From Lt. Barker (RESERVE)
				There are about 685 lap tents which we left full, and also are	
			burying 11,000 gallons reservoir Latrine satisfactory I visited Latrine of gains of Pint Group, not satisfactory. I visited Latrine at FOSSE 10	Reserve
			(Scarpe) – in good condition	Reserve

Army Form C. 2118.

Sanitary Section

WAR DIARY
or
INTELLIGENCE SUMMARY.
(Erase heading not required.)

Place	Date	Hour	Summary of Events and Information	Remarks and references to Appendices
BOUFFLERS	13/9/16		Major visited BUNVIGNY and BOUVIGNY WOODS. 3 units in NOULETTE and saw Hutons of R.F.A. (223rd) Brigade, R.F.A. (1st group), 179th Machine Gun Company, Trench Mortar group, 1 Company 4th Berkshires, 1 Company Hood Batt. (1) There was a French latrine very close to an officers cook house, arrangements were made for having it removed to some distance away (It was not a permanent structure). (2) Notice to be put up as well in Artillery H.Q. (R.F.A.). (3) New officers latrine & latrine sent up to send at Bour Grenay. Machine Gunners at Trace 10.	RWK
"	14/9/16		Sgt. Tate visited BULLY GRENAY. In evening 3 visited NOULETTE WOODS and inspected HAWKE Battalion. 3 visited BULLY GRENAY at request of M.O. 1 HAC. United Visiting one of the Battalions and made a visit to staff Capt. 190th Brigade with reference to the making of some permanent Sanitary arrangements for the area. Saw H.O's of 317th and 223rd Brigade R.F.A. Major visited Saens - aux - GOUELLE.	RWK RWK

T2134. Wt. W708—776. 500000. 4/15. Sir J. C. & S.

Army Form C. 2118.

SANITARY SECTION

WAR DIARY
or
INTELLIGENCE SUMMARY.
(Erase heading not required.)

Place	Date	Hour	Summary of Events and Information	Remarks and references to Appendices
BOYEFFLES	15/9/16		Went out to VERDREL, Sgt TATE to ARLAIN-sy-NAZAIRE. I went to COUPIGNY and saw Head Quarters, NELSON Transport, 223rd Brigade (C Battery). Also No 3 Temp. Dis. Train (37th Div.) and 3rd FIELD AMBULANCE Orderlies no of men. Inspected men at BARLIN & latrines etc.	
	16/9/16		I visited HERSIN-COUPIGNY — with reference to reports from Empersed Plant. Sgt Tate visited N°. [?] section as unit supplies. Latrines sent to FOSSE 10.	rept.
	17/9/16		Col F Lamville RAMC. 37th Div. Came in to see me with reference to taking on my area. Medical Unit Officer ordered/reviewed Coy "A" "Coy J". The Sanitary Section will be relieved by the Sanitary Section of the 37th Division on the morning of the 19th. Rec'd. Details of relief should be arranged by the O/C. 3 units concerned. On a/c from 3 went to BULLY GRENAY. Latrines sent up to Bully that night.	rept.
	18/9/16		I went to Bruay with Sgt Tate to see O.C. 34th Div Sanitary Section as arranging relief. Motor Lorry with stores and men sent on	rept.

T2134. Wt. W708—776. 500000. 4/15. Sir J. C. & S.

Army Form C. 2118.

SANITARY SECTION

WAR DIARY
or
INTELLIGENCE SUMMARY.
(Erase heading not required.)

Instructions regarding War Diaries and Intelligence Summaries are contained in F. S. Regs., Part II. and the Staff Manual respectively. Title pages will be prepared in manuscript.

Place	Date	Hour	Summary of Events and Information	Remarks and references to Appendices
BOYEFFLES.	17/9/16 (cont.)		to BRUAY. Men recalled from BULLY TRENAY. The "Temporary Major" men also came from BULLY and in attached temporally to SANITARY SECTION. Remainder of photos after packed ready for completion of run in following day. YMR.	
BOYEFFLES to BRUAY	18/9/16		Men for FOSSE 10 again at BOYEFFLES Lorry with remainder of etc. move to BRUAY. Men move via HERSIN and BARLIN — picking up men of San Sect. en route and same BRUAY 1 P.M. 3 on section of 24 Division arrived afternoon. I went on to BARLIN for orders. Received instructions to fix men up in BRUAY for the night. Got lorriskers of 24 th Div. San Sect. men put up in their quarters.	
BRUAY.	20/9/16		I went to enquire of O.C. Sanitary Sections at Lillers — D.M.S. 1st Army. Men billeted with 3rd Field Ambulance for the night. I went to OURTON and arranged of billets for San Sect — and made arrangement to move in in following morning. A.D.M.S. at [Labeur] at OURTON. RMT.	
BRUAY	21/9/16		Sanitary Sect. moved to OURTON in morning — men employed by	

Army Form C. 2118.

WAR DIARY
or
INTELLIGENCE SUMMARY.
(Erase heading not required.)

SANITARY SECTION.

Place	Date	Hour	Summary of Events and Information	Remarks and references to Appendices
OURTON	21/9/16 (cont)		Mid-day. Stores unloaded and sanitary arrangements made for Sanitary Section. No office could be obtained - temporary one made in stables.	
OURTON	22.9.16		Local sanitary work - Latrine hut for Gen. HdQr. War Section. Erection of Officers, Signal Officers and Military Foot Police. Two incinerators built also two urinals. Main sent up to G.H.Q. and DIEVAL (Dinner Batt. and 1st Q.M. Batt.) Visited La Comté (1 Kone), MAINICOURT (NELSON), La THIEULOYE (Worcester Pioneers B.W.) Also saw M.O. of DRAKE Batt. (FREVILLERS) re water etc. etc. Received orders to go to La Grange to inspect Sanitary Work Shop of 61st Division. Drew money and hayer men of Section. Ford Ambulance on man attached for my use/men. Local work in village of OURTON. Men to DIEVAL on BEUVIN (2 a.m. pm). I went to La TORTUE - saw very large and interesting workshop run by Sanitary Section of 61st Division.	
OURTON	23.9.16			
OURTON	24/9/16		Church Parade in morning. Local work. Kit inspection in afternoon. Pte Johnson J.W. M2/12197 A.S.C.(M.T.) - one of attached drivers - sent to 3rd Field Ambulance at BRUAY - diagnosis R.U.O. Ford car sent to pick up my mud artillery man on La COMTÉ road.	

Army Form C. 2118.

WAR DIARY
or
INTELLIGENCE SUMMARY.
(Erase heading not required.)

SANITARY SECTION.

Instructions regarding War Diaries and Intelligence Summaries are contained in F. S. Regs., Part II. and the Staff Manual respectively. Title pages will be prepared in manuscript.

Place	Date	Hour	Summary of Events and Information	Remarks and references to Appendices
OURTON	25/9/16		Pte Ferrand sent to make reports on urine cats at LA COMTÉ, LATHIEULOYE, MAGNICOURT, ROCOURT, & DIEVAL.	
			Lieut MOSS to FREVILLERS (DRAKE BN. & 1 CANAD. BDE.)	
			Pte LEES goes daily to B.H.Q. Corpl. ATKINSON & ten men daily to DIEVAL.	
			Some local improvements in village of OURTON.	
			I visited OLLENCOURT (4th Bedfords), BAILLEUL-AUX-CORNAILLES (7th R. Fusiliers), OSTREVILLE (10th R. Fusiliers) and MARQUAY (1/1 H.A.C.). Also HANGE BATHS at LATHIEULOYE.	RWF
26/9/16			Men sent to SALONNE RICOUART (39th Brig R.F.A.) and La COMTÉ (223rd Bais, R.F.A.) also to examine urine cats at BEUGIN and BAJUS. I went to BRUAY and purchased some extra life required for the carpenter. Local man in OURTON taking cats made by M.M.S. Vet Sect. Has to get extra for sanitary work.	
			Men and 190th Brigade to examine urine cats. I visited BRUAY and made arrangements to send extra men than temporally, local man in OURTON.	RWF
27/9/16			I saw M.O.'s of 317th Brigade, 223rd Brigade R.F.A. also No. 2 & 4 Coys. Div. Engineers, also INVALIDES, and Mobile Vetr Train, also 77th Field Ambulance.	RWF
			Men as usual to DIEVAL, etc. and OURTON.	RWF

Army Form C. 2118.

WAR DIARY
or
INTELLIGENCE SUMMARY.
(Erase heading not required.)

SANITARY SECTION.

Instructions regarding War Diaries and Intelligence Summaries are contained in F. S. Regs., Part II. and the Staff Manual respectively. Title pages will be prepared in manuscript.

Place	Date	Hour	Summary of Events and Information	Remarks and references to Appendices
OURTON	29/9/16.		Men to H.Q. for return. MEYAL and OURTON Wells out of 3rd Field Ambulance examined. Men inspected for scabies, gas helmets, dentistry &c. Parade in evening in full marching order.	
OURTON	30/9/16.		Latrines and grease traps sent to D.H.Q. Routine inspection carried out by Men, (and local work). 2 men to MAISNIL and La THIEULOYE (LOWE Batch). 9 visited 2nd Field Ambulance at MAISNIL-SU-BOIS, Incinerators and sanitary arrangements inspected.	

Oct 1st 1916

R.F.K[...] R.N.
Sanitary Section
O/C

"Confidential"

V696

Sanitary Section.
63rd (R.N) Division
November 1st/1916.

War Diary
of
Sanitary Section
63rd (R.N.) Division

From October 1st to 31st 1916.

R.M. Knowles.
Temp. Surgeon R.N.
O/C SANITARY SECTION, ROYAL NAVAL DIVISION.
No. 4
Date 1/11/16

To D.H.Q.
63rd (R.N) Division
Despatched Nov. 1st/1916.

Army Form C. 2118.

SANITARY SECTION, ROYAL NAVAL DIVISION.

WAR DIARY
or
INTELLIGENCE SUMMARY.
(Erase heading not required.)

Instructions regarding War Diaries and Intelligence Summaries are contained in F. S. Regs., Part II. and the Staff Manual respectively. Title pages will be prepared in manuscript.

Place	Date	Hour	Summary of Events and Information	Remarks and references to Appendices
OURTON.	Oct 1st		Church parade in morning. Order received to discharge men unfit to march 6 to 8 miles to nearest Field Ambulance.	Orders
"	Oct 2nd		Two "temporary unfit men" who had been attached to Sanitary Section were discharged to 3rd Field Ambulance. Operation order No 5 received. "Sanitary Section will travel with Lorry and all its personnel by march route. O.C. Sanitary Section accompanying." Wagon packed ready to move off.	Order No 132.
	Oct 3rd		Further instructions received "Sanitary Lorry is to proceed to CANETTE MONT to the O.C. Sanitary Section to consult with O.C. Supply Column at that time to leave OURTON and ante to follow, in ask not to interfere with her traffic. Or is probable but not certain that the Sanitary personnel will travel on Wednesday by train. Later information will be sent when received." Lorry left OURTON at 5.30.a.m. with 2 drivers, and three men and an extra groom and horse, and two men & leaders also left by rail - attached to '8' Coldm for march. Remaining personnel fell in Division Square ready etc. etc., starting by to move early next morning. Orders received to be at entraining station LIZZY-St-FOCHEL by noon next day.	Nil

T2134. Wt. W708—776. 500000. 4/15. Sir J. C. & S.

Army Form C. 2118.

SANITARY SECTION, ROYAL NAVAL DIVISION

WAR DIARY
or
~~INTELLIGENCE SUMMARY.~~
(Erase heading not required.)

Instructions regarding War Diaries and Intelligence Summaries are contained in F. S. Regs., Part II. and the Staff Manual respectively. Title pages will be prepared in manuscript.

Place	Date	Hour	Summary of Events and Information	Remarks and references to Appendices
OURTON	Oct 3rd		to join up with 3rd Field Ambulance entraining in Train "A" Series 3.	
OURTON	Oct 4th		Men marched from OURTON at 7.45 A.M. via LA COMTÉ & MAIZICOURT - joining up with 3rd Field Ambulance en route. Arrived LIGNY-tr-FOUWEL at 11 A.M. Did not entrain until 9.30 P.M. - train left at 10.30 P.M. arrived at ACHEUX at 7.30 A.M. next day	R.V.K
	Oct 5th		Marched from ACHEUX to FORCEVILLE - to Company Billet. Long was the arrival. Also two men and bicycles. Horse and man arrived late in the day. Some of the stores unpacked - latrines etc. fixed up. Received orders to send 1 N.C.O. and 1 Man to 1st Bn.R.M. Headquarters, also 1 N.C.O. and 4 men to take over Divisional Baths. Pte Leer S/4161 discharged to 1st Field Amb.	
FORCEVILLE			Ambulance suffering from burned Wrist (left eng.) Sergt Price and 1 man went to 1st Bn.R.M. Headquarters } Sanitary Work L.Cpl Ladd and 1 man " " " " " Our Headquarters } Corpl Platt and 4 men. " " ACHEUX to take over Baths -	R.V.K.
	Oct 6th		I visited LEALVILLERS and saw A.D.M.S. and new A.D.M.S. + D.A.D.M.S. - also drew money to pay men. Sanitary Section marched to mens mobile killer - men for stores, Officers.	

WAR DIARY
or
INTELLIGENCE SUMMARY.
(Erase heading not required.)

Army Form C. 2118.

SANITARY SECTION, ROYAL NAVAL DIVISION.

Place	Date	Hour	Summary of Events and Information	Remarks and references to Appendices
FORCEVILLE	Oct 6th		Carpenters ships and men billets. Father Long Chaplain arrived.	
FORCEVILLE	Oct 7th		Signals received re infection cases — (1) Scarlet Fever in 1/1 H.A.C. at VARENNES. (2) Diptheria in No 26 Coy. German Prisoners camp near VARENNES. I visited H.A.C. and prisoners camp during the morning and found that all necessary precautions had been taken. Work of clearing up billets, latrines etc. Lance Corporal Moss supervised local sanitary work in village of FORCEVILLE. Fell on return.	RNR
FORCEVILLE	Oct 8th		I proceeded in direction of excreta commencing behind billets. I visited Hedauville and saw Town Major. 2 men went to HEDAUVILLE on inspection work. Serjt Tate paid visits locally in FORCEVILLE. Men paid.	RNR
	Oct 9th		I visited D.A.D.M.S, in office at ACHEUX. 2 men to HEDAUVILLE, 2 men on local work at FORCEVILLE. I visited 1st Q.M. Ward at VARENNES, c/o of Ambulance — also visited W Field Ambulance and 3rd Field Ambulance. Visited Men at Divisional Baths at ACHEUX.	RNR
"	Oct 10th		Saw Sanitary Officer of Rl Division at his headquarters was in an area	RNR

T2134. Wt. W708—776. 500000. 4/15. Sir J. C. & S.

Army Form C. 2118.

SANITARY SECTION,
ROYAL NAVAL
DIVISION.

WAR DIARY
or
INTELLIGENCE SUMMARY.
(Erase heading not required.)

Place	Date	Hour	Summary of Events and Information	Remarks and references to Appendices
FORCEVILLE	Oct 10		and arranged with him as to who should look after HEDAUVILLE.	
	Oct 11		1 Man sent out inspecting materials. Local inspection from those went from R.E. dump, men LEAUVILLERS - VAREVNES went round village of FORCEVILLE; also visited HEDAUVILLE and arranged with Staff-Captain to send me two men to be attached to 155th Brigade for Sanitary duties, also new Tran Major of new A.D.M.S. and what for a week's) my men to be returned to me from the batts. Went on to inspect billets occupied by ANSON Batt. or regiment of M.O. - found it undesirable for men to live in and suggested that Tran Major should be apprised on the matter. Motor Lorry lent to pick Field Ambulance to get medical stores. RNDK	
"	Oct 12		Men sent to HEDAUVILLE & VARENNES. One man sent out inspecting materials. Also visited MAILLY + ENGLEBELMER; saw Brig/Captain of 190th Brigade and arranged to send men (two) to be attached to Brigade; also visited NELSON and DRAKE Batts. Two men returned from duty at the baths at ACHEUX.	
"	Oct 13		Working party invited by Tran Major for cleaning up FORCEVILLE and visited the HAWKE + HOOD Batts. and arranged to have visitors visits.	

Army Form C. 2118.

WAR DIARY
or
INTELLIGENCE SUMMARY.
SANITARY SECTION
(Erase heading not required.)

Place	Date	Hour	Summary of Events and Information	Remarks and references to Appendices
FORCEVILLE	Oct 13th (cont)		Dr having erected 1000 lin, sent to send working party to Itture Bat. Men working locally. Several urinals repaired.	
	Oct 14th		Lt-Col had returned from A.D.S. Lt-Col Hen made Acting Corporal and sent with Pte Jackson to 190th Bde H.Q. & Sanitary Section. Visited A.D.S. at MAILLY also 4th Bedfordshires & 1st Brighton. Latrine tip made and sent down to HAWRE Officers. Pu Fielder superintending building of Latrines. Latrines tips also made for Officers Mess R.A.M.C., A Coy & 317th Bde R.F.A. The Sanitary round wells in Artillery area in bad repair - Inspector sent to Town Major and the R.E's were put on and repair has been effected. Runt in afternoon at [illegible]	Rupt
	Oct 15th		HEDAUVILLE and VARENNES inspected. Men have bitten [illegible] at ACHEUX.	Rupt
	Oct 16th		Lt-Corpl Hen made acting Corpl: sent with Pte Hunt to 158th Brigade H.Q. for Sanitary duties. Visited 139th Bde. H.Q. with reference to sending men of Sanitary Section to work with Brigade. H/Sh Long lent to 1st F.A. to force Medical attendance.	Rupt
	Oct 17th		Corpl Alderson who had returned from leave on previous day - now with Pte Greenwood to 159th Brigade H.Q. & visited A.D.S. at MESNIL on	

Army Form C. 2118.

WAR DIARY
or
INTELLIGENCE SUMMARY.
(Erase heading not required.)

Instructions regarding War Diaries and Intelligence Summaries are contained in F. S. Regs., Part II and the Staff Manual respectively. Title pages will be prepared in manuscript.

SANITARY SECTION

Place	Date	Hour	Summary of Events and Information	Remarks and references to Appendices
FORCEVILLE	Oct 17th		went up the line to leave park. On return to FORCEVILLE found orders to move to VERANNES. Long packed and arrived en route to VERANNES.	
VERANNES	Oct 18th		An return for office in Mayor at VERANNES. I went to HEDAUVILLE and saw SANITARY OFFICER of 51st Division who arranged to take over his messes billets and office. Long and me moved over to	RWK
HEDAUVILLE	Oct 19th		HEDAUVILLE. Mills Long sent to A.D.M.S. Local inspection. Clean up their mess billets and fix up horses lines – sanitary arrangements. Orders received for Long to be fitted up to the returns which wounded cases in event of active operations.	RWK RWK
"	Oct 20th		Long sent to 2nd/2nd Field Ambulance at ACHEUX to draw Medical Stores. Ford car returned to 2nd Field Ambulance. Sacriancula is C.O's camp being recommended to their it mild incinerate FECES. I inspected 2nd R.H. camp with M.O. in reference to the large number of cases of P.U.O. their have been occurring in the unit. The conditions in the camp were good and their was no obvious thing the occupants of a particular strain of militia troops and from have been shown to 3 Ford	
"	Oct 21st			

Army Form C. 2118.

SANITARY SECTION

WAR DIARY
or
INTELLIGENCE SUMMARY
(Erase heading not required.)

Instructions regarding War Diaries and Intelligence Summaries are contained in F. S. Regs., Part II. and the Staff Manual respectively. Title pages will be prepared in manuscript.

Place	Date	Hour	Summary of Events and Information	Remarks and references to Appendices
HEDAUVILLE	Oct 21		Ambulance to Mesnil Station. In the event of active operations 2 auxy men assist at the station. Lorry has been fitted with removable seats. Inspected the collecting station and also one the pits by which nothing could come to the camp. Drew money and paid men.	
	Oct 22		Lorry lent to 3/1 F.A. Men on local work, and supervision carried and burial of dead horse.	
	Oct 23		Incinerator in Sgts camp finished. Queen stop. Urinals made also latrine buckets for collecting station. Sized up 9 m????d works bad at P.24.C.2.9. and made arrangements to hand over cleaned out, with M.&O. in charge of pumping station. Routine inspection work etc.	
	Oct 24 Oct 25		Pte Fletcher sent up to Divisional Collecting Station; also wood, 52 gall tank etc Pte Plevin sent to R.E.s at ACHEUX to where Englund Platt who is to proceed to ENGLAND on 10 days leave. Routine work. Englund Platt on leave. Routine work.	
	Oct 26		Received instructions to open tank at P.24.C.2.9. cleaned out. Party went up	

Army Form C. 2118.

WAR DIARY
or
INTELLIGENCE SUMMARY
(Erase heading not required.)

SANITARY SECTION.

Instructions regarding War Diaries and Intelligence Summaries are contained in F. S. Regs., Part II. and the Staff Manual respectively. Title pages will be prepared in manuscript.

Place	Date	Hour	Summary of Events and Information	Remarks and references to Appendices
October 28th HEDAUVILLE	Oct 28th		and work completed in afternoon. I visited O.A.C. at FOREEVILLE, sanitation satisfactory. I also visited General Collecting Station.	Risk
	Oct 29th		Case of MUMPS reported by M.O. 1st R.M. I visited the hut in the afternoon and made arrangement to have it fur out of bounds and disinfected by men of Sanitary Section. Local work — HEDAUVILLE.	
	Oct 30th		I visited Royal Nav in VARENNES - everything satisfactory. Also visited Field Ambulance. Rubin inspection made by Sanitary Section.	Rept
	Oct 29th Oct 30th		I visited camps recently vacated by 7th Royal Fusiliers and 10th Dublins near Invernain Arden in camp reused by Dublins HQD Group 2, an HAWKE Coys into HEDAUVILLE.	
	Oct 31st		I visited MESNIL and huddo nets ATT,MS. Incinerator in camp founded. Park arranged for, to clean up round camps in the morning. I also noted the sanitary arrangement in the billets — arrangements made to use main hut between Aven ann hut from Sanitary Collecting Station. P.G. Fletcher	RMMcnab.

SANITARY SECTION,
ROYAL NAVAL DIVISION.

"Confidential"

140/262
Vol 7

> COMMITTEE FOR THE
> MEDICAL HISTORY OF THE WAR
> Date 3 JAN 1917

Sanitary Section
63rd (RN) Division
December 1st/1916

War Diary
of
Sanitary Section
63rd (RN) Division
From 1st November to 30th November 1916

o/o A.D.M.S.
63rd (R.N.) Division

R.H. Vramols
Surg. R.N. O.C.
Sanitary Section
63rd (RN) Division

Despatched Dec 1st/16.

WAR DIARY or INTELLIGENCE SUMMARY

Army Form C. 2118.

SANITARY SECTION
63rd (R.N) DIVISION

Place	Date	Hour	Summary of Events and Information	Remarks and references to Appendices
HEDAUVILLE	Mar. 1st		Party obtained from Labour Company to clean up & white wash HEDAUVILLE. Mule Lines sent to ENGLEBELMER to fetch lime for incinerators. I visited VARENNES and 1st R.M. Camps. Routine inspection work.	RMR
"	Mar 2nd		Brick incinerators commenced for burning of excreta. Working party again obtained for cleaning up. I visited Divnl C.O.S. also visited ENGLEBELMER. Latrines chiefly of deep pit type.	RMR
"	Mar 3rd		Work on incinerators in camp in progress, also working party cleaning up. 5 riveted iron pattern latrine seats sent up to camp at HEDAUVILLE. Engineers have built many huts in front which obstructs. Re Wells & Sanitary section short (M/F Form. 51.4) RMR
"	Mar 4th		Divisional B[att]s started at HEDAUVILLE. Report received from A.D.M.S. stating there is to be a Sanitary Advisor to Town Majors at HEDAUVILLE & AUX TOUR. Major with reference to the Latrine Lines at Billets in HEDAUVILLE was away with Town Majors. 4 new latrines made at ENGLEBELMER.	SMR
"	Mar 5th		Temporary Baths and drying room erected in ENGLEBELMER by 188th Brigade. I visited MESNIL (7th Royal Fusiliers) and also HAMEL (11th H.A.C.) Muda

WAR DIARY or INTELLIGENCE SUMMARY

Army Form C. 2118.

SANITARY SECTION

Place	Date	Hour	Summary of Events and Information	Remarks and references to Appendices
HERISSART	Mar 5		Arrangements to send Latrine buckets up to a.t. Inspected with S.A.D.M.S. "R.B" men at ENGLEBELMER.	
	Mar 6		Inspected "R.B" men at VARENNES and PUCHEVILLERS with S.A.D.M.S. Visited Nissen Butts at VARENNES & HERNE of PUCHEVILLERS. Also erected camp and butts at PUCHEVILLERS.	RWR
	Mar 7		Pte Webb promoted acting (unpaid) Lance Corporal – in charge of HERISSART butts. Visited butts at ACHEUX. Latrine buckets sent up to MESNIL & HAMEL. Drew Money and Paid Men.	RWR
	Mar 8		Men in hospital until O/C Divisional Laundry this day a week. Unused S.A.P. camp fixed up. Found Latrine repairs wanted by carpenter. Visited huts with D.A.D.Q.M.G. Sent in report to Fus. Commandant as to repair of ten wells, h. villages. 3 visited ENGLEBELMER with S.A.D.M.S. and new Bridge Butts.	RWR
	Mar 9		Local work in HERISSART. Visited MESNIL & Q 21D ref mts for public latrines as arranged with R.E. to have public Latrines at Q 25 c 6.9, Q 25 c 4.9 and N.7 & SB.R.D.F.E DUMP. Saw M.O. 1st WORC	RWR

Army Form C. 2118.

WAR DIARY
or
INTELLIGENCE SUMMARY.
(Erase heading not required.)

SANITARY SECTION.

Place	Date	Hour	Summary of Events and Information	Remarks and references to Appendices
HEDAUVILLE	Nov 9th		Battalion in MESNIL.	
	Nov 10th		I visited ENTLEBEHER as inspected No 1, No 2, & No 3 Companies Engineers. Reported on Sanitary Condition of No 1 Company as inspected by H.Q. 10th D.S.E. (satisfactory). Saw M.O. Above Battalion. Visited Guide Camp and Sanitary & Washing station. Arranged to send Sgt tin & parts of Dunn Offices to inspect Latrine screen urine carts, also with Tait at Q 24 c 2.5. Latrine Inspection in W. Stafford (Pioneer Batt) which he can into camp at HEDAUVILLE. Enquired about return from ENGLISH leave.	
	Nov 11th		I visited local sanitary arrangements with Staff Sergt Tate. Washing point for Salvay Company found to be unsatisfactory. Return Guide over to Sanitary Officer 4. Northstafford (Pioneer Batt) and went round camp and with M.O.	
	Nov 12th		I went up to Amiens Collecting Station (3rd Field Ambulance); remained in Section with the exception of men left behind to look after stores here + office: - attaching by to proceed to Amiens collecting – and annex Field Ambulance. Pte Rumford I S/2335 proceeded on English leave (10 days) xxxxx	

2333. Wt. W2344/7454 700,000 5/15 D.D.&L.   A.D.S.S./Forms/C. 2118.

WAR DIARY
or
INTELLIGENCE SUMMARY.
(Erase heading not required.)

Army Form C. 2118.

SANITARY SECTION

Place	Date	Hour	Summary of Events and Information	Remarks and references to Appendices
HEDAUVILLE	Nov 13th		Remainder of section (ten men detailed to remain behind at HEDAUVILLE) proceeded to EMARTIN SEARCH @ 31.b.7.7. at 6 A.M.	
	" 14		M/M Long-litter with next convoy. "walking wounded" cases.	
	" 15		Active Operations in progress. Section arrived 3/Full Ambulance.	
	Nov 16th		M/M Lorry carrying "walking wounded" were attacked. 1 of 159th, 189th & 190th Brigades returned and men who were attached. Section returned to Wilcre at HEDAUVILLE from morning action.	
			E/Martin search.	
	Nov 17th		Section moved with men from HEDAUVILLE at 1 P.M. Arrived SARTON at 3.15 P.M. Billets arranged for the night.	
SARTON	Nov 18th		Left SARTON at 10 A.M. arrived DOULLENS and billets than for the night.	
DOULLENS	Nov 19th		Left DOULLENS and arrived YVRENCH in the evening. Billets fixed up.	
YVRENCH	Nov 20th		Latrines made for section + Urinal. gnomometer erected. Cpl. Bishop in Lorry.	
"	Nov 21st		Incinerator completed. Officers latrine made. Inspection.	

Army Form C. 2118.

WAR DIARY
or
INTELLIGENCE SUMMARY.
(Erase heading not required.)

SANITARY SECTION

Place	Date	Hour	Summary of Events and Information	Remarks and references to Appendices
YVRENCH	Nov. 22nd		Local inspection work	Pmt
RUE	Mar 23rd		Left YVRENCH for RUE – arrived 3 o'clock P.M. Men billeted and offices arranged.	Pmt
"	Mar 24th		Men wkr changed to kilter position – Stean urinals and other Latrine Wkr. Latrines & Urinals made. Local inspection work.	Pmt
"	Mar 25th		9 visited Signal Survey &c. Latrine Bucket inducted for. 9 visited with WORCESTER M.O. all billets of his battalion and arranged provisional alt. to public Latrines. Repair men in to ADMS. Empl. Lad & Men engaged in making map of village.	Pmt
"	Mar 26th		Rue inspection – Latrine inspection. Sgt Price in local inspection work. 9 visited 15 gt Brig. H.Q. and arranged to send men for Sanitary work. Also saw M.O. Oxon Batt.M. Latrine for RAMLI Pan made.	Pmt
"	Mar 27th		9 visited 155th B.H.Q. and arranged to send men for Sanitary duties. Received note from H.Q. Horse Batt; asking for a man to keep builts incinerator. Pte Ruhys S/3335 returned from English leave. Gas Respirators Pmt.	

2353 Wt. W2544/1454 700,000 5/15 D.D.&L. A.D.S.S./Forms/C. 2118.

Army Form C. 2118.

WAR DIARY
or
INTELLIGENCE SUMMARY.
(Erase heading not required.)

SANITARY SECTION

Place	Date	Hour	Summary of Events and Information	Remarks and references to Appendices
RUE	Nov 27th (cont) Nov 28th		No materials for latrines or urinals have arrived yet. I visited 190th Bgd H.Q. + arranged to send men to instruct men. Visited H.A.C. and went round men of the Hawke billets. Gave good men daily to collect refuse from billets. Pte Fielder sent to L. Entry. I visited Le Rutoy as saw H.O. [Howe]. Cpl Lord & Pte Hewitt sent to H.Q 188th Brig for duty.	
	Nov 29th		Cpl Wm. L. Cuff, 13th + Pte Jackson to 190th Brigade. I visited Hawke Batt: Nelson Batt. + 2nd F.A. Arranged with WORCESTER Officer i/c on to alts & latrines in RUE. Local inspection	
	Nov 30th		Visited G Company Anson Batt who Howe Batt: Arranging for fatigue party for Worcesters in the afternoon.	

R J A Crombie
Temp Surg R.N.
S/C

SANITARY SECTION,
ROYAL NAVAL DIVISION.
No. ......
Date 1/12/16

"Confidential"

Sanitary Section,
63rd (R.N) Division,
January 1st/1917.

War Diary
of
Sanitary Section
63rd (R.N) Division
From December 1st to 31st/1916.

COMMITTEE FOR THE MEDICAL HISTORY OF THE WAR
Date 31 JAN 1917

R.W.N.Mawle
Temp. Surg. R.N.
O.C. Sanitary Section
63rd (R.N) Division

O/o A.D.M.S.
63rd (R.N) Divn.
1.1.17.

WAR DIARY or INTELLIGENCE SUMMARY.

Army Form C. 2118.

SANITARY SECTION

Place	Date	Hour	Summary of Events and Information	Remarks and references to Appendices
RUE.	Dec 1st		Routine Inspection. Our present sanitary improvements are being held up owing to lack of material.	RUE
"	Dec 2nd		M/Cr Lorry sent to ROMAINE to draw wood etc. Smiths NUNNON rej. some reported cases of measles amongst the civilians. Saw M.O. of 4th Rifle Bgd. in regard to the matter. Inspected unit cooks and traced it to its source - (from a stream). In afternoon J marked WINKLE and 1st RFA.	
			J marked ARRY (ANSON Bn. HQ - Suffk Rgt).	RUE
	Dec 3rd		J marked 1st + 2d R.M. Bns. and saw their sanitary arrangements with the M.O.s of the units, also attended + Weds occupied by these units. Saw Town Major of PONTHOLE. Enfield Platt + 2.O.R. rejoined section from	RUE
			View We of ACHEUX	
	Dec 4th		J marked NOYELLES - Routled + 10th RDF. - saw Town Major. 3/FA, 1/40th	RUE
	Dec 5th		Madame Gr. Roy or NULETTE, who accuses one of them, with curls, Nanny known as Meer fail. Visited locally to RUE in morning,	RUE
			HAWKE letter in afternoon.	
	Dec 6th		J marked BONELLE saw 31st + 293 RFA also TAC. Routine inspection	

Army Form C. 2118.

WAR DIARY
or
INTELLIGENCE SUMMARY.
(Erase heading not required.)

SANITARY SECTION

Place	Date	Hour	Summary of Events and Information	Remarks and references to Appendices
RUE	Dec 7th		Visited DRAKE and HOOD Batts. Saw Town Major at CROTOY. Latrine Inspection. Local work in progress.	
"	Dec 8th		Visited A.S.+D. Engrs, Comm. Batt with Town Major. Work locally in RUE. Public Latrines commenced in RUE.	
"	Dec 9th		Visited HOWE Batt at FAVIERES in cinemas. Inspected 2 latrines. One public latrine completed. Sites of new latrines arranged. Unit commenced work. Local inspection. Bricks to commence construction. Latrine for Divisional Section completed.	
"	Dec 10th			
"	Dec 11th		Visited HAWKE Batt. – saw M.O. 2nd Public latrine in RUE completed – this started. Local inspection. Anchors not Purseys not with M. Letrine as necessary.	
"	Dec 12th			
"	Dec 15th		Visited MOUVION, NOYELLES and VOLETTE. Saw Town major MOUVION. Went and NOYELLES with Capt. Baker R.A.M.C. - also m.o. to Town-Majr. Also visited and inspected railhead. 3rd Public Latrine in RUE finished. Inspected 3r method working.	
"	Dec 16th		Visited VRON. – New area recently taken over Little Progress	

Army Form C. 2118.

WAR DIARY
or
INTELLIGENCE SUMMARY.
(Erase heading not required.)

SANITARY SECTION

Instructions regarding War Diaries and Intelligence Summaries are contained in F.S. Regs., Part II. and the Staff Manual respectively. Title pages will be prepared in manuscript.

Place	Date	Hour	Summary of Events and Information	Remarks and references to Appendices
RUE	Dec 15th		Visited HOWE Batt. at VERCOURT and inspected Billets etc. also M.O. 4th Latrine & RUE emptied. The incinerator burning seems to have been out of use — as no coal in Arcumble.	Rev—
"	Dec 16th		Visited San Supply Column and 15th Fld G.P.S. & 100th T.M.B. at ARRY, also No 2 Ry San Train at CANTERBME No 3 Coy or LARRONVILLE Met M.O. Said train.	Rev.
"	Dec 17th		Visited 94 Bty at VRON and Amm Batt. at VILLERS San M.O.C Also saw O/C Signal Company of will men. He now here uses Iron will latrine "May to be used by troops"	am
"	Dec 18th		Visited LE CROTOY and saw How Batt. & R.F.A. also Tim Maga. Visited Batts, latrines etc. Spoke many from Field Cashier Then paid.	etc
"	Dec 19th		Visited NOUVION FAVIERES and saw Park & see BAC also Town Major. Recommended them a cook here should be moved Local workman and sentries work in mud.	R.M.C.
"	Dec 20th		Visited NOUVION, NULETTE & SAILLY BRAY — saw sanitary conditions etc. Inspected water carts. Local work.	Rev—

Army Form C. 2118.

WAR DIARY
or
INTELLIGENCE SUMMARY.
(Erase heading not required.)

SANITARY SECTION

Place	Date	Hour	Summary of Events and Information	Remarks and references to Appendices
AVE	Dec 21st		I went to III Corps H.Q. at CRECY to meet A.D.M.S. Sanitation 5th Army. Sanitary questions discussed. 5th Army Order 263 "The Sanitary Section will be given definite Sanitary Areas – and work under Corps administration – as Army troops." Was shewn map of new area – which shews power area with scattered villages.	
	Dec 22nd		I visited VRON & saw M.O. 1st & 2nd Rly. & inspected into cost. Saw M.O. Sanitary Train and WDS of H.Q. Sanitary.	
	Dec 23		Visited school of Instruction at NOUVION. Saw Tim Major and Capt Horn etc 31st Army RFA.	
	Dec 24		Visited locally and referred site of Divn Laundry, also D.A. & Q.M.G. Visited Nelson & Howtha Battalions. Man of Leicesters went to the School in afternoon to hear Small Box Properties [?] lecture and explain.	
	Dec 25th		Christmas day. Only necessary intins not done.	
	Dec 26th		Visited VRON w/ case of suspected diphtheria – also 1st FA at NEWPORT or FERMIN, also visited BECQUEREUE (– a section of ?A.C.) Received orders to send men of Sanitary Section to School of Instruction at NOUVION.	

2353 W¹. W2544/1454 700,000 5/15 D. D. & L. A.D.S.S./Forms/C. 2118.

Army Form C. 2118.

WAR DIARY
or
INTELLIGENCE SUMMARY.
(Erase heading not required.)

SANITARY SECTION

Place	Date	Hour	Summary of Events and Information	Remarks and references to Appendices
R.N.E.	Dec 27th		Visited School of Instruction at NOUVION - & Enf WW detailed for duty to school. Went round with O.C. Saw Town Major - NOUVION. Visited NOVELLES with Capt BAKER R.A.M.C. - saw Town Major & Staff Capt 190th Bry. Visited PONTHOILE	R.W.K
	Dec 28th		& MORLAY - saw M.O. 223rd Brig R.F.A. - also visited FAVIERES & saw Town Major. Map of new area received & copied. Visited L. Ent H.Q. & saw D.A.D.M.S. Visited went to RUE in afternoon.	R.W.K
	Dec 29th		Went with A.D.M.S. to CANDAS to see incinerator at German camp. Visited Mpt in route to ADMS. found work being carried out at RUE as pmenty always	R.W.K
	Dec 30th		I visited SAILLY BRAY - 7th R.F. a/ com 1 Brewry. Spend time gth L 3/FA. at NOLETTE.	R.W.K
	Dec 31st		Visited L.BVIT du CROES and inspected billets and sanitation of BOMB SCHOOL as a company of 1st R.M. (Nunley 2 ndC) - also saw Town Major 1 St QUENTIN. none.	R.W.K

R.W.Knyvett
Surgn R.N.

SANITARY SECTION,
ROYAL NAVAL
DIVISION.

No. ....
Date 31/12/16

"Confidential"

FROM.
Sanitary Section
63rd (R.N) Division.

140/1943 9519

COMMITTEE FOR THE
MEDICAL HISTORY OF THE WAR
Date 13 MAR. 1917

War Diary
of
Sanitary Section
63rd (R.N) Division.
From January 1st to 31st/1917.

R.M.Knowles.
Temp. Surgeon. R.N.
O.C
Sanitary Section
63rd (R.N) Division

To
Officer i/c.
A. G's Office
3rd Echelon
63rd R.N. Division

1/2/17.

Army Form C. 2118.

WAR DIARY
or
INTELLIGENCE SUMMARY.
(Erase heading not required.)

SANITARY SECTION
63 (RN) DIVISION

Place	Date	Hour	Summary of Events and Information	Remarks and references to Appendices
RUE	Jan 1st		I went to ABBEVILLE to meet Sanitary Officer of 2nd Division. Used motor lorry. Various working sites of new Sanitary Areas. Men of section.	RWK
	Jan 2nd		I went to see ADMS of 15th Division at BUIGNY. Saw Town Major NOUVION re Inspective Visits for Headquarters of Sanitary Section. Routine inspections	RWK
	Jan 3rd		I visited with Staff Sergt Tose mess and Bn ENY of LITTRE and arranged to send on M.C.O.'s and men. Paid men.	RWK
	Jan 4th		Visited locally - RUE in morning. Visited VRON in afternoon. Saw Staff Captain and Town Major. Large incinerator has been erected by Infant head capable of burning all refuse and excreta of village, 12 ones Flying Incher before has been erected and other, are in course of construction. Pte Attwood J. S/4137 to 2nd Field Amb. Pte Jackson S/4093 awarded "3 days attg" of pay in charge by A.C.H. Found drinking men in an Estaminet L/Cpl Kirk to hospital 3rd Field Ambulance.	RWK
	Jan 6th		Visited St Firmin, saw Batt etc; L/Cpl Richmond sent down to NOUVION	RWK

2353 Wt W2544/1454 700,000 5/15 D. D. & L. A.D.S.S./Forms/C. 2118.

Army Form C. 2118.

WAR DIARY
or
INTELLIGENCE SUMMARY.
(Erase heading not required.)

SANITARY SECTION

Place	Date	Hour	Summary of Events and Information	Remarks and references to Appendices
RUE	Jan 7th		Went round RUE locally - saw Laundry, sanitary arrangements etc. Visited LARRONVILLE, CANTEREME etc.	
"	Jan 8th		Y visited II'd Echelon Headquarters at New Sanitary Area. Saw Corps Supply Officer. Visited FORREST L'ABBAYE and NOUVION - saw Town Majors. Arranged for billets in NOUVION for section - also officer etc. Corporal Atkinson recalled from 189th Brigade. Pte Hunt from 105th Brigade. He & Cpl Pink exchanged with Sgt SEA.	Rue
"	Jan 9th		Sgt Price + Pte Hunt sent to BUIGNY. Corporal Rixborough and Pte Hatton to L. TITRE. Position unknown. Pass moves from Field Substance.	Rue
-	Jan 10th		Pte Luce regrad section from 1st Field Substance. Return return and location sent in to A.D.M.S.	Rue
-	Jan 11th		9 visited NOUVION, L TITRE, HAUTVILLERS and BUIGNY. Men at L TITRE and BUIGNY. Corporal Wilson arranged for accommodation at NOUVION.	Rue
-	Jan 12th		I visited NUYELLES, 91 LAVIERS, FONTEIL ERARD BUIGNY and NUVION with Sgt YATES. Corporal Leak + Pte Fylde rejoind H.Q. of Section at RUE.	Rue
RUE	Jan 13th		Sanitary Section moved to NOUVION. Pte Haulman rejoined section from ship 63. (A.N) Dim. Corporal Platt, Pte Greenwood + Fernand left at RUE - to work with	Rue
NOUVION				

Army Form C. 2118.

WAR DIARY
or
INTELLIGENCE SUMMARY.
(Erase heading not required.)

SANITARY SECTION.

Place	Date	Hour	Summary of Events and Information	Remarks and references to Appendices
NOUVION	Jan 13th		Town Major. 63rd (RN) Divisn W/F to Div. Pte Jackson returned to Sanitary Section from NOYELLES. Return was drawn from Sanitary School of Instruction at NOUVION.	Punk
"	Jan 14th		Visited locally with Enfield Mos in morning - chose site of Latrines. Went to CRECY to see D.A.D.M.S. II Corps: was informed that I was to be relieved. Enfield Ltd and Dammar to work with Town Major at PONTHOILE.	Punk
"	Jan 15th		I visited BUIGNY and met round with Sgt. Rice re sanitary arrangements. Men building incinerator at NOUVION. Long report re refuse - refuse not exported. instructions	Punk
"	Jan 16th		I visited Le Titre and met round with Enfield Blakeney. Remonstrated privately to Town major. Went to NOYELLES to see M.O. B.A.C. Sir Brown re latrines and WCs. Am I W.C. at SAINT-RIQUIER. Rupert with Gasoline (A.?cwm.? Panks Signal Monington on in connected from lion 4 wks ago). Maj. g prepared sanitary arrangements committee (Town Major, Pres. perpetually amputated owing to frost + snow. Cold mm. Visited (with M.O. A/Canadian) - prepared notes for latrines in NOUVION. Work in incinerator	mm
"	Jan 16th		Visited BUIGNY and A.D.M.S. office in morning. NOYELLES to on B.A.C.	mm

Army Form C. 2118.

WAR DIARY
or
INTELLIGENCE SUMMARY.
(Erase heading not required.)

SANITARY SECTION

Place	Date	Hour	Summary of Events and Information	Remarks and references to Appendices
NOUVION	Jan 19th		51st Division and M.O. at Work on Sanitary arrangements of militia. BONELLE CAMP (1/4 Gordons) PONTHOILE + MORLAY (1/19th Royal Scots) saw M.O. and Town Major, LE CROTOY (1/7th Argyll + Suthers) + RUE (Minimum detachments of R.G.A.) also saw Town Major. Routine work by the rest of the section.	MKK RWK
"	Jan 20th		Attended meeting of Sanitary Officers at ABBEVILLE. Surgeon Genl Dr. Maher lect. section. Pte Erews returned from English leave.	RWK
"	Jan 21st		Visited PONTHOILE (T.M. Pvt.), NOYELLES (H.Q. 9 B.C.) and NOLETTE afternoon. Lecture to T.M. Pvt. Minimum which lectr on visited A/Scout Price on leave to England.	amy
"	Jan 22nd		Visited FAVIERES (1/4 Seaforth), LE TAUTOY (Pioneer Park + T.M.M.) and RUE (T. Major). CRECY to trans. S.S office - meeting in afternoon.	amy
"	Jan 23rd		Visited artillery at FORT LE FRAND + Gr LAVIERS, also BUIGNY (Arms office) From L'ABBAYE (2/7 Warwick) seen men along with M.O.	RWK
"	Jan 25th		afternoon met Supd MOS. HAUVILLERS - went round with M.O. (1/5th Gordon Highlanders). Gave lecture at 6.30 Squadron School of Instruction on "Sanitation" + inst.	MKK
"	Jan 26th		Visited locally, billets etc - saw M.O. 1/6th Argyll + Sutherd - inspection of Minor offrs.	amy

2353 Wt. W2544/1454 700,000 5/15 D.D.&L. A.D.S.S./Forms/C.2118

Army Form C. 2118.

WAR DIARY
or
INTELLIGENCE SUMMARY.
(Erase heading not required.)

Instructions regarding War Diaries and Intelligence Summaries are contained in F. S. Regs., Part II and the Staff Manual respectively. Title pages will be prepared in manuscript.

SANITARY SECTION

Place	Date	Hour	Summary of Events and Information	Remarks and references to Appendices
NOUVION	Jan 26th		Cow of difference. Visited H.Q. Canhan / Sm: Train at ST NICHOLAS DESARTS. Visited L.Emp Westn in hospital at ABBEVILLE.	
	Jan 27th		Visited CAREY - saw Emp. Obhaman, she saw DESERTS, IV Emp. Visited ARRY in afternoon (V.E.H) saw M.O.	
	Jan 28th		Routine work of section. Reports received from men outside saw RUNELLE Camp ? and talk at PONTHOILE. also visited Le CROTOY.	
	Jan 29th		Saw ADMS at NOYEVY. visited H.Q. 1st Corps, Commandant & Head Nurse. Staff Engr Tpl visited NOUVION locally. Routine work.	
	Jan 30th		Saw An 2 Emp. Gen Traw at ROMAINE. Local Inspection work in morning at NOUVION. Meeting at IV Emp. office in afternoon - topics Invalidin / Army "influenza" - special reference to Dessertern. Dress Army from IV Enfs. cashes and past men.	

R.W. Thomson
Sup Surgeon R.N.

[Stamp: SANITARY SECTION, ROYAL NAVAL DIVISION. 1/2/17]

"Confidential"

Sanitary Section
63rd (R.N.) Division

COMMITTEE FOR THE
MEDICAL HISTORY OF THE WAR
Date 4 APR 1917

War Diary
of
Sanitary Section
63rd (R.N.) Division
From Feby 1st to 28/1917.

F. Carry Capt.
O.C.
Sanitary Section
63rd (R.N.) Division.

H/o A.G's Office
3rd Echelon
63rd (R.N.) Division.
March 3rd/1917.

MESSAGES AND SIGNALS.

Army Form C. 2121.

TO: A.D.M.S. 13th Corps

Sender's Number: SS/254
Day of Month: 3rd

AAA

Enclosed herewith "War Diary" of Sanitary Section 63rd (RN) Division aaa Forwarded to you under cover for despatch to A.G. Officer 3rd Echelon aaa

From: 63rd (RN) Divl Sanitary Section

D.A.G.
 Base.

 Forwarded.

 J. Kendrew
 Captain, D.A.D.M.S.
 for D.D.M.S. XIII Corps.

5/3/17.

Army Form C. 2118.

WAR DIARY
or
INTELLIGENCE SUMMARY.
(Erase heading not required.)

SANITARY SECTION

Instructions regarding War Diaries and Intelligence Summaries are contained in F.S. Regs., Part II. and the Staff Manual respectively. Title pages will be prepared in manuscript.

Place	Date	Hour	Summary of Events and Information	Remarks and references to Appendices
NOUVION	Feb 1st		Routine work. I visited Le TITRE reference case of Diphtheria at Brigade H.Q.	nil
—	Feb 2nd		Made arrangements for disinfection. Saw Tom Major.	nil
—	Feb 3rd		I visited MORLAY; saw new Major PONTHOILE and inspected former billets. Met with officer in charge to view same. Hy Price returned from leave.	nil
—	Feb 4th		Coffee NOUVION (Lt Army Water Office). Visited me. Gave instructions as to mile survey of area. Lt/Engl. Reid returned from hospital to section. Staff Sgt Tate and I went to RUE, LE TITRE, BUIGNY + PONTHOILE ref mile survey.	nil
—	Feb 5th		— instruction given to M.E.O.'s in their area. Received instructions from Sgt Dinnin to take me C in C in area where 51st Division have area. Marched up as well to forward area. Sgt/Engl Tate to ST OMIFAST to see the P.W. then Decan- but they had already moved our work. 51st Division have area. I went to PIRECY ran against SIV Coy + one who enjoyed Officers.	nil
—	Feb 6th		Work continuing ref: mile survey. I visited BONELLE	nil
—	Feb 7th		I visited RUE and saw Tom Major also WCOs etc.	nil
—	Feb 8th			nil

Army Form C. 2118.

WAR DIARY
or
INTELLIGENCE SUMMARY.
(Erase heading not required.)

SANITARY SECTION

Place	Date	Hour	Summary of Events and Information	Remarks and references to Appendices
NOUVION	Feb 9th		Visited FORREST L'ABBAYE, & LAMOTTE BULEUX. Men sent to CANCHY & NEUILLY L'HÔPITAL. Ration van men out of this area visited	
	Feb 10th		Received visit from D.A.D.M.S. (Sanitation) V Army: instructed not to move any men out of this area visited when orders received from XIII Corps	
	Feb 11th		Q went to Le CROTOY re rats money. Capt TRAYER R.A.M.C. arrived with FORD Car as asst. to him in duties.	
	Feb 12th		Visited RUE with Capt TRAYER. new van taken over. Major and ans. went to Rin. Visited SAILLY-le-SEC.	
	Feb 13th		Visited Le TITRE, HAUTVILLERS, BUFFNY, went to ABBEYVILLE and able to draw money from Field Cashier. L.Cpl. Hinx &?? by Artillery Field Visited Le CROTOY, NOYELLES & NOLETTE with Capt TRAYER R.A.M.C.	
	Feb 14th		R.Q. Mannion to Le TITRE to his refuge. Work since now completed & majority To Sailly-le-Sec as to Le TITRE of M.O/p went off to D.A.D.M.S. V Army (Sanitation). Wind & maps enclosed —	
	Feb 15th			
	Feb 17th		Inspected NOUVION with Deputy Mayor R.A.M.C.	

Army Form C. 2118.

WAR DIARY
or
INTELLIGENCE SUMMARY.
(Erase heading not required.)

SANITARY SECTION

Instructions regarding War Diaries and Intelligence Summaries are contained in F. S. Regs., Part II. and the Staff Manual respectively. Title pages will be prepared in manuscript.

Place	Date	Hour	Summary of Events and Information	Remarks and references to Appendices
NOUVION	Feb 18th & 19th		Routine work.	
	Feb 20th		Visited PONTHOILE and NUBLIES. Working hard just up for us I expect. Visited MAESIERET & see Field Cashier XIII Corps - he told you where I arrived. Visited PROUVILLE & LONGVILLERS. Last I month's water Survey sent to this I'th Army	
	Feb 21st		Natal then received I Ponetion Pack on NOUVION this Corp & dep RAMC arrived P.M. to-day to take command of Sanitary Section.	
	Feb 22nd		I handed on command of Sanitary Section to Lieft Walter RAMC. this morning.	

R.W.K[...] R.N.
[signature]

2353 Wt. W2544/1454 700,000 5/15 D.D.&L. A.D.S.S./Forms/C. 2118.

Army Form C. 2118.

WAR DIARY
or
INTELLIGENCE SUMMARY.
(Erase heading not required.)

SANITARY SECTION

Place	Date	Hour	Summary of Events and Information	Remarks and references to Appendices
	Feb 22.		Took over command of 63rd (RN) Div Sanitary Section.	
	23.		Met with NORMAN (inspector) re Sanitary arrangements. T/C	
			Went with ABBEVILLE to make enquiries recruits for Section.	
			Inspected Sanitary arrangements at LE TITRE, HAUTVILLIERS, PONTHOILE, ROMAINE, NOYELLE, HAMEL. Paid Section.	
Hebert	Feb 24		Inspected Sanitary arrangements RUE, ARRY, ST QUENTIN, LE CROTOY, RUSSELMONT, LA BASSÉE, FAVIÈRES. Saw Town major at RUE & LE CROTOY T/C	
	Feb 25		Inspected Sanitary arrangements NOYELLES, NEUFETRE, SAILLY LE SEC. Sat RMO of artillery behind at cellar place. T/C	
	Feb 26		Saw General XIII Corps at DOULLENS & FOSS Carlist re men used to Division at DOULLENS to have extra Clothing taken off Section. T/C	
	Feb 27		Wrote to DONVAST & GYER CHART re men used Ration supplies T/C to men orders to move to DONVAST in Kuef not received T/O	
	Feb 28		Interview Town major Minion re Slimming Sanitary arrangements O/C Routine.	

F. J. Carey Capt.

SANITARY SECTION,
63 (ROYAL NAVAL)
DIVISION.
No. 2.514.

"Confidential"

Sanitary Section
63rd (R.N.) Division

Vol XI
140/2043

COMMITTEE FOR THE
MEDICAL HISTORY OF THE WAR
Date 11 MAY 1917

"War Diary"
of
Sanitary Section
63rd (R.N.) Division.
From March 1st to 31st/1917.

H. Caley Capt. R.A.M.C.
O.C.
Sanitary Section
63rd (R.N.) Division

T/o Officer i/c
A. G's Office
3rd Echelon
63rd (R.N.) Divn
April 1st/1917.

Army Form C. 2118.

WAR DIARY
or
INTELLIGENCE SUMMARY.
(Erase heading not required.)

Place	Date	Hour	Summary of Events and Information	Remarks and references to Appendices
NOUVION	1917 March 1.		Section made preparation to move to DOMVAST tomorrow. Summary OC to Capt TRAVER marched to DOMVAST & made arrangements for billeting section. No maps in the village. OC appointed temporary Town Major of DOMVAST. H.Q.	
DOMVAST	March 2.		Moved to DOMVAST completed billy. OC went to ST RIQUIER to interview Town Major but he was not available. T.G. OC Cast Town Major at ST RIQUIER. Arranged for new & exchanged schools & 1st & 2nd Divisional School as a Divisional Rest Home all at ST RIQUIER. Called on Area Commandant. He was not available.	
Do	March 3.		Arranged to draw rations at ST RIQUIER. Inspected sanitary arrangements & half village of DOMVAST. There are 25 villages in the Central Sub Area. Arrangements made for 2 men the billets at CANCHY, 3 at DRUCAT, 2 at FROYELLES, 1 at DOMVAST, 2 at ST RIQUIER, 2 at GAPENNES, 1 at QUESCHART. First 4 parties selected & despatched today. H.Q.	

Army Form C. 2118.

WAR DIARY
or
INTELLIGENCE SUMMARY.
(Erase heading not required.)

Place	Date	Hour	Summary of Events and Information	Remarks and references to Appendices
DOMVAST	March 3		On march the section yesterday, 3 men were left in hospital at RUE 1 at SAULY-LE-SEC.	
Do.	March		O.C. went to CRECY. Whilst there places were inspected. O.C. to GUESCHART. had a field cadet. Arrangements for 1 man to 6 weeks' instruction to school (2nd Swain) there. O.C. to CAPENNES. Arranged for two men to be billeted there, some not there. O.C. to YVRENCH, saw Town Major + General Officer 1 Division. 2 men detailed, went to ST RIQUIER	H.C.
Do.			CAPT TRAYER took 1 man to GUESCHART in Ford Ambulance. O.C. inspected billets of DOMVAST. Arrangements made to collect ambulances + equipment (gap etc. other things + place them in Town Major Office.	H.C.
Do.	March 16		O.C. (early) FRAYELLES, 18 horses in trough + buying chargers delivered to several dumps + instruction issued for dealing with horse Recom'd visit from Training Area Commandant. ST RIQUIER.	H.C.
Do.	Sunday		O.C. + CAPT TRAYER inspected units of LAMOTTE-BULEUX + checked the water supply.	H.C.

WAR DIARY or INTELLIGENCE SUMMARY

Army Form C. 2118.

SOMMARY SECTION

Place	Date	Hour	Summary of Events and Information	Remarks and references to Appendices
Domart Sur...	March 8		Arrived in billets. Water supply of village arranged. Arrangements made for collection of stores brought by lorries & lying above in each village. Lorries taken to Tournier's store — O.C.	
Do	March 9		O.C. examined wells, detailed daily supply of ERQUELLES. O.C. Carried on with water supply. O.C.	
D°	March 10			
D°	March 11			
D°	March 12		O.C. to DOULLENS. Collected stores. Received monument. Home on Col. XIII Corps. Interview from Camp Commandant Long & DOULLENS. Arms & equipments — informed that interim transfer S.B. Athenies J. Fontaine.	
D°	March 13		O.C. examined billets. Checked survey of BRUCAT, Parlanche	
D°	March 14		Billets NEUILLY L'HOPITAL. CAPT TRAYER checked survey of DOMVAST	
D°	March 15		Billets FONTAINE-SUR-MAYE.	
			Word received from CAPT TRAYER to rejoin his ambulance. Ord ambulance to remain with section.	
			Notification received that 17th Divisional Artillery moving tomorrow am 16 to 26th. Received instruction to notify O.C. Divisional Arrangements on stages occupied.	

Army Form C. 2118.

WAR DIARY
or
INTELLIGENCE SUMMARY.
(Erase heading not required.)

Place	Date	Hour	Summary of Events and Information	Remarks and references to Appendices
BONVAST	March 16		N.O. sent to ACQUET to arrange re 17th Divisional Artillery passing through village of ACQUET, CUMANVILLE, LANNOY. N.O. stationed at BUSSCHAR. Returns to Supreme BELINVAL, LEBRAND, LE PETIT for same purpose. Talks to On arrival for one of Section from 3/1st Motor Ambulance Convoy.	F.J.C.
Do	March 17		Capt TRAYER returned to his unit, taking four ambulances with him, in aid of 13th mother post Army convoys. Make survey of village of CORNEDOITE & LA PLESSIEL (completed). O.C. inspected both these Villages.	F.J.C.
Do	March 18		Orders received this in future Donkey trains of ambulances are to the Army troops. This section is to take over Rue over, & are to East of DOMVAST area.	F.J.C.
Do	March 19		Make survey of GUESCHART & DUVILLE stopped by O.C. Village of ACQUET, LANNOY inspected.	F.J.C.
Di	March 20		Inspection of ST RIQUIER. NEUVILLE & DUEUX new showings. Survey of ST RIQUIER to incorporate Cantonments in ST RIQUIER. R.E. (Field Company) Australians are here to value army stones to area	F.J.C.

Army Form C. 2118.

WAR DIARY
or
INTELLIGENCE SUMMARY.

SANITARY SECTION

(Erase heading not required.)

Place	Date	Hour	Summary of Events and Information	Remarks and references to Appendices
DONVAST	March 21		Visited ACQUET refuse hutment of 17th Divisional Artillery — not yet of their use. Completed water surveys of BRAILLY & CANCHY.	O/C
Do	March 22		NEUF MOULIN, L'HEURE & NOYELLE-SUR-CAUSSE inspected. Water surveys of their village now about complete.	O/C
Do	March 23		MARCHÉVILLE, BELINVAL LE GRAND, BELINVAL LE PETIT inspected. Water surveys complete.	O/C
Do	March 24		DOMVAST cleans up. Army stores by 12th Field Co., Australian R.E.	O/C
Do	March 25		AGENVILLERS & YVRENCHEUX inspected. Water Camp about complete.	O/C
Do	March 26		Sanitary report for the month end of to 14th army.	O/C
Do	March 27		More work	
Do	March 28		Inspected JAEMES for completion of water survey.	
Do	March 29		Previous inspect. to now St Cecilia Abbeville. Inspected well of ONEUX & NEUVILLE — water survey of these villages now complete. Push on of surveys.	O/C
Do	March 29		Inspected YVRENCH for completion of water survey.	O/C
Do	March 30		O/C visited R.V.E. Saw Town Major. The Australian R.E. are like hounds.	

WAR DIARY
or
INTELLIGENCE SUMMARY.

Army Form C. 2118.

Place	Date	Hour	Summary of Events and Information	Remarks and references to Appendices
Pommier	March 30 (continued)		Men chiefly to another Army. Received complaint that Cavalry Reserve Train at Army not disposing of manure correctly. Saw O.C. of that unit & arranged to have him more diligently to tackle manure. Survey of all sources of water making supply in the Capt'l Area complete. All notices nailed up. Will be requested to remove to 5th Army. Received warning from 7th Army Div to hold unit in readiness to move to another area at short notice. F.O.	
Do.	March 31		Reported unit moving displaced to 7th Army to-day. Assume Field Ambulance reported from units here to replace the one already here, which returns to that unit.	

H. Carey Copeman
O.C.

SANITARY SECTION.
63/ROYAL NAVAL
DIVISION.
Date. 1.4.17.

63RD DIVISION

53RD MOBILE VETY SECTION
MAY 1916 – APR 1919

63RD DIVISION

"*Confidential*"

Magnicourt.
30th June 1916.

War Diary

of

53rd Mobile Veterinary Section.

from

30th May

to

30th June 1916.

To/
The A.G's Office.
3rd Echelon.

Wilmot R. Pinnell
Capt. A.V.C.
O.C.
53rd Mobile Vety Section.

Army Form C. 2118.

WAR DIARY
or
INTELLIGENCE SUMMARY

(Erase heading not required.)

Instructions regarding War Diaries and Intelligence Summaries are contained in F.S. Regs., Part II. and the Staff Manual respectively. Title Pages will be prepared in manuscript.

Place	Date	Hour	Summary of Events and Information	Remarks and references to Appendices
Woolwich	30.5.16	6.30A.M.	The M.T.S. entrained for Southampton, arriving at	Passed over
Southampton	"	1.40P.M.	Embarking on S.S. "S". Panceras" at 3.P.M. Sailed at 6.45 P.M. arriving at	amp strength [7/4]
Le Havre	31.5.16	5.15A.M.	Disembarked at 8.30 A.M. marched to the Rest Camp (N° 1.) Received instructions	
			to proceed to the Rouen station at 4 O'clock 1.6.16. left Camp at 3.30P.M.	
Rouen			Entrained at 5.30 P.M. for Rouen arriving at Rouen at mid-night	
Hallencourt	2.6.16	8.30A.M.	Detrained and marched to tarrive at	Bills & Nels
	"	11.30A.M.	Where we took over the silicha arrangel for us	got 1 1/4
			Started duties with the Divisional Trains Train were sent	manoeuvres
"	6.6.16		Received sic Sick Horses	
"	7th		Evacuated 1 "	to the 22nd Field Veterinary Hospital
"	8th		Horses received Nil	
"	9th		Received seven Sick Horses	
"	10th		Evacuated six "	to the 29th Field Veterinary Hospital
"	11th		Received three "	
"	12th		" one "	Train Point
"	13th		" two "	
"	14th		" one "	
"	15th		Evacuated eight "	to the 29th Field Veterinary Hospital
"	16th		Received instructions to proceed at 10 A.M. to Rail Head Abbeville manoeuvres	
"	17th			
Abbeville	"	12.30P.M.	Entrained at 3.P.M. arriving at	
Brucy	18th	1.A.M.	Entrained and marched to Magnicourt arriving at	

2449 Wt. W14957/M90 750,000 1/16 J.B.C. & A. Forms/C.2118/12.

Army Form C. 2118.

WAR DIARY
or
INTELLIGENCE SUMMARY

(Erase heading not required.)

Instructions regarding War Diaries and Intelligence Summaries are contained in F. S. Regs., Part II. and the Staff Manual respectively. Title Pages will be prepared in manuscript.

Place	Date	Hour	Summary of Events and Information	Remarks and references to Appendices
Hugueseaul	June 18	9. A.M.	Billets for men very poor. Received sick horses	
"	19"	"	"	
"	20"	"	"	
"	21"	"	one "	
"	22"	"	four (3) "	
"	23"	"	two four (2) "	
"	24"	"	four "	
"	25"	"	two "	
"	26"	"	four "	
"	27"	"	two "	
"	28"	"	five " Evacuated Jenkins. Sent Hodges to the 22nd Vety Veterinary Hospital	
"	29"	"	Nil "	
"	30"	"	Nil "	
"	"	"	two "	
"	23rd June		Evacuated Engels & Sergt Horas to the 22nd Vet Vety Hospital	
"	21st June 10.5 3.0"		One NCO & one Pte forced to attend a sick horse thrown from a wagon which was exchanged for a three thougk by returned 2nd Inst. from 21st to date have done Veterinary duties Company 2, 3 & 4. D.T. for V.O. Health & conduct of men excellent.	

Confidential

War Diary
53rd Mobile Rly Section
from ~~1st July 1916~~
to ~~31st July 1916~~

JULY 1916

To A.G's Office.   Wilmot L. Quinnell
3rd Echelon.   Capt RE
                              OC 53rd M.V.S
———
2. 8. 16

63
53 M.V.S.
Vol 1
July

WAR DIARY or INTELLIGENCE SUMMARY

Army Form C. 2118.

(Erase heading not required.)

Instructions regarding War Diaries and Intelligence Summaries are contained in F. S. Regs., Part II. and the Staff Manual respectively. Title Pages will be prepared in manuscript.

Place	Date	Hour	Summary of Events and Information	Remarks and references to Appendices
Mudros	1st July		3 Sick Horses received. Gave the officers of the Division from a Practical Demonstration. Elementary anatomy having a P.M. on a Horse. 2.15 - 15. 3 - 4.5. 7 P.M.	
"	2nd "		2 Sick Horses received. Scanned for Divisional Train Horses assured for Remounts.	
"	3rd "		2 " " " "	
"	4th "		9 " " " "	
"	5th "		10 " Evacuated 1 Horse brought in by Boat from Harbin	
"	6th "		7 " (received)	
"	7th "		6 " "	
"	8th "		2 Horses Received. Gave a Practical Demonstration to N.C.Os & Officers of Divisional Train	
"	9th "		17 Sick Horses Evacuated to N.º 2 Field D.P Hospital	
"	"		3 " "	
"	10th "		9 " "	
"	11th "		11 " "	
"	12th "		22 " Evacuated to N.º 2.8 Field D.P Hospital (received)	
"	"		13 " "	
"	13th "		11 " 1 Horse brought in by Boat from Bryas. Was mobilised to take the Veterinary Charge of the Divisional Train. R.N.D

Army Form C. 2118.

WAR DIARY
or
INTELLIGENCE SUMMARY

(Erase heading not required.)

Instructions regarding War Diaries and Intelligence Summaries are contained in F. S. Regs., Part II and the Staff Manual respectively. Title Pages will be prepared in manuscript.

Place	Date	Hour	Summary of Events and Information	Remarks and references to Appendices
Thuzinent	14th July		29 Sick Horses Evacuated to No. 22. Field Veterinary Hospital.	
"	"		Sergt. Rearden A.V.C. reported here for temporary duty under instructions from Private Pollinor A.V.C. and Driver Stockering A.S.C. were recruits to Central Remounts	
"	15th "		17. Sick Animals received.	
"	16th "		21 " " Evacuated to No. 22nd Field Veterinary Hospital.	
"	"		14 " " received	
"	17th "		10 " " " including one brought in by float from 63rd R.N.D.	
"	18th "	1 P.M.	Received instructions to proceed to Barlin	
"	"	5 P.M.	Started for Barlin taking over with us 21. Sick Horses belonging to Horsemoiff	
"	"		16 travel.	
Barlin	"	7.30 P.M.	Arrived. Taking up the quarters of the 1/2 London Mtd 6 Fd. Sy Station who were for preceding to Fresnicourt.	
"	19th "		6. Sick Animals received.	
"	20th "		7. " " "	
"	21st "		12. " " "	
"	22nd "		9 " " 34 Sick Animals Evacuated to No. 13 Field Vet Hospital.	
"	23rd "		20 " " "	
"	24th "		8 " " 37. Sick Animals Evacuated to No. 13 Field Vet Hospital.	

2449 Wt. W14957/M90 750,000 1/16 J.B.C. & A. Forms/C.2118/12.

Army Form C. 2118.

WAR DIARY
or
INTELLIGENCE SUMMARY

(Erase heading not required.)

Instructions regarding War Diaries and Intelligence Summaries are contained in F. S. Regs., Part II. and the Staff Manual respectively. Title Pages will be prepared in manuscript.

Place	Date	Hour	Summary of Events and Information	Remarks and references to Appendices
Barton	25/July		19 Sick Animals received.	
"	26"		18 " " "	
"	27 "		11 " " "	
"	28"		44 " " Evacuated to No. 13 Field Veterinary Hospital.	
"	29"		11 " " received	
"	30"		3 " " " Sergt. Bolton. A.V.C. admitted to 3rd Field Ambulance	
"	"		Float sent out to Penrose, to bring in lame horse.	
"	31/July		9 Sick animals received. Pte. Saunders A.V.C. admitted to No. 3. Field Ambulance.	

W.H.A. Dimmell Capt AVO
O.C. 53rd Mobile Veterinary Section
63rd (RN) Division

2nd August 1916

```
                    C O N F I D E N T I A L.
                    ************************

                         WAR     DIARY

                              of

                    53rd Mobile Veterinary Section.

                         (63rd (R.N) Division).


                         VOLUME  No.  3.


            From.  1st August, 1916  to  31st August, 1916.
```

Wilmot R. Quinnell.
Capt. A.V.C.
Commdg, 53rd Mobile Vety. Section.

Army Form C. 2118.

WAR DIARY
or
INTELLIGENCE SUMMARY

(Erase heading not required.)

53rd Mobile Veterinary Section
63rd (RN) Division

Place	Date	Hour	Summary of Events and Information	Remarks and references to Appendices
Berlin	August 1st		SS/M 12855 Acting L/Corporal Lewis promoted to Paid L/Corporal. SS/No 9152 L/Corporal Herbert promoted to Acting Sergeant. SS/No 6321 Private M°Carthy promoted to Acting S/Corporal. SS/No 9991 Private Lewis " " " "	
"	Aug 2nd		Admitted to 3rd Field Ambulance	
			Cpl Ind & 4 men proceed to No 13 Field Veterinary Hospital, 36 Sick Animals evacuated to " " " " including 5 skin cases. SS/No 3893 Pte Sanders discharged from 3rd Field Ambulance and reports for duty August 2nd 1916. Pte Baffin and Flood proceed to Sans En Gohelle Wks & Rest house returns from " " " "	
"	Aug 4/		Sgt Bolton discharged from 3rd Field Ambulance & reports for duty Aug 16. Cpl Yard & 4 men's returns from No 13 Field Veterinary Hospital Sedin Paid.	
"	Aug 5th		SS/No 9955 Pte Lewis J.E. Admitted to No 3 Field Ambulance. Pte Boyle & 4 " Proceed to Sans En Gohelle " " " Wks & Rest house returns from " " " "	
"	Aug 6th		SS/No 7981 Corporal Lewis L.E. Discharged from No 3 Field Ambulance for duty 6th August 1916. O/C Proceeds to Headquarters 63rd (RN) Division for Distribution of Remounts.	

Army Form C. 2118.

WAR DIARY
or
INTELLIGENCE SUMMARY

53rd Mobile Veterinary Section
63rd (RN) Division

(Erase heading not required.)

Place	Date	Hour	Summary of Events and Information	Remarks and references to Appendices
Barlin	Aug 7th		8.6 to 11.50: Pte Reaves & E. sent to Casualty Clearing Station from 3 Field Ambulance. Col. McCarthy & L then proceeds to 10/13 Field Veterinary Hosp; 31 sick Animals evacuated to 13th Field Veterinary Hospital including 2 Run cases & 1 Remount to Calais	
"	Aug 8th		NIL	
"	Aug 9th		L/Cpl. McCarthy and L hier returns from 13th Field Veterinary Hospital	
"	Aug 10th		Pte Boyle and L/Cpl proceeds to 189th Infantry Bde 63rd (RN) Div for 1 Sick horse. Pte Boyle returns from 189th Bde 63rd (RN) Bri: with 1 sick horse. Proceeds to Divl Batn 63rd (RN) Bri: Transport Lines with 1 horse for 1 sick horse. Pte Boyle returns from Divl Batn with 1 sick horse	
"	Aug 11th		NIL	
"	Aug 12		NIL	

WAR DIARY or INTELLIGENCE SUMMARY

Army Form C. 2118.

53rd Mobile Veterinary Section
63rd (R.N.) Division

Place	Date	Hour	Summary of Events and Information	Remarks and references to Appendices
Barlin	July 31		Cpl Loss & 3 men proceed to 13th Field Veterinary Hospital. 19 sick Animals Evacuated to " " including 3 Glanders Cases. T/4/043309 Dvr Dilston T. reports from 1st Base M.T. Depot, A.S.C. for duty. Section Paid	
"	Aug 1st		Pte Boyle proceeds to 37th Divisional Train Headquarters A.S.C. for two injured horses July 31st. Pte Boyle Returns from " " " with two injured horses	
"	Aug 15th		Cpl Loss & 2 men returns from No.13 Field Veterinary Hospital	
"	Aug 16		S/84 Oreben & Pte proceed to R. Battery 316 Bde. R.F.A. Boyeffles. " " " returns from " " " " One Sick Horse. M2870 Dvr Stocking A.S.C. reports for duty from Mew Stationary Base Hospital Le Havre 16th August 1916.	
"	Aug 17th		O/C Visits Company's & Divisional Train & Event and Horse Proceeds to 1st London Paid. for 3 Sick Animals. " " " returns from " " " Two sick horse & Mule " " " Proceeds to 188th Machine Gun Company for Sick horse " " " returns from " " " " " " Sick Horse	

2449 Wt. W14957/M90 750,000 1/16 J.B.C. & A. Forms/C.2118/12.

Army Form C. 2118.

WAR DIARY
or
INTELLIGENCE SUMMARY

(Erase heading not required.)

53rd M. Vet. Section
O.C. 2 of (R.N.) Division

Month of August, 1916.

Place	Date	Hour	Summary of Events and Information	Remarks and references to Appendices
Barlin	August 18th		S/S Bolton & 5 men proceed to No 13 Field Veterinary Hospital SS Sick Animals Evacuated to " " "	
"	Aug 19		O/C Proceeds to Headquarters Company.	
"	Aug 20		Dr Gossett & float proceed to 1st Field Ambulance for Sick Horse returning from " " " with No 69m	
"	Aug 21st		Col Gnd & 2 men Proceed to No 13 Field Veterinary Hospital 24 Sick Animals Evacuated to No 13 " "	
"	Aug 22.		Float sent to be repaired by Headquarters Company. O/C proceeds to Ho's 2 & 3 Inf. Divisional Train Section Point.	
"	Aug 23.		Col Gnd & 2 men return from No 13 Field Veterinary Hospital SS No 3384 Pte Y. S. Scott reported for duty from Do 9 Veterinary Hospital	
"	Aug 24		SS 9947 Pte Pollard to Y. proceeds to Railway Operating Division Infantry tr. List Rd Freeman SS No. 3793 Pte Sanders admitted 3rd Field Ambulance SS 145970 Dr Stocking Evacuated to No 6 Cavalry Clearing Sta O/C Proceeds to Ho's L & 9 Coy. Divisional Train	

2449 Wt. W14957/Mgo 750,000 1/16 J.B.C. & A. Forms/C.2118/12.

Army Form C. 2118.

WAR DIARY
or
INTELLIGENCE SUMMARY   33rd Mob Vety Section
(Erase heading not required.)   (Bde 4) Division

Instructions regarding War Diaries and Intelligence Summaries are contained in F. S. Regs., Part II. and the Staff Manual respectively. Title Pages will be prepared in manuscript.

Place	Date	Hour	Summary of Events and Information	Remarks and references to Appendices
Barlin	July 25		Dispatch of Horse Puchers to B. Battery 333 Bde R.F.A.	
"	"		" " " " " " "	
"			1 Sick Horse	
"	Aug 26		Cpl Shepard Saddler, 9 Rifles & Section	
"	Aug 27		Sgt Dalton No 3157 Admitted to 3rd Field Ambulance	
"	Aug 28		Cpl Hardy & 2 men agreed to No 13 Zulu Veterinary Hospital 16 Sick Animals Evacuated " " " " including 3 Skin cases. and 1 Remount case. SS No 3157 Sgt Dalton sent to C.C.S. from No 3 Field Ambulance	
"	Aug 29		SS No 10193 Pte Pinnels to Perform the duties of cooks from 28.8.16 SS No 10439 Pte Soper whilst Pte Auty from 28.8.16	
"	Aug 30		S.S. No 11357 Pte Rede Admitted to Hospital 30. Inst. Cpl McCarthy & 2 Men returns from 13th Field Hosp	

Army Form C. 2118.

WAR DIARY
or
INTELLIGENCE SUMMARY

(Erase heading not required.)

Instructions regarding War Diaries and Intelligence Summaries are contained in F. S. Regs., Part II and the Staff Manual respectively. Title Pages will be prepared in manuscript.

Place	Date	Hour	Summary of Events and Information	Remarks and references to Appendices
Bavlin	Aug 31/16	3 PM	Inspection of Section by a D.V.S. DDVS. A.D.V.S. and a K.S. Officer. Genl. Moore expressed himself well pleased with the work of M.Y. Section	53rd Mobile Vety Section 63rd W Division
"	"		SE. 11351 Pte J. Keep sent to 6th C.C.S. from 3rd Australians	

Mhnall
Capt A.V.C

Vol 3

CONFIDENTIAL.

WAR   DIARY

of

53rd Mobile Veterinary Section.

From 1st September, 1916   To 30th September, 1916.

VOLUME.   4.

[signature]
Captain. A.V.C.
Commdg, 53rd Mobile Vet. Section.

Army Form C. 2118.

WAR DIARY
or
INTELLIGENCE SUMMARY
(Erase heading not required.)

53rd Mobile Vety Section

Place	Date	Hour	Summary of Events and Information	Remarks and references to Appendices
Dublin	1/Sept		Driver one man & one horse proceeded to H.Q. Battery 27 Div. to Curragh. GIR Horse Section Paid	
"	2 Sept		NIL	
"	3 Sept		Driver one man & one horse proceeded to Hare S. One of Curragh 1 horse. One man & one horse proceeded to Keller Bath.	
"	4 Sept		Driver one man & one horse proceeded to D/Rd Section Headquarters RA/ SCR Curragh	
"	5 Sept		Issued 1 ord & 8 men returned from Ho'd Ercol Vety Hospital Curragh. One man & Mrs. proceeded to 130th Battery RFA. II Corps AB No 2893. 16 Services relieves to duty from 3rd V. Ambulance AB No. 0428. 16 L. Cpl returning to duty from Tackeny Hospital Amiens, Anderry. Kowed Lonko for Curragh AB No. 579. Smith Cpl to Franklin & Does 8	
"	6 Sept		NIL	
"	7 Sept			
"	8 Sept		SP Sexton & 13 mules proceeded to 8th of Vety Reserve in Charge of Sick Animals. Staff Sgt. proceeded to D/Battery 28 Div. 16 Sept in Charge of sick horses.	

WAR DIARY
or
INTELLIGENCE SUMMARY

Army Form C. 2118.

53 Mobile Vety Section

Place	Date	Hour	Summary of Events and Information	Remarks and references to Appendices
Duba	9th Sept		S.S. no 10351 McKechnie on duty to H.Q. Ambulance. Driver one man & two horses proceeded to V.M. Royal Services See Horses	
"	10th Sept		Driver one man two horses proceeded to Port Sudan to see horse. One man & two horses proceeded to San En Gilea to dispose of sick Cattle returns from No 3 F. Vety Hospital 86 Sergeant to hen	
"	11 Sept		Surgeon one man & two horses proceeded to 1st & 9 Baty R.F.A. to inspect sick horse. Driver, one man & two horses proceeded to Section Park	Flooded out, to take home
"	12 Sept		Davis one man & two horses proceeded to R Baty R.F.A to see 1 sick horse. Driver one man & two horses proceeded to Royal Marines for sick horse	
"	13 Sept		Sgt Gard proceeded to No 13 Field Vety Hospital to arrange a horse of instruction in the method of telegraph Repair along the desert elapsing machine. Cpl McCathy & 3 men proceeded to 13 Field Vety Hospital in charge of 33 sick animals	

Army Form C. 2118.

WAR DIARY or INTELLIGENCE SUMMARY

3rd Mobile Vety Section

Place	Date	Hour	Summary of Events and Information	Remarks and references to Appendices
Bailin	15th Sept.		Driver McKay #T/223 proceeded to B/Ech for duties since.	
"	16th Sept.		No.335 Saddler S. Ruperts in place of No.351 Sgt. Ballis who proceeded to No.9 Vety Hospital. Sgt. No.579 J Stinard C/C SS relieves him on Stationary Dept for a period of 9 months.	
"	16th Sept.		Driver McKay #T/223 See to the instructions Capt. W.E. Greisal proceeded to England on 9 days leave. Capt. J.C. Brown took over temporary command of Section.	
"	17th Sept.		Dark Rath H/o & Capt Horse A.V.S. Inspects Saddler & public of section.	
"	18th Sept.		Driver McKay #T/223 proceeded to Dep. of 3/3 Bde Arty. Tri Sect. Horse Amm. One man since proceeded to No. 3 D.R.S. in his from.	
"	19th Sept.		Cpl. Ford & then proceeded 135 J Vety Hospital in charge of 3 sick animals. Driver McKay #T/223 proceeded to Headquarters 89th Bde. 8 am on orders for 1 sick since section Ford.	

WAR DIARY
or
INTELLIGENCE SUMMARY

(Erase heading not required.)

Army Form C. 2118.

Instructions regarding War Diaries and Intelligence Summaries are contained in F. S. Regs., Part II. and the Staff Manual respectively. Title Pages will be prepared in manuscript.

53rd Mobile Vety Section

Place	Date	Hour	Summary of Events and Information	Remarks and references to Appendices
Denton	20th Sept	11.00 P.M.	Section Departs from Barlin	
		1.00 A.M.	Section Arrives at Denton.	
"	21st Sept		Driver, one man & float proceeded to W. Stuart. Drain Pres. Ayn. Hestin to collect 1 Sick Horse	
			No. T4/043397 Dvr Atkinson Awarded 7 days C.C. prejudicial to good order & military discipline	
"	22nd Sept.		Driver, one man & float proceeded to D/223 Bde RFA for Sick Horse	
			Driver one man & float Proceeded to A/317 Bde R.F.A for Sick Horse	
			Cpl Ford & 6 men returns from 13th F. Vety Hospital	
"	23rd Sept		OC Inspected Saddles, Rifles, & Identification & gas helmets of Section	
			Driver, one man & float Proceeded to Hawke Battn for Sick Horse	
"	24th Sept.		Cpl Lewis & 1 man proceeded to 13th F Vety Hospital in charge of 12 sick Animals	
"	25th Sept.		Driver, one man & float proceeded to Hennicourt A/a H. S. Coy. A.S.C for 1 sick Horse	
			Driver, one man & float. proceeded to St Martin 149th Bde R.F.A for 1 sick Horse.	
			Cpl Lewis & 1 man returns from 13th F. Vety Hospital	

2449 Wt. W14957/M90 750,000 1/16 J.B.C. & A. Forms/C.2118/12.

WAR DIARY or INTELLIGENCE SUMMARY

53rd Mobile Vety Section

Place	Date	Hour	Summary of Events and Information	Remarks and references to Appendices
Hulluch	26th Sept		One No man & 1 mule proceeded to A.S.C. Btl Stables to report sick horse. One x Corporal & two proceeded to 13 Field Vety Hospital. Rank of B/ Sect Admiral.	
"	27th Sept		One x 1 N.C. & four Men proceeded to Rouen Base for sick horse. Section paid. Capt N.C. Quinnell returns from England & takes over command of Section. 1 August R.S.	
"	28th Sept		He visits long days & R.S. Cpl Levin & two men proceeded to 13 F Vety Hospital in charge of 13 sick animals. Driver one man & four proceeded to No 3 Cav Bde S. Henin for 1 sick animal. USA ambulance ASC proceeded to Chelers on manoeuvres but aimed Sgt Walker & 3 Men proceeded to Lyonville & Hindermes for Drivers.	
"	29th		1 Walker & 2 Men returns from Sevelins. Driver one man & four proceeded to 3/3 Res Bde C Sqn for 1 sick horse.	

Army Form C. 2118.

WAR DIARY
or
INTELLIGENCE SUMMARY

(Erase heading not required.)

53rd Mobile Vety Section

Place	Date	Hour	Summary of Events and Information	Remarks and references to Appendices
Nurlu Sept.	30th		Sgt Andrews & 3 men NCO returning from Chateau Tom Hanover Area to F Section. Cpl Foster & 3 men returning from 18th Field Vety Hospl. SS. 20491 Smith Harry G. for duty from No 22 Field Veterinary Hospital. T/04339 Pte Wilkinson awarded 28 days Field Punishment No. 1. Offence:- drunkenness &c. (3) Feigning a convulsion whilst on active service :- duly founded over to the R.P.M. 63 (RN) Division and was founded.	

Wilmot C Emmerich
Capt f A.V.C.
O.C. 5"/3"rd = Mobile Veterinary Section
63rd (R.N.) Division.
1st October 1916.

CONFIDENTIAL.

WAR   DIARY

of

53rd Mobile Veterinary Section.
63rd (R.N) Division.

From 1st October, 1916   to   31st October, 1916.

VOLUME   5

Wilmot R. Dinnell
Captain A.V.C.
O.C., 53rd Mobile Vety. Section.

Army Form C. 2118.

WAR DIARY
or
INTELLIGENCE SUMMARY

(Erase heading not required.)

333rd (North Ichmary) Infpn

Place	Date	Hour	Summary of Events and Information	Remarks and references to Appendices
Onston	1st Oct 1916	8 P.M.	1 N.C.O. & man proceed to No. 13. Field Dy/Hospital in charge of 13 Sick Animalizments	
"	2nd "		Nil.	
"	3rd "	8 P.M.	1 N.C.O + 3 men proceed to No 13. Field Dy/Hospital in charge of 29 Sick animals (including 2 Mares & 2 Jacks) evacuated	
		7.30 P.M	S.E. 6289. Pte Wheeler W. proceeds to England on special leave	
		9 A.M.	Section leaves Onston arrives at Frevent	
Frevent	4th "	6.30 P.M	& billets open field.	
"	4th "	5.30 A.M.	Section leaves Frevent for Leaturlier arriving	
Leaturlier	"	11 P.M.	& billetted from in Barn & horses open field	
"	5th "		Besides Sectional Routine Duties under the lines of L Signal Co; 10th Durham Fusiliers at Ht Beaufort.	

Army Form C. 2118.

WAR DIARY
or
INTELLIGENCE SUMMARY

(B)

(Erase heading not required.)

53rd Mobile Veterinary Section

Place	Date	Hour	Summary of Events and Information	Remarks and references to Appendices
Lentilleres	Oct 6th		Besides Sectional Routine duties, inter-Relieves of Signal Co; 10th Dublin Fusiliers at H.S. Belfort.	
"	7th	8-30 A.M.	Section leaves Lentilleres, arriving at	
Hedauville	"	9-30 A.M.	Billetted. Then Forces in Open Field.	
			Men & Horses proceed with flow to collect Sick Horse Trouville.	" Betnt — Beaussart
"	8th		" " " " " " "	" "
"	9th		N.C.O. & 2. Men proceed to No. 22. Bde H.F. Hospital in charge of 19. Sick Horses evacuated.	
"	10th		Men & Horses proceed with float to collect a Sickhorse Forceville	
"	11th		Nil.	
"	12th		N.C.O. & 2 Men proceed to No. 22 Bde H.F. Hospital in charge of 18. Sick Horses evacuated.	
"	13th		Men & Horses proceed with float to collect a Sick Horse Forceville	

Army Form C. 2118.

Instructions regarding War Diaries and Intelligence Summaries are contained in F. S. Regs., Part II. and the Staff Manual respectively. Title Pages will be prepared in manuscript.

WAR DIARY
or
INTELLIGENCE SUMMARY

(Erase heading not required.)

53rd Mobile Veterinary Section

Place	Date	Hour	Summary of Events and Information	Remarks and references to Appendices
Heelourille	20 14		S/E 6289. Pte. Wheeler W. returned from England from hosp.	
"	"		Man & own horses with 79 float worth a sick Horse Prisoners Heelourille	
"	15		Nil	
"	16		Man & own horses with 2 hrs to collect a sick Prisoner	
"	"		N.C.O. & 2 men horses to No. 22 Base Vet. Hospital in charge of 17 sick animals evacuated	
"	17		Man & own horses with float to collect a sick horse Prisoners Frevits	
"	18		" " " " " kto " " "	
"	19		N.C.O. & 2 men horses to No. 22 Base Vet. Hospital in charge of 20 sick animals evacuated	
"	"		Besides Sectional routine duties, visited daily from this date the lines of Mult of 189th Brigade to the end of month.	

Army Form C. 2118.

WAR DIARY
or
INTELLIGENCE SUMMARY

(Erase heading not required.)

53rd Mobile Veterinary Section

Instructions regarding War Diaries and Intelligence Summaries are contained in F. S. Regs., Part II. and the Staff Manual respectively. Title Pages will be prepared in manuscript.

(D)

Place	Date	Hour	Summary of Events and Information	Remarks and references to Appendices
Hedauville	March 20th	—	Manoeuvres (forces) with flock to collect sick Horses	Manoeuvres
"	"	—	" " " " " " "	Forceville
"	"	—	" " " " " " "	Englebelmer
"	21st	—	" " " " " " "	Englebelmer
"	"	—	" " " " " " "	Hérissart
"	22nd	—	" " " " " " "	Forceville
"	"	—	" " " " " " "	Hedauville
"	"	—	N.C.O. & 2 men proceed to No. 22 Base Vety Hospital in charge of 17 Sick Animals for Evacuation.	
"	"	—	From forces proceed with flock to collect sick Horses Crooked	Trépune
"	23rd	—	" " " " " " "	
"	24th	—	N.C.O. & 2 men proceed to No. 22 Base Vety Hospital in charge of 17 Sick Animals for Evacuation	
"	"	—	2nd Sick Animals evacuated.	

Army Form C. 2118.

WAR DIARY
or
INTELLIGENCE SUMMARY

(Erase heading not required.)

33 rd / 7 th / 6 (Veterinary Section)

Place	Date	Hour	Summary of Events and Information	Remarks and references to Appendices
Hedouville	Oct. 25th	—	Man & Driver forces with floyd to collect horses to 1st Western S.E. 10428. Pte Skyper I admitted 2nd Field Ambulance wounded	
"	"	—	NCO & 2 men forced to No 22 Bn & Y.C.B. hospitals in charge	
"	26th	—	of 18 sheb Animals evacuated.	
"	"	—	7 No SE 8334 Pte Tretheler A. reported sick from No 10. Stationary Hospital where he was admitted on 24/9/16	
"	"	—	No S.E. 11904 Pte: Slaney J.W.} Join Section from } No 7. Bn o Veterinary	
"	"	—	" " 5789 " Irvine W. } Hospital,	
"	27th	—	No SE. 1058 Dr. Burton J. admitted 2nd Field Ambulance	
"	28th	—	NCO & 4 men to proceed to No 22. Bn o V.F. Hospital in charge of 33 sick animals evacuated	

WAR DIARY
or
INTELLIGENCE SUMMARY

(Erase heading not required.)

Army Form C. 2118.

53rd (2nd/1st the Welch in. my) Section

Place	Date	Hour	Summary of Events and Information	Remarks and references to Appendices
Heilwooll	Oct 28		No S.E. 10357. Pte; Krejo J.) admitted 2nd A.S.C. 1/4044.3397. Driver Attendant) Field Ambulance	
	29th		No S.E. 7889. Pte Tnockton. W.) admitted 2nd No S.E. 5189. " Tyno. W.) Field Ambulance Then Driver proceed with Pvt to attend 28 Sick horses to Aberwith	
	30th		Wire received form O in C at 7 P.M. at Towyn that No S.E. Pte Allen. A. (One commanding sent to Abercyth with Horses on 29 inst) was murder arrest with Escort conducting Pack.	

Army Form C. 2118.

WAR DIARY
or
INTELLIGENCE SUMMARY

(Erase heading not required.)

53rd Mobile Veterinary Section

Place	Date	Hour	Summary of Events and Information	Remarks and references to Appendices
Hedauville	31st		N.C.O.s & E 579. S/S Cooke F.W.) admitted to N.º 1 Field " " 3384. Pte Scott. F.) Ambulance. N.C.O. & 1 man to escort to N.º 22. Bwsjais Hospital i/c charge of 16 Sick animals. Summary of Horses & mules dealt with by the Section during the month :- Evacuated - 210. Treated - 30. Joined - 7. } 256 Sick - 5. Lost - Destroyed - 3 W.H.H. Grimmond Capt. A.V.C.	

Vol 5

<u>Confidential</u>

<u>War Diary</u>

<u>— of —</u>

<u>53rd Mobile Veterinary Section</u>

<u>63rd (RN) Division</u>

<u>From 1st November 1916 to 30th November 1916</u>

<u>Volume 6</u>

<u>C.E. Neill   Capt</u>
AVC

Army Form C. 2118.

WAR DIARY
or
INTELLIGENCE SUMMARY

(Erase heading not required.)

Instructions regarding War Diaries and Intelligence Summaries are contained in F. S. Regs., Part II. and the Staff Manual respectively. Title Pages will be prepared in manuscript.

Place	Date	Hour	Summary of Events and Information	Remarks and references to Appendices
Adainville	2.11.16		One man Driver and Stoat proceeded to Forceville for one days leave S.E 2892 Pte Sanders R and A.S.C No 297 Driver Scott admitted to No 1 Field Ambulance	
	3.11.16		One N.C.O and escort return from Abeville with S.E No 96 Pte Allen G. who moved in the N.C.O and three men proceeded to N°22 Base Veterinary Hospital	
	3.11.16		One man Driver and Stoat proceeded to Havenes for 1 days leave	
	4.11.16		A man Driver and Stoat at proceeded to Havrincourt & Havenes for 1 days leave 1 N.C.O and three men proceeded to No Base hospital No 16 of No 31 Field Hosp 1 N.C.O and three men returning from 22nd Base hospital	
	5.11.16		One man a driver and Stoat proceeded to Havrincourt for 1 days leave S.E No 96 Pte Allen G. admitted 21 days S.S field punishment for drunkenness and breaking out of Adainville Station One N.C.O and three men return from Base Veterinary Hospital	
	6.11.16		One man a Driver and Stoat proceeded to Engleterre for 1 days leave S.E 11036 Pte Davies J S.E 10692 " N° William H } Joined the section from N°9 base hospital S.E 11951 " Salisbury J	

2449 Wt. W14957/M90 750,000 1/16 J.B.C. & A. Forms/C.2118/12.

Army Form C. 2118.

WAR DIARY
or
INTELLIGENCE SUMMARY

(Erase heading not required.)

Place	Date	Hour	Summary of Events and Information	Remarks and references to Appendices
Abbeville	7.11.16		N.C.2893 Pte Sanders R. rejoined the section from 2nd Field Ambulance. 1 N.C.O and three men returned from Base Veterinary Hospital	
	8.11.16		1 foreman Driver and 1 Shoot-proceeded to Havre on to 1 Sick horse. 1 N.C.O and 7 men proceeded to 22nd Base Veterinary Hospital /o 43 Sick animals. N.C. 11904 Pte Murray S admitted to 2nd Field Ambulance. N.C. 11953 Dr Forest H Rejoins Section from 3rd Field Ambulance	
	9.11.16		Nil	
	10.11.16		1 horse shoer and Shoot-proceeded to Havre for 2 Sick horses. 1 N.C.O and 2 men proceeded to 22nd Base Veterinary Hospital. /o 24 Sick horses	
	11.11.16		1 horse Driver Shoot-proceeded to Abbeville for 1 Sick horse. 1 N.C.O and 5 men return from 22nd Base Veterinary Hospital	
	12.11.16		1 N.C.O and 4 men proceeded to 22nd Base Veterinary Hospital /o 21 Sick animals. 1 N.C.O and 3 men proceeded to England to arrive Remount Station	
	13.11.16		1 N.C.O and 2 men return from 22nd Base Veterinary Hospital	
	14.11.16		1 N.C.O and 4 men proceeded to 22nd Base Veterinary Hospital /o no Sick animals	

Army Form C. 2118.

WAR DIARY
or
INTELLIGENCE SUMMARY

(Erase heading not required.)

Instructions regarding War Diaries and Intelligence Summaries are contained in F. S. Regs., Part II. and the Staff Manual respectively. Title Pages will be prepared in manuscript.

Place	Date	Hour	Summary of Events and Information	Remarks and references to Appendices
Abbeville	15.11.16		N.C. 984 Pte Claxton A.J.) Return from No 5 Convalescent Home Depot S.E. 1557/H " Dixon R) 1 N.C.O. and 4 men return from 23 no Base Veterinary Hospital	
	16.11.16		1 N.C.O and 4 men Return from attenuand Dressing Station at Eryhehelmer	
	17.11.16		1 horse & driver and staff proceeded to Eruyny's for 1 sick horse 1 N.C.O & 4 men return from 22nd Base Veterinary Hospital	
		5 P.M	Section handed over 83 sick Animals for Evacuation to No 28 Mobile Vety Section	
		8 P.M	leaving 6 men behind to assist in the Evacuation Section arrives at Argoeuves	
Argoeuves	18.11.16	10 am	Section leaves Argoeuves	
Saigneville		4 P.M	Section arrives at Saigneville	
	19.11.16	10 am	Section leaves Saigneville	
		1 P.m	Section arrives at Tenvillers	
Tenvillers	20.11.16		S.E. 9168 Serjt Shone. J reports for duty from No 14 Base Veterinary Hospital	

WAR DIARY or INTELLIGENCE SUMMARY

Army Form C. 2118.

(Erase heading not required.)

Place	Date	Hour	Summary of Events and Information	Remarks and references to Appendices
Yvrencheux	22.11.16	9.45 A.M.	Section leaves Yvrencheux	
Mesnil Gonguet	22.11.16	2 P.M.	Section arrives at Mesnil Gonguet	
		10 A.M.	Section leaves Mesnil Gonguet	
		2 P.M.	Section arrives at St. Riquier. Temporary Cpl. Dummett leaves Section for England. No 303 S/Sergt Andrews A.1 leaves Section for No 14 Base Veterinary Hospital for duty. L.N.G. O. 1 man return to Yvrencheux & Candas to collect 700 kms for Base	
Brigny St. Maclou	23.11.16	10.20 A.M.	Section leaves St. Riquier	
		2 P.M.	Section arrives at Brigny St. Maclou. Captain K. Broad arrives and takes over duties of O.C.	
	24.11.16	10 A.M.	Section leaves Brigny St. Maclou. L.E. Pte Stimson W.A. joins Section for duty from No 2 Base Veterinary Hospital	
		2 P.M.	Section arrives at Javonville	
Javonville	25.11.16		Capt C.E. Neill arrived from 315th Brigade R.F.A. Reputation Duties & takes Command of the 53rd Mobile Vet Section. Capt J.E. Broad leaves the Section to resume his ordinary duties. 6 men return from Base Veterinary Hospital, after awaiting transfer from 29 M.V.S.	
	25.11.16	Continued	L.N.G. O. 1 man return from 22nd Base Veterinary Hospital	
	26.11.16			

Army Form C. 2118.

WAR DIARY
or
INTELLIGENCE SUMMARY

(E)

(Erase heading not required.)

Instructions regarding War Diaries and Intelligence Summaries are contained in F. S. Regs., Part II. and the Staff Manual respectively. Title Pages will be prepared in manuscript.

Place	Date	Hour	Summary of Events and Information	Remarks and references to Appendices
Canneville	27.11.16		Nil	
	28.11.16		Nil	
	29.11.16		1. A.D.V.O. and his men proceeded to 23rd Base Veterinary Hospital in charge of 51 sick animals. S.E. 7522 Pte Stevenson W.A. admitted to 1st Field Ambulance	
	30.11.16		SE 7522 Pte Stevenson W.A. evacuated to 7th Canadian Hospital	

Eg Kaill Capt. R.C.A. Section
O.C. 13th Mobile Veterinary
30.11.16

Vol 6

<u>Confidential</u>

53ʳᵈ Mobile Veterinary Section

January 2ⁿᵈ 1917

<u>War Diary</u>
of
<u>53ʳᵈ Mobile Veterinary Section</u>

From
<u>December 1ˢᵗ 1916</u>
to
<u>December 31ˢᵗ 1916</u>

To A.G.'s Office
3ʳᵈ Echelon

J. C. Broad
Capt A.V.C.
53ʳᵈ Mobile Veterinary Section

WAR DIARY of 53rd Mobile Veterinary Section

Army Form C. 2118.

INTELLIGENCE SUMMARY

(Erase heading not required.)

Place	Date	Hour	Summary of Events and Information	Remarks and references to Appendices
Sarraville (Rue)	1916 Dec 1		Section. 1 Hr. foot drill. 1 N.C.O. & 2 men returned from 22nd Base Veterinary Hospital. 5 sick animals admitted.	
	" 2		1 N.C.O. & 3 men proceeded to 22nd Base Veterinary Hospital in charge of 22 sick animals. O.C. to sick railhead. Inspection of Section by A.D.V.S. 4 sick animals admitted.	
	" 3		General inspection of horses, stables, men by O.C. 1 N.C.O. & 3 men returned from 22nd Base Vety. Hospital. 1 N.C.O. Driver Ford proceed to de Baal des Boers for 6 sick animals. On return journey Ford axle broke; Ford left on road. O.C. proceeds to railhead. 12 sick animals admitted.	
	" 4		SE/15774 Pte Dixon admitted to 1st Field Ambulance; Section had 1 hr. football. A.D.V.S. visited Section.	
	" 5		SE/15774 Pte Dixon evacuated to 1st Canadian Hospital, & was struck off strength of Section. 1 hr. mounted drill for Section. Rifle inspection. 14 sick animals admitted.	
	" 6		1 N.C.O. & 3 men proceeded to 22nd Base Vety. Hospital in charge of 18 sick animals. O.C. proceeded to SE/10692 Lt. McMillan proceeded to England on leave. railhead. 9 sick animals admitted.	

WAR DIARY of 53 Mobile Veterinary Section

INTELLIGENCE SUMMARY

Army Form C. 2118.

(Erase heading not required.)

Place	Date	Hour	Summary of Events and Information	Remarks and references to Appendices
Lamonville	1916 Dec 7		Section had 1 hr foot drill: rifle inspection. 2 sick animals admitted.	
	-8-		1 N.C.O., limbered wagon & driver proceeded to Ordnance dump for Stores. 4 sick animals admitted.	
	-9-		Section had 1 hr. mounted drill, 1 hr rifle drill. 5 sick animals admitted.	
	-10-		1 N.C.O. 1 private proceeded to H.Q. Coy. Divisional Train to arrange about horses for evacuation. General inspection of billets, harness river &c. to 10.0b. P. Hain, joined Section from Vet. Convalescent Horse Depot.	
	-11-		1 N.C.O. 1 private proceeded to 22" Base Vet. Hospital in charge of 23 sick animals. O.C. proceeded to railhead. 9 sick animals admitted.	
	-12-		S.E./8334 Pte Webster proceeded to 3" Field Ambulance. 1 N.C.O. 2 men returned from Base Vet. Hospital. Inspection of Section by D.D.V.S. 5th Army. 1 man & driver, with limbered wagon proceeded to coal dump for fuel. 1 sick animal admitted.	
	-13-		1 hr riding drill for Section. 1 N.C.O. + 1 man proceeded to Noreuil to number horses belonging to 317 Brigade, R.F.A. ready for evacuation. Section's blankets sent to Steriliser.	

Army Form C. 2118.

WAR DIARY of 53rd Mobile Veterinary Section

or

INTELLIGENCE SUMMARY

(Erase heading not required.)

Instructions regarding War Diaries and Intelligence
Summaries are contained in F. S. Regs., Part II.
and the Staff Manual respectively. Title Pages
will be prepared in manuscript.

Place	Date	Hour	Summary of Events and Information	Remarks and references to Appendices
Lamorville	1916 Dec 13 (cont'd)		No. 235/ Sgt Wilson F. proceeded to England on leave. 4 sick animals admitted.	
	" 14		1 N.C.O. + 2 men proceed to No. 22. Base Vety Hospital by road, in charge of sick animals, assisted by R.F.A. Conducting party returned same day. 3 sick animals admitted.	
	" 15		1 hours riding drill for Section. 2 sick animals admitted.	
	" 16		Section departs from Lamorville at 1.30 p.m., arriving at Fauvres at 3.0 p.m. SE/6332 L/Cpl McCarthy admitted to 2" Field Ambulance. (was taken ill whilst on duty) SE/8324 Pte Webster evacuated to S.A. General Hospital. 6 sick animals admitted.	
Fauvres	" 17		O.C. proceeded to Foova Dall's at midnight to meet cole car. Limbered wagon + driver proceeded to Rue for fuel. A.D.V.S. visited Section. 6 sick animals admitted	
	18		16 sick animals evacuated to 22" Base Vety Hospital. 1 N.C.O + 2 men in charge L/Cpl McCarthy returned to duty from hospital. Capt Neal proceeded to Eng Base on leave: Capt Broad took over Section. 4 sick animals admitted	

WAR DIARY of 53 Mobile Veterinary Section

INTELLIGENCE SUMMARY

Army Form C. 2118.

(Erase heading not required.)

Instructions regarding War Diaries and Intelligence Summaries are contained in F. S. Regs., Part II. and the Staff Manual respectively. Title Pages will be prepared in manuscript.

Place	Date	Hour	Summary of Events and Information	Remarks and references to Appendices
Favieres	1916 Dec 19		Limbered wagon & driver proceeded to Rue to draw forage & stores. 1 N.C.O. & 2 men returned from 22. Base Rly. Hospital. Lt. McMillan SF/1062 returned from leave. 34 sick animals admitted.	
	" 20		Section had their rifle drill. A.D.V.S. visited Section. Limbered wagon & driver proceeded to Rue for stores.	
	" 21		Limbered wagon & driver proceeded to coal dump to draw fuel. General inspection of billets, stables & equipment by O.C. O.C. visits railhead & evacuates. 5 sick animals admitted.	
	" 22		1 N.C.O. & 4 men proceeded to 22. Base Rly. Hospital in charge of 38 sick animals. O.C. proceeded to railhead with evacuating party. 2 sick animals admitted.	
	" 23		Limbered wagon & driver & N.C.O. proceeded to Abbeville to draw drugs, with instructions of A.D.V.S. 1 N.C.O. & 4 men proceeded to 22. Base Rly Hospital in charge of 33 sick animals. 8 animals admitted.	

WAR DIARY or INTELLIGENCE SUMMARY

Army Form C. 2118.

of 53rd Mobile Veterinary Section

Place	Date	Hour	Summary of Events and Information	Remarks and references to Appendices
Laviero	1916 Dec 24		Limbered wagon & driver & 1 N.C.O. returned from Abbeville with dogs.	
	" 25		1 N.C.O. & 5 men proceeded to 22nd Base Vety Hospital in charge of 37 sick animals: evacuated by road. 1 N.C.O. & 4 men returned from 22nd Base Vety Hospital. 5 sick animals admitted. Several inspections of units by A.D.V.S. & O.C.	
	" 26		Sergt Shore & 5 men returned from 22nd Base Vety Hospital. Daily routine as usual until 12.30 p.m. Section paraded at 4.30 p.m. to water & feed. Limbered wagon & driver proceeded to Rue to draw stores. 1 hr. marching drill for Section. Sergt Wilson & 2 men returned from leave.	
	27		5 sick animals evacuated to 22nd Base Vety Hospital, in charge of 1 N.C.O. & 3 men. 74/14990 S. Fossett from France proceeded to No 5 Base Vety Hospital for new foot, by instructions of A.D.V.S. also to Rest Base Vety Stores for 1 Vety. Chests Vet (25lb). 4 sick animals admitted.	

WAR DIARY of 53rd Mobile Veterinary Section

Army Form C. 2118.

or

INTELLIGENCE SUMMARY

(Erase heading not required.)

Place	Date	Hour	Summary of Events and Information	Remarks and references to Appendices
Laventie	1916 Dec 28		Sgt Watson + 3 men returned from 22nd Base Rly Hospital. Sgt Fossett returned with men floral & drugs from Base Rly Hospital. 10 sick animals admitted. Section had 1 hr riding exercise. Rifle inspection. 4 sick animals admitted.	
	" 29		Snow. Wheeled wagon proceeded to de Cathy to draw forage. A.D.V.S. visits.	
	" 30		Laventie. 10 sick animals admitted. 32/1953 Sgt Herbert proceeded to No 2 Base Rly Hospital for duty, by instructions of A.V.C. Base Records.	
	" 31		1 N.C.O. + 3 men proceeded to 22nd Base Rly Hospital in charge of 27 sick animals. O.C. visit returned. General inspection of billets, stables & equipment by O.C. 19 sick animals admitted.	

T Broad. Cpl A.V.C.
for O.C. 53rd Mobile Veterinary Section

Confidential   53rd Mobile Veterinary Section

Volume 8.

War Diary
of
53rd Mobile Veterinary Sect:

From   January 1st 17

To   January 31st 17

To/
The A.G's Office
  3rd Echelon
    Base

C.E. Neill Capt. A.V.C.
O.C. 53rd M.V.S

Army Form C. 2118.

53rd Mobile Veterinary Section
63rd (R.N.) D

WAR DIARY
or
INTELLIGENCE SUMMARY

(Erase heading not required.)

Instructions regarding War Diaries and Intelligence Summaries are contained in F. S. Regs., Part II. and the Staff Manual respectively. Title Pages will be prepared in manuscript.

Place	Date	Hour	Summary of Events and Information	Remarks and references to Appendices
Faviers	1-1-17		Limber and driver proceeded to Rue to draw forage and Stores. That and driver & 1 N.C.O proceeded to 22nd Base Veterinary Hospital Abbeville with one sick horse. Two sick animals evacuated to 32nd Base Veterinary Hospital. Rifle inspection by acting O.C at 9 a.m. Where and animals admitted. One animal destroyed cast. The charger belonging to the Iron Major clipped. One horse belonging to No 2 Company transferred from Cox Reaper.	
"	2-1-17		Float driver and N.C.O return from Base Hospital Abbeville. Float driver and driver proceed to 6 Bonvalle for sick horse. Float & driver proceeded to Rue for sick horse. S.S. Sgt No 3 Sgt Longstone reported for duty from No 9 Base Veterinary Hospital. Twenty six sick animals evacuated 22nd Base Vet J Hospital 10 of 1 NDD & 7 man. One animal destroyed suffering from Influenza Icteria. On way seven animals returned	
"	3-1-17		Acting O.C (Capt n Broad) and One N.C.O's proceeded to Base Vets & 2 ... Base Vet's Hospital for a riot animal. Capt'n Broad course of inoculation. Float and driver proceeded to Rue for a riot animal. Capt'n Broad returned from Leave and took over Command of Section. O.C returned from Leave Section (how pretty severene the inoculation) acting O.C leaves Section	
"	4-1-17		Float and driver proceed to Rue for sick horse. One N.C.O and 10 men proceeded to Joncville to join the 53rd M.V.S for duty under instructions from the D.D.V.S. O.C inspects men, billets, and equipment. Two sick animals admitted	
"	5-1-17		Limber and driver proceed to 1/23 for pay. Seven sick animals Evacuated from C.R.E. clipped and taken over.	

Army Form C. 2118.

53rd Mobile Veterinary Section
53rd (W.N.) D

WAR DIARY
or
INTELLIGENCE SUMMARY
(Erase heading not required.)

Instructions regarding War Diaries and Intelligence Summaries are contained in F. S. Regs., Part II. and the Staff Manual respectively. Title Pages will be prepared in manuscript.

Place	Date	Hour	Summary of Events and Information	Remarks and references to Appendices
Varieres	6.1.17		All animals inspected by A.D.V.S. & O.C. Sick animals evacuated to 32nd Base Vet Hospital, 16 N.C.O. and 1 man. O.C. proceeded to Rashead.	Cholera
"	7.1.17		Orders and drivers proceeded to Rue for fuel and stores. N.C. party. Re-Barrage reported for duty from 58 Base Veterinary Hospital. Twenty one horse animals evacuated to 23rd Base Vet Hospital 16 one N.C.O and 3 men. O.C. attended published. One horse showing symptoms Strangles & Ulcerative Catarrh, and other sick animals admitted. Two animals developed cheast	
"	8.1.17		of army and two horses promoted to 41st Company for train for busters lines. Sick animals admitted	1NCO
"	9.1.17		A.M. 7.5 visited section. Orders and drivers proceeded to Rue for stores. 13 sick animals evacuated and two men returning from 23rd Base Vet Hospital. Three sick animals admitted 6.23rd Base Vet Hospital 16 1.N.C.O and his men 2 billets by A.D.V.S. + A.D.V.S. + O.C. One sick	
"	10.1.17		Inspection of animals, harness + billets by A.D.V.S. + O.C. One N.C.O. and two men return from 23rd Base Vet Hospital	
"	11.1.17		4.00 P.S. visited section. Six sick animals evacuated to 23rd Base Vet Hospital. 16 of one man. O.C. attended at Railhead. Sheep and cows proceeded to Hazren for sick horse. Three animals discharged.	
"	12.1.17		Orders and drivers proceeded to Rue for stores. Rifle inspection by O.C. and N.C.O. No sick animal admitted. Inspection of section lines by O.C.	

2449 Wt. W14957/Mgo 750,000 1/16 J.B.C. & A. Forms/C.2118/12.

Army Form C. 2118.

53rd Mobile Veterinary Section
63rd (R N) D

WAR DIARY
or
INTELLIGENCE SUMMARY
(Erase heading not required.)

Instructions regarding War Diaries and Intelligence Summaries are contained in F. S. Regs., Part II. and the Staff Manual respectively. Title Pages will be prepared in manuscript.

Place	Date	Hour	Summary of Events and Information	Remarks and references to Appendices
Javiens	13.1.17		Section made preparation for moving. At 10.20 am. N.S. left billet for place of assembly of convoy, where they were inspected by General Phillipo. Convoy moved off at 11.30 am and after having several halts en route arrived at Bucquoy St. Vaast at 6 P.M. Sick animals were evacuated by road to 22nd Base Vet: Hospital from billets to Louez. 2 N.C.O. and 1 man.	
Bucquoy St Vaast	14.1.17		Section of 1 officer, 9 N.C.O.s, 3 sanitary, place of assembly, and proceeded to Koyleu on Chaussee where it arrived at 4 P.M. Sick animals to 22nd Base Vet: Hospital 16 in no. One N.C.O. proceeded to Neuilly l'Hospital for sick load left by Royal Dublin Fusiliers animal found to have to meet 22nd Base Vet: Hospital. Sires to Silent V.	
Koyleu on Chaussee	15.1.17		Section left Koyleu on Chaussee at 8.20 am for place of assembly of convoy to Bennaville where it arrived at 3.30 p.m. 06 stated at 9 am and proceeded to Bennaville with Gun belonging to No 3 Company on their way at horse on Chaussee Fontes where horses for feed. Cut the billet occupied by our section at Jonas proceeded to Hamville. Sick animals to No of Division the third animal reserve animals too of which we believe belonged to 51st Division	
Bonnaville	16.1.17		Stations and billets made and spaces for inspection of horses. Three sick animals evacuated to 22nd Base Vet: Hospital. O6 started Parked.	
Harienco	17.1.17		Section left Bonnaville at 8.20 a.m. for place of assembly horses convoy at 5 p.m. and proceeded to Hamenes where it arrived at 5 p.m.	
Harienco	18.1.17		Inspection of section by O.C. the section visited by A.D.V.S.	

WAR DIARY or INTELLIGENCE SUMMARY

Army Form C. 2118.

53rd Mobile Veterinary Section
63rd (R.N?D.)

Place	Date	Hour	Summary of Events and Information	Remarks and references to Appendices
Marieux	19.1.17		O.C. & one NCO proceeded to Beauquesne to see horse left by 763 Company. Car train. Horse shot and NCO sent for. This case which was conveyed to 3/1st F.S. Coy. was for destruction.	
Toutencourt	20.1.17		Section proceeded from Marieux at 9 a.m. for Toutencourt, where 17 animals sent in from by sick animals were taken over by the 63rd M.V.S. 38 sick animals admitted by 32 sick animals evacuated to 22nd Base Vet. Hospital. 16 NCO and 6 men O.C. attended.	
"	21.1.17		Railways, Kenher & chimes proceeded to fuel dumps. Heat and chimes collected. NCO attended 12 sick animals admitted 1 from Englebelmer	
"	22.1.17		45 sick animals evacuated to 23rd Base Vet. Hospital 16 NCO and 5 men. Italians Railways. Italians clawey proceeded to Eng. Citerneg for a sick horse. He proceeded. S.E. M.P.S.1 Pte. Newbury proceeded on leave to England. 17 horse animals admitted	
"	23.1.17		Timbers & clinker proceeded to fuel dump. Rifle inspection at 9 am by O.C. and saddlery at 3 p.m. 36 sick animals admitted. 1 NCO & 6 men return from 22nd Base Vet. Hospital	
"	24.1.17		Forty seven sick animals evacuated to 23rd Base Vet. Hospital 16 of NCO & men. 1 NCO and 5 men return from 22nd Base Vet Hospital. Four sick animals admitted Heat & chimes collected 1 sick animal at Englebelmer. S.E. No. 23469 Shoeing Smith	
"	25.1.17		Murphy A. reported for duty from 803 Base Vet. Hospital, A.O.M.S. praster section Kirby G. proceeded to Nos Base Vet Hospital. Th. No. 1498 Shoeing Smith one horse slipped for A.D.M.S. Twenty eight sick animals admitted.	

Army Form C. 2118.

65th Mobile Veterinary Section
63rd R.W.D.

WAR DIARY
or
INTELLIGENCE SUMMARY
(Erase heading not required.)

Place	Date	Hour	Summary of Events and Information	Remarks and references to Appendices
Forceville	26.1.17		28 sick animals evacuated to 22nd Base Veterinary Hospital ½ . 1 N.C.O and 3 men detailed for this belonging to 5 M.4 Company Train. Head and dinner proceeded to Chaufayes for sick animal. One N.C.O and 5 men return from 22nd Base Veterinary Hospital. Two sick animals admitted.	
"	27.1.17		One N.C.O and 3 men return from 32nd Base Veterinary Hospital. Proceeded to 6 R.E. dump Engelbelmer for material for erecting stables. O.C. and all animals in section for Colegne Stables. Two sick animals admitted. Vaccines for sick lines. A.D.V.S. visited section.	
"	28.1.17		O.C. and 1 N.C.O proceeded to 6 R.E. dump Engelbelmer 6 arrange stabling. 3 heat and driver collected one sick horse from Engelbelmer Curtin and driver proceeded to said dump. Section said Eight sick animals admitted.	
"	29.1.17		Timber driver and men proceeded to Engelbelmer for stabling material. Heat and driver collected one sick horse from Bailly. 1 N.C.O and two men return from 22nd Base Veterinary Hospital. O.C. inspected rifles and Saddlery. One sick animal admitted.	
"	30.1.17		Timber and driven straw while from Acheus. 2 N.C.O.s proceeded to R.E. dump Engelbelmer for purpose of company material for stabling. Found inspection of men and kits by O.C. Eight sick animals admitted.	
"	31.1.17		Twenty two sick animals evacuated to 22nd Base Veterinary Hospital ½ . One N.C.O and two men in charge. One N.C.O and four men proceeded to Acheus on detachment. Ten sick animals admitted.	

(Sd.) J.S. Neill Capt. A.V.C.
53rd M.V.S

Confidential

[stamp: 53RD MOBILE VETERINARY SECTION. No..... Date. March 1st 17.]

Volume. 9.

War Diary

of

53rd Mobile Veterinary Section. 63rd (RND)

From. February 1st 1917.

To. February 28th 1917.

To.

The A.G's Office.

3rd Echelon.

J. C. Road. Capt. A.V.C.

O.C. 53rd M.V.S.

Army Form C. 2118.

WAR DIARY
or
~~INTELLIGENCE SUMMARY~~

(Erase heading not required.)

53' MOBILE VETERINARY SECTION

Place	Date	Hour	Summary of Events and Information	Remarks and references to Appendices
Forceville	1917 Feb. 1		Section inspected by D.D.V.S., A.D.V.S. and O.C. Winter and Snow proceeded to Arbeux to draw water. 27 animals evacuated.	
	" 2		~~Snow & hay inspected~~ SE/6981 Cpl Lewis proceeded on leave to England. Rifle inspection by O.C. All animals in Section examined for contagious disease and found free. I.V.C.O. returned from Base Veterinary Hospital. 5 animals evacuated.	
	3		Hay & oats collected rck from four Orderlies; limber wagon & mess carried on working to 3' Field Ambulance. 1/Cpl Spalding I.V.C. proceeded for duty from C. Bathop. 223. Sgt - T.S.A. 4 animals evacuated.	
	4		Hay & oats proceeded to No 3 Coy 63' R.I. Divisional Train for rations to brake. 1/Cpl Hoar Inspection of rifles by O.C. at 9.0 am. Inspection of ordinary tackle at 9.30 am. 2 animals evacuated.	
	5		Hay & oats collected rck from Englebelmer. SE/9251 Pte Charlton sports off base. Winter & Snow proceeded to field dump. 15 animals evacuated.	

2449 Wt. W14957/Mg0 750,000 1/16 J.B.C. & A. Forms/C.2118/12.

Army Form C. 2118.

WAR DIARY
or
INTELLIGENCE SUMMARY

(Erase heading not required.)

53" MOBILE VETERINARY SECTION

Instructions regarding War Diaries and Intelligence Summaries are contained in F. S. Regs., Part II. and the Staff Manual respectively. Title Pages will be prepared in manuscript.

Place	Date	Hour	Summary of Events and Information	Remarks and references to Appendices
Forceville	1917 Feb 5		Section visited by D.D.V.S. Mules & other animals sectional for vetting for R.E. Coys	
	" 7		at Engleburn. All animals kept in Section inspected for contagious disease.	
	8		One stabling discharged from 3rd Field Ambulance. 1 west Cow at Roselle	
	9		Mules & other horses to Colou to this sector. 1 sick animal admitted	
			Capt Neill A.V.C. relinquishes command of 53rd Mobr Veterinary Section	
			Capt Brow A.V.C. R/posted O.C. Mules & other horses to D.A.D.V.S.	
	10		for sector. Mules & other horses wash from Pobeux. General inspection of billets, men	
			& equipment by O.C.	
	11		Sergt Spaling N.C. despatched to No. 2 Base Veterinary Hospital for duty O.C.	
			proceeded to H.Q. Coy 63 (R.N. Division) Farm to inspect sick horses. 1 rejoined active	
	12		32 cars of wage evacuated to 28 Base Veterinary Hospital in charge of N.C.O.	
			and 3 men O.C. attended meeting. 38 animals admitted Section hard.	

Army Form C. 2118.

WAR DIARY
or
INTELLIGENCE SUMMARY
(Erase heading not required.)

53' MOBILE VETERINARY SECTION

Instructions regarding War Diaries and Intelligence Summaries are contained in F. S. Regs., Part II. and the Staff Manual respectively. Title Pages will be prepared in manuscript.

Place	Date	Hour	Summary of Events and Information	Remarks and references to Appendices
Locvill	1917 Feb 13		ADVS visited Section. Rif. inspection of O.C. 5 sick animals evacuated.	
	14		O.C. inspects sick animals & billets. A/Veg/Sgt. Boyle attached to 1 Cav/Field Amb. General Hospital. 48 sick animals evacuated to 22 Base Veterinary Hosp. O.C. attends sick in charge of 1 NCO and 5 men + 2 sick animals evacuated.	
	15		Stables + horse parade. 2 stray horses 32/793 & Denim gunner. 26 animals evacuated.	
	16		Rifle inspection by O.C. ADVS visited Section. 9 sick animals evacuated.	
	17		32 sick animals evacuated to 22 Base Veterinary Hospital in charge of 1 NCO and 3 men. O.C. worked with road. 1 NCO and 5 men returned from 22 Base Veterinary Hospital. 3 sick animals evacuated.	
	18		Inspection of billets by O.C. 1 officer 9 men arr'd 10.00 from D.V.O.S. 1 NCO and 3 men return from 22 Base Veterinary Hospital. Medical inspection of NCOs and men for scabies. O.C. visits Melawille to arrange lines & billets & shelter. 31 sick animals evacuated.	

2449 Wt. W14957/Mgo 750,000 1/16 J.B.C. & A. Forms/C.2118/12.

Army Form C. 2118.

WAR DIARY
or
INTELLIGENCE SUMMARY
(Erase heading not required.)

53' MOBILE VETERINARY SECTION

Place	Date	Hour	Summary of Events and Information	Remarks and references to Appendices
Toeuvilles	1917 Feb 19		21 sick animals evacuated to 22" Base Veterinary Hospital in charge of 1 NCO and 3 men. O.C. attended railhead. There rec'd Brevet of Thouxville 26 sick horses, 3 sick animals admitted.	
	20		A.O.V.3. visited Section. O.C. & 1 NCO proceeded to Bergicourt Road to inspect sick horse belonging to 7th Btn. 63 Res. Division from animal was destroyed. 9 sick animals admitted	
	21		22 sick animals evacuated to 22" Base Veterinary Hospital in charge of 1 NCO and 3 men. O.C. attended railhead. 1 NCO and 3 men return from Base Veterinary Hospital. 14 sick animals admitted.	
	22		O.C. inspects all animals on section lines for contagious disease. 19 sick animals admitted.	
	23		23 sick animals evacuated to 22' Base Veterinary Hospital in charge of 1 NCO and 3 men. Section visited by General Dame, A.D.M.S., and A.D.V.S. S.E./ 9153	

Army Form C. 2118.

WAR DIARY
or
INTELLIGENCE SUMMARY
(Erase heading not required.)

53 MOBILE VETERINARY SECTION

Place	Date	Hour	Summary of Events and Information	Remarks and references to Appendices
Hedauville	1917 Feb 23 cont		Sergt Herbert A.V.C. reported from No 2 Base Veterinary Hospital for duty. 2 animals discharged cured. 15 sick animals admitted.	
	24		Stable dresser proceeded to Engelbelmer for fuel. 1 N.C.O. and 3 men returned from 22° Base Veterinary Hospital. Inspection of billets and men by O.C. 4 sick animals admitted.	
	25		A.D.V.S. visited section. Rifle and lx respirator inspection by O.C. Section had half-hour gas drill. A small time-rick built by section for purpose of making quicklime for veterinary purposes. SS/9163 Sergt Chase A.V.C. discharged to No 2 Base Veterinary Hospital for duty. 7 sick animals admitted. Vaccinepure.	
	26		1 N.C.O and 3 men returned from 22° Base Veterinary Hospital. Ambulance driver proceeded to Engelbelmer for fuel. 3rd sect animals admitted. 4 animals discharged cured.	

Army Form C. 2118.

WAR DIARY
or
INTELLIGENCE SUMMARY

(Erase heading not required.)

53ʳᵈ MOBILE VETERINARY SECTION

Instructions regarding War Diaries and Intelligence Summaries are contained in F. S. Regs., Part II. and the Staff Manual respectively. Title Pages will be prepared in manuscript.

Place	Date	Hour	Summary of Events and Information	Remarks and references to Appendices
Neuville	1917 Feb 27		A.D.V.S. visited Section. O.C. examined all animals on October Lines for contagious disease. 9 clipping machine heads sharpened for 9³¹ˢ Sqⁿ R.F.A. Inspection of billets by O.C. 5 sick animals admitted. 1 animal discharged cured.	
"	28		13 sick animals evacuated to 22 Base Veterinary Hospital in charge of 1 N.C.O. and 1 man. O.C. took rations. Section cooker carted by Neuton Battalion sent to disinfect stabling in village vacated by 22ⁿᵈ Base Veterinary Hospital. 1 N.C.O. and 3 men returned from 22 Base Veterinary Hospital.	

Broad
Capt. A.V.C.

Confidential   Headquarters 63rd (RN) Div

53rd Mobile Vety Section

31st March 17

Vol 9

War Diary (Volume 10)

of

53rd Mobile Vety Section 63rd (RN) Div

From

1st March 1917

To

31st March 1917

T/o

The HQ³ Office

3rd Echelon

S. Broad Capt AVC

O/c 53rd Mobile Vety Sect

Army Form C. 2118.

53RD MOBILE VETERINARY SECTION.
No. ....
Date ....

WAR DIARY
or
INTELLIGENCE SUMMARY
(Erase heading not required.)

Instructions regarding War Diaries and Intelligence Summaries are contained in F. S. Regs., Part II. and the Staff Manual respectively. Title Pages will be prepared in manuscript.

Place	Date	Hour	Summary of Events and Information	Remarks and references to Appendices
HEDAUVILLE	MARCH 1		Limbered waggon and driver received ADVS office stores from Engelbelmer to Hedauville. Limbered waggon & driver proceed to Supply dump for rations. O.C. visited 9" Labour Coy R.E. horses. A.D.V.S. visited Section.	
	2		2 animals found straying admitted.	
	3		Limbered waggon & driver proceed to Supply dump for rations, also to find stray horses of 9/o Labour Bn. O.C. and gas helmet drill for 1/2 hr. SE/10404 & Curkhot admitted to 3rd Field Ambulance. 1 NCO & 3 men returned from 21" Base Vety Hospital. O.C. visits ADVS office.	
	4		Limbered waggon return, proceed to Supply dump for rations: Head & chest proceed to Engelbelmer. 10 catt/1 sick horse. 10 sick animals admitted. Inspection of 9/96 by O.C.	
	5		Limbered waggon return proceed to Supply dump for rations. ADVS visits Section. O.C. inspects all animals on lines for contagious disease. Inspection of cattle by O.C. Limbered waggon & driver proceed to Supply dump for rations. 15 sick animals evacuated to 22" Base Vet + Hospital in charge of 1 NCO and 1 man. O.C. attends railhead. 23 sick animals admitted.	

WAR DIARY or INTELLIGENCE SUMMARY

Army Form C. 2118.

53RD MOBILE VETERINARY SECTION.

Place	Date	Hour	Summary of Events and Information	Remarks and references to Appendices
HEDAUVILLE	MARCH 6		Limbered waggon & driver proceeded to Supply dump for rations. O.C. proceeded to Varennes to cast horse of 11 Marshals Batt. S/Sjt. D. Wheatland reported for duty from No 1 Base Vety Hospital.	
	7		9 sick animals admitted. Limbered waggon & driver proceeded to Supply dump for rations. 22 sick animals evacuated to 22° Base Vety Hospital in charge of 1 NCO & 2 men. O.C. attended rail head. 1 NCO & 1 man returned from 22 Base Vety Hospital. Rifle inspection by O.C. 17 sick animals admitted.	
	8		Limber waggon & driver proceeded to Supply dump for rations. 4 horse cleft of for D/223 By. R.F.A. 3 sick animals admitted.	
	9		Limbered waggon & driver proceeded to Supply dump for rations. 18 sick animals evacuated to 22 Base Vety Hospital in charge of 1 NCO & men. 4 surplus pack animals admitted & inspect animals of 11 Marshals Batt. 9 sick animals admitted. O.C. visited Varennes & Acheville to inspect animals of 11 Marshals Batt. O.C. visited A.D.V.S. office.	
	10		Limbered waggon & driver proceeded to Supply dump for rations. Driver with return proceeded	

Army Form C. 2118.

53RD MOBILE VETERINARY SECTION.

No. ....
Date. ....

WAR DIARY
or
INTELLIGENCE SUMMARY

(Erase heading not required.)

Instructions regarding War Diaries and Intelligence Summaries are contained in F. S. Regs., Part II. and the Staff Manual respectively. Title Pages will be prepared in manuscript.

Place	Date	Hour	Summary of Events and Information	Remarks and references to Appendices
MEDADVILLE	MARCH 10 (con/t)		1st Pat. Cy Divisional Train for G.S. wagon. Men to R.E. dump at St Rivelle for materials for stabling. 1 NCO + 1 man returned from 22 Div. Vet. Hospital. 9 sick animals admitted. Inspection of section by OC.	
	11		Supped stables wagon + drove proceeded to Chippy dump for rations. 1 N.C.O. + 1 man returned from 22 Div. Vet. Hospital. Inspection of 9.00 Returned to O.C. 9 gas killed animals for H.L. Inspection of Stables by OC. Vetns paid. 9 sick animals admitted.	
	12		Stables & wagon + drivers proceeded to Chippy dump for rations. ADVS proceeding to England on leave. O.C. takes on his duties. 31 sick animals evacuated to 22 Div. Vet. Hospital. in charge of 1 NCO + 3 men. 1 hour (Sound) issued to APM.	
	13		Stables + wagon + drivers proceeded to Chippy dump for rations. 19 surplus animals admitted. OC cents carries stabullen + Private Hopfer from J "Mounted + Battalion" g. taken Batt. R.E. Inspector of rifles in section by OC.	

2449 Wt. W14957/M90 750,000 1/16 J.B.C. & A. Forms/C.2118/12.

WAR DIARY or INTELLIGENCE SUMMARY

(Erase heading not required.)

Army Form C. 2118.

53RD MOBILE VETERINARY SECTION.

Place	Date	Hour	Summary of Events and Information	Remarks and references to Appendices
HEDAUVILLE	MARCH 14		Ambulance waggon & driver proceeded to Supply dump of Raincheval to meet supplies from No 1 Corps (Rear) Batt'y & 1st 1 Row to be handed to troops field O.R.E.	
			24 sick animals evacuated to 32 Base Vety Hospital. Received from No 22 Base Vety Hospital Field Staff of Mobile waggon and 1 N.C.O. 2 men for upkeep of Supplies received. Animals admitted.	
	15		Ambulance waggon & driver proceeded to Supply dump for return. Ambulance waggon & driver proceeded to field dump to No 4 Coy Div Train to collect 1 N.C.O. now Ambulance waggon & driver proceeded to feed sharps. 5 men attached G.S. school for instruction. 11 sick animals admitted.	
	16		Ambulance waggon & driver proceeded to Supply dump for return. 27 sick animals evacuated to 22 Base Vety Hospital in charge of 1 N.C.O. + 3 men. SE/41636 Pte Adams J reported for duty from No 14 Base Vety Hospital. 1 sick animal admitted.	
	17		Ambulance waggon & driver proceeded to Supply dump for return. How returns proceeded to No 2 Coy Divisional Train for 1 sick horse. Inspection of billets received by myself & O.C.	

2449 Wt. W14957/M90 750,000 1/16 J.B.C. & A. Forms/C.2118/12.

WAR DIARY or INTELLIGENCE SUMMARY

Army Form C. 2118.

53RD MOBILE VETERINARY SECTION.

Place	Date	Hour	Summary of Events and Information	Remarks and references to Appendices
HEDAUVILLE	MARCH 18		Ambulance waggon & driver proceed to Supply dump for rations. 7 animals trans fered to 2/1 (W.R.) Mobile Vet. Section. to Division. prior to 63 (R.N) Division moving. 2 N.C.O. and 3 men returned from 22 Div Vet Hospital. Stores packed ready for move.	
	19	9.15 am	Capt. A. O'Neill assumed charge of Section, as O.C. proceeded to D.H.Q. during move. Section moved off from Hedauville.	
HARPONVILLE		2.0 pm	Section arrived at Harponville. 1 horse collected from 1st Field Ambulance at Warloy. 2 transfers to H (W.R.) M.V.S. at Forceville	
BEAUVAL	20	7.30 am	Section moved off from Harponville	
		1.30 pm	Section arrived at Beauval	
BONNIERES	21	9.30 am	Section moved off from Beauval	
		3.30 pm	Section arrived at Bonnieres	
	22	10.15 am	Section moved off from Bonnieres	

Army Form C. 2118.

53RD MOBILE VETERINARY SECTION.

No..............
Date............

WAR DIARY
or
INTELLIGENCE SUMMARY

(Erase heading not required.)

Instructions regarding War Diaries and Intelligence Summaries are contained in F.S. Regs., Part II. and the Staff Manual respectively. Title Pages will be prepared in manuscript.

Place	Date	Hour	Summary of Events and Information	Remarks and references to Appendices
	MAR/18			
HERLIN-LE-SEC	22	2.0 p.m.	Section arrived at Herlin le Sec at 2.0 p.m. to visit animals actively sick.	
	23		Lines & stead washed, saddlery cleaned & inspected. Rifles inspected by O.C. & sick animals attended.	
		9.45 a.m.	O.C. visited Horse of 190" Brigade Enquiry.	
	24		Section received order from Herlin-le-Sec . 1 N.C.O. left at M. BERNARD AUCHY-AU-BOIS.	
PERNES	25	3.0 p.m.	Section arrived at PERNES.	
		8.40 a.m.	Section moved off from Pernes	
ESTREE BLANCHE		2.30 p.m.	Section arrived at Estree Blanche – 8 sick animals evacuated to 22 Div. Mob Hospital in charge of 1 N.C.O.	
	26	9.0 a.m.	Section moved off from Estree Blanche	
ROBECQ		3.0 p.m.	Section arrived at Robecq.	
	27		Saddlery, rifles inspected by O.C. O.C. visits visits to inspect Horses for evacuation	
	28		Capt. A. O'Neil proceeded to No. 3 Co Divisional Train to resume duty. Capt. C. Brown M.A.V.C. Section. O.C. visited units of 190" Brigade & notified at Allier in circulation of Horses. A.D.V.S. visited Section.	

2449 Wt. W14957/M90 750,000 1/16 J.B.C. & A. Forms/C.2118/12.

Army Form C. 2118.

WAR DIARY
or
INTELLIGENCE SUMMARY
(Erase heading not required.)

53RD MOBILE VETERINARY SECTION.
No............
Date............

Instructions regarding War Diaries and Intelligence Summaries are contained in F. S. Regs., Part II. and the Staff Manual respectively. Title Pages will be prepared in manuscript.

Place	Date	Hour	Summary of Events and Information	Remarks and references to Appendices
ROBECQ	MARCH 29		1 N.C.O. + 6 men despatched to 3rd Canadian Division M.V.S. for duty for such time as 53 Div. Div. Artillery is administered by that Division. Lieut.Colf Waggon & film evacuated; supervision of British Saddlery & Stores by O.C. H.Q. O.C. cocks awards of "A" "B" Groups.	
	30.		24 sick animals evacuated to No 13 Base O.C. Hospital in charge of 1 N.C.O. + 2 men. O.C. attended rainout. 1 N.C.O. + 1 man proceeded to Estairs - Gen. H.Q. Anoubra to collect 3 sick Horses left by 1st Ford Ambulance & Armor Bn: 1 m NCO for Divisional Gas School under restrict 82 Relief & instructional Purpose. 1 N.C.O. returned from No 22 Base Cty Hospital. O.C. visits A.D.V.S. O.C. inspected billets & saddlery; All Horses on turn for contagion disease.	
	31		1 N.C.O. in charge of 1 N.C.O. attended gas school for setting of Gas Helmets. O.C. interviewed butcher from Allen with regard to purchase of carcases and animals to be destroyed.	

R.Broad
C/L A.V.S.

Confidential   53rd Mobile Vety Section.

Vol 10   63rd (RN) Division

            30th April 1917

War Diary

of

53rd Mobile Veterinary Section

from

1st April 1917

To

30st April 1917

Volume — XI

To

The A.G's Office

3rd Echelon

J. Broad Capt AVC

O/C

53rd M.V.S.

Army Form C. 2118.

53RD
MOBILE VETERINARY
SECTION.

No..............
Date.............

WAR DIARY
or
INTELLIGENCE SUMMARY
(Erase heading not required.)

Instructions regarding War Diaries and Intelligence Summaries are contained in F.S. Regs., Part II. and the Staff Manual respectively. Title Pages will be prepared in manuscript.

Place	Date	Hour	Summary of Events and Information	Remarks and references to Appendices
A/Poseop	1917 April 1		A.D.V.S. visited Section. O.C. visited units of 190 Inf. Bgde. Capt Watson at war proceeded to Auchy and Bois aux Lebres Patrol to collect 2 horses left by 10 Royal Welsh Fusiliers. 14 sick animals admitted.	
	2		Steadiness rifle inspection by O.C. A.D.V.S. visited section. O.C. visited units of 190 Inf Bgde. O.C. lectures to transport Officers & NCOs on Stable Management. Post Section died for 48 hour. 14 sick animals admitted.	
	3		6 sick animals died, 1 sick animal destroyed. All corpses skinned & hides despatched to Base. Limbers & drawn processed to Allen Station with hides. 32 sick animals evacuated to 13 Base NCH Hospital in charge of 1 N.C.O. & 4 men. O.C. attended ... A.D.V.S. & D.D.R. visited Section.	
	4		O.C. inspected billets stabs. S.E. 12956 Sgt Ryan A.V.C. posted for duty until such time as he can report for duty to D.A.C. Working party of 1 N.C.O. & 19 men from 1st HAC reported for burying dead horses. 1 sick animal admitted.	

2449 Wt W14957/M90 750,000 1/16 J.B.C. & A. Forms/C.2118/12.

Army Form C. 2118.

53RD
MOBILE VETERINARY
SECTION.

No............
Date...........

WAR DIARY
or
INTELLIGENCE SUMMARY

(Erase heading not required.)

Place	Date 1917	Hour	Summary of Events and Information	Remarks and references to Appendices
Robecq	April 5		Numbered wagon & Drawn proceeded to coal dump for fuel. Supplied A/13 return packs & later to 1st HAC. Salvage dump. Working party from 1st HAC reported for duty.	
	6		O.C. visited units of 190 Inf. Bde. 89th. O.C. inspected all horses & mules for contagious diseases	
	7		Vehicles cleaned and oiled. S/mo at packes ready to move next day.	
	8		Section departed from Robecq at 8.30 am to arrive at Warlingham J march at 9.25 am. Section march with & under orders of 10th of 11th Divcoit (Pioneer Bn). Arrived at Bruay at 2.30 pm. A.D.V.S. visited Section. 3 sick animals admitted.	
	9		SE 12950' Lt. Regan A. departed hospital for duty to Dymbert 63 (?) D.A.C. 1 N.C.O. & 1 man left in charge of 10 sick animals for "23" Base Vet. Hospital. O.C. attended restored. O.C. visited A.D.V.S. & units. 1 N.C.O. returned from 13" Gen. BM Hospital.	
	10		Sno. behind clock for 1/2 hour. Inspection of saddlery, rifles & billets by O.C. O.C. visited units of 190 Inf. Bde. A.D.V.S. visited Section	

Army Form C. 2118.

53RD MOBILE VETERINARY SECTION.

No...........
Date...........

WAR DIARY
or
INTELLIGENCE SUMMARY
(Erase heading not required.)

Instructions regarding War Diaries and Intelligence Summaries are contained in F. S. Regs., Part II. and the Staff Manual respectively. Title Pages will be prepared in manuscript.

Place	Date	Hour	Summary of Events and Information	Remarks and references to Appendices
	1917			
Bruay	April 11		Section departed from Bruay at 10.15 am. under orders of 190" Inf. Bde. arrived at 06 Caute at 1.15 pm.	
La Caute	12		A.D.V.S. visited Section. O.C. visited units of 190" Inf. Bde. Quartermaster & driver proceeded to coal dump for fuel.	
	13		7 sick animals admitted & evacuated to 3 Canadian M.V.S. at Berlin. O.C. visited units of 190" Inf. Bde. O.C. visited sick horse at Maquence at 9.30 pm.	
	14		O.C. visited sick horse at 6.15 am. Rode to Aubigny for two hours to watch Section departed from La Caute & then proceeded to Aguiers, sat on Bluth at 9 am. M.V.S. & feed stores, then proceeded to Aguiers.	
Aguiers	15		39 sick animals admitted. An advanced collecting post established at 5.30 pm. Fatigue party from 1st (P.B.) Labour Coy. attached to bury dead animals 2 N.C.O.s by 44" M.V.S.	
"	16		10 sick animals admitted. O.C. visited advanced collecting post. 40 sick animals evacuated to 22" Base Vety Hospital. 2 N.C.O.s & men from 1st P.B. Labour Coy. attached to bury dead animals. O.C. attended meeting at "A.D.V.S." Fatigue party 16 sick animals admitted.	

Army Form C. 2118.

53RD
MOBILE VETERINARY
SECTION.

WAR DIARY
INTELLIGENCE SUMMARY
(Erase heading not required.)

Place	Date	Hour	Summary of Events and Information	Remarks and references to Appendices
	1917			
Aguiera	Apr 17		Section dispatched for Aguiera at 11.0 a.m. arrived at Marœuil at 2.30pm. Apr 17 Field where took	
Marœuil	Apr 18		on the journey	
	19		3 sick animals admitted. Sec hitted out for R.V. Rifle inspection by OC	
			Subcharges upon Drivers proceed to first dump. Dentally inspection by OC. 1 NCO & men return for	
	20		3rd Canadian M.V.S. 1 N.C.O & men return for 22 Bde DAC hospital. 53 sick animals admitted	
			2. 32nd Sqd Herd A 93/1 Bde AFA attached to Section for Board on evacuation attached. A.D.V.S. +	
			1st Field Ambulance. 5 sick animals dehors. dismount. 8 sick animals admitted	
	21		OC sited place for Advanced Bathing Pool	
			Lieut Sealsto No. 3 Coy Cdn Rail. Btns was sited opend 40 sick animals admitted	
	22		63 sick animals admitted. A.R.T Canadian M.V. in charge of 1 N.C.O 2 men. Returned	
			Bathing Pool established. 7 dismounts loaned. 63 sick animals admitted. 1 N.C.O & 5 men	
			Rept for duty for 63 (2/v) D.A.C.	

Army Form C. 2118.

53RD MOBILE VETERINARY SECTION.

No............
Date............

WAR DIARY
or
INTELLIGENCE SUMMARY

(Erase heading not required.)

Army Form C. 2118.

Place	Date	Hour	Summary of Events and Information	Remarks and references to Appendices
Marceuil	1917 Apr 23		Horse ret received from Res 3 Bde Clu Train. 6 dead animals buried. 1 no Bwn rec'd to 3rd MVS.	
			16 sick an evacuated. 57 sick animals evacuated to 3rd MVS. 23 sick animals admitted.	
			O.C. visits collecting post.	
	24		2 dead animals burned. 47 sick animals evacuated to 3rd MVS. 55 sick animals admitted. Horse	
			& driver proceeded to Vth Corps RFA for sick horse. O.C. visited advanced collecting post.	
	25		50 sick animals evacuated to 3rd MVS. 23 sick animals admitted. O.C. visited new Collecting Post.	
	26		3 sick animals evacuated by float to 3rd MVS. 80 sick animals admitted.	
	27		57 sick animals evacuated to 3rd MVS. 44 sick animals admitted. O.C. visited Res Wksley Sec.	
	28		57 sick animals evacuated to 3rd MVS. Los relieved ans for ½ hour. 29 sick animals admitted.	
	29		66 sick animals evacuated to 3rd MVS. 26 sick animals admitted. 1 N.C.O. v 12 men	
			attend for Clu. Train. 10 very dead horses. O.C. inspects billets.	
	30		27 sick animals evacuated to 3rd MVS. 1 sick animal treated. and to oi 1st MVS.	
			Section departed from Marceuil at 10.30 a.m., and arrived at Mingoval at 2.0 p.m. O.C.	
			visited ADVS.	

R. Broad
Cpl M.A.V.C.

Confidential   53rd Mobile Vety Section

63rd (RN) Division

31st May 1917

War Diary

— of —

53rd Mobile Veterinary Section

— from —

1st May 1917

— to —

31st May 1917

Volume XII

To

The A.G's Office

3rd Echelon

H W Fenn Capt AVC

O/c 53rd M.V.S

WAR DIARY or INTELLIGENCE SUMMARY

Army Form C. 2118.

53RD MOBILE VETERINARY SECTION.

Place	Date	Hour	Summary of Events and Information	Remarks and references to Appendices
MINGOVAL	1917 May 1		Head and down proceeded to No 8 Mobile Workshop for repair to ironwork. DADVS & ADVS visited Section to select 5 horses for issue to units, under authority QMG Eshlis 6314 (Q.A.1). Inspection of saddlery by OC.	
"	2		1 N.C.O. & 2 men proceeded to Lovillers to meet 4 sick horses left at La Comté by 21st MVS. 1 horse left by party at Lovillers as too lame to travel. OC visited at an afternoon. OC visits units.	
	3		OC visits ADVS. Gas helmet parade & drill for ½ hour. Inspection of billets by OC. Auster & dm proceed to Ordnance for stores. 4 sick animals admitted.	
	4		8 sick animals evacuated to 22 Base Vety Hospital, exchange of 1 NCO. OC attend railhead. Head brought for No 6 Mobile Workshop after repair. ADVS visited Section	
	5		O.C. visited units. 1 set of Saddlery complete handed over to ADVS. Ambulance wagon repainted by Section. Saddlery (stables oats) inspection by OC.	
	6		3 sick animals admitted. ADVS visited Section. O.C. visited units. SE 12355 Corp¹ Ford J.S. rejoin Section from Hospital. 3 sick animals admitted.	

WAR DIARY
or
INTELLIGENCE SUMMARY

(Erase heading not required.)

Army Form C. 2118.

53RD MOBILE VETERINARY SECTION.

No..........
Date..........

Place	Date	Hour	Summary of Events and Information	Remarks and references to Appendices
MINGOVAL	1917 May 7		Ambulance wagon & driver proceeded to Ordnance for stores. Head repaired by Section. OC visited ADVS.	
	8		S/Sgt 12255 Corpl Foot J.S. proceeded to No 3 MVS for duty. S/Sgt 644 Sgt Wheathead admitted to hospital. Saddlers inspection & drill for 1½ hour.	
	9		4 sets of saddlery complete handed to DADOS. Sergt Dobson + 1 man proceeded to TOURS to fetch 1 found horse. OC visited units. 1 sick animal admitted.	
	10		Ambulance wagon + driver proceeded to coal dump for fuel. T/4 142950 S/Sgt Forrest P. admitted to 3rd Field Ambulance. OC visited ADVS.	
	11		1 NCO proceeded to CAUCOURT to collect mule. On return by motor boat, 7 sick animals evacuated to 22° Base Vet Hospital in charge of 1 NCO. OC attends conference. 1 animal evacuated to No 3 MVS. 1 sick animal admitted.	
	12		Head & driver proceeded to CALONNE RICOUART, to collect our loose box wagon. Stay for the night. OC visited units. Rifle inspection by OC. 5° sick animals returned for duty.	
	13		Head & driver returned from CALONNE RICOUART. OC visited ADVS units. 1 NCO returned from Base Vet Hospital. 7 sick animals admitted. OC inspected billets.	

WAR DIARY or INTELLIGENCE SUMMARY

Army Form C. 2118.

53RD MOBILE VETERINARY SECTION.

Place	Date	Hour	Summary of Events and Information	Remarks and references to Appendices
MINGOVAL	1917 May 14		13 sick animals evacuated to 22" Base Vety Hospital in charge of 1 NCO & horses. OC attended purchase of horses visited SE 644 Vet Wheathew.	
	15		OC visited units. OC visited Wheathew & joined Section from hospital.	
	16		ADVS visited Section. OC visited Fouilloy to inspect sick horse left by sick unit, unknown, not inhabited. 4 sick animals admitted.	
	17		ADVS & OC visited Fouilloy to arrange destruction & burial of horse left behind. OC visited units. Who was carried out by party from Section. 1 NCO returned from 22 Base Vety Hospital. 3 horses (found) sent to 63 (Rx) Divisional train.	
	18		OC visited units. Gas officer & 3 NCOs attended Section for instruction in fitting of gas masks for horses. ADVS visited Section. Limber & lorry proceeded to cart dump for fire. 3 sick animals admitted.	
	19		7 sick animals evacuated to 22" Base Vety Hospital in charge of 1 NCO. OC attended veterinary proceeded to ANZIN with ADVS to select site for Section.	
	20		OC visited units. Section packed up ready to move.	
			Section departed from MINGOVAL at 8.30 am.	
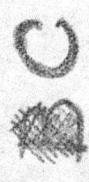 ANZIN	21	1.30pm	Section arrived at ANZIN at 1.30pm Stables up billets. OC visited ADVS. Inspected & saddlery refits by OC. 1 sick animal admitted.	

Army Form C. 2118.

53RD MOBILE VETERINARY SECTION.

WAR DIARY
or
INTELLIGENCE SUMMARY
(Erase heading not required.)

Instructions regarding War Diaries and Intelligence Summaries are contained in F.S. Regs., Part II. and the Staff Manual respectively. Title Pages will be prepared in manuscript.

Place	Date	Hour	Summary of Events and Information	Remarks and references to Appendices
ANZIN	1917 May 22		Inspection of gas helmets by O.C. + ½ hour drill. 3 animals admitted.	
	23		ADVS. visited Section. 3 sick animals admitted.	
	24		Sewlon Iron pressed to coal dump for fuel. ADVS. evicted Section for purpose of instructing and NCOs in fitting of gas masks for horses. 7 sick animals admitted. + 8 animals admitted for feeding up.	
	25		O/C visited A.D.V.S. Floet & drew to Science for cl. off for Section animals. 6 sick animals admitted.	
	26		O.C. to proceed to England on leave for 10 days. Capt. H. Yeam ADC. 63 Std. Vet. takes over command. 17 sick animals evacuated to 3rd M.V.S. No. 85891, Capt Irwin is exchanged for No. 1225 "S" Corp. Ford F. M. from 3rd M. V.S. Both 3.3 m.s.no.'s thee Heuri 2 January to 3rd M. V.S. with 2 sick animals. A.D.V.S. visits Section.	
	27		3 sick animals admitted.	
	28		Rifle Inspection + gas helmet parade inspected by O.C. Gas helmet drill half an hour.	

2449 Wt. W14957/M90 750,000 1/16 J.B.C. & A. Forms/C.2118/12.

Army Form C. 2118.

WAR DIARY
or
INTELLIGENCE SUMMARY
(Erase heading not required.)

53RD MOBILE VETERINARY SECTION.
No..........

Place	Date	Hour	Summary of Events and Information	Remarks and references to Appendices
ANZIN	1917 May 29		Flood driver proceeded to 3rd M.V.S. with 1 Sick Animal. 3 Sick animals Admitted.	
	30		12 Sick Animals dispatched to 3rd M.V.S. for evacuation. No 2062 Private Hann H. dispatched to the same for duty. 2 Sick animals admitted.	
	31		For a conv. of army A.P.V.S. Mobile Section. 2 Sick animals admitted. 1 N.C.O. & No 8 Mobile Sections wagon & driver to coal dump on fore. Workshops opened Heat wave Epiz. trodon 3 Sick animals admitted	

Capt. H.V. Fenn A.V.C.
53rd M.V.S.

Confidential

53rd M. Vety Section
63rd (RN) Division
Date. June 30th 1917.

War Diary

— of —

53rd Mobile Veterinary Section

— from —

1st June 1917.

— to —

30th June 1917.

Volume 13.

To.
  A.G.S. Office
    3rd Echelon.

Confidential

A O'Neill Capt. a Vc
O.C. 53rd M. Vety Section

Army Form C. 2118.

(A).

WAR DIARY
or
INTELLIGENCE SUMMARY
(Erase heading not required.)

53RD MOBILE VETERINARY SECTION.
No. ....
Date ....

Instructions regarding War Diaries and Intelligence Summaries are contained in F. S. Regs., Part II. and the Staff Manual respectively. Title Pages will be prepared in manuscript.

Place	Date	Hour	Summary of Events and Information	Remarks and references to Appendices
Aujus	1/June 1917		Billets and Sanitary inspection by O.C.	
"	"		O.C. Visits D.A.D.V.S.	
"	"		1 Sick Animal admitted	
"	2 June		S.E. No 4591. Pte Burns R.A.V.C. proceeded to England on Leave 10 days.	
"	"		6 Sick Animals admitted	
"	"		D.A.D.V.S. Visits Section	
"	3 June		Horses and Driver two journeys to No 3 M.V.S. Evacuees with 2 Sick	
			Animals	
"	"		Horses and Driver to 293rd Coy. Army Col. for one Sick Animal	
"	4 June		Horses and Driver to 3rd M.V.S. with 2 Sick Animals (two journeys)	
"	"		12 Sick Animals Evacuated to No 3 M.V.S. and 2 Ideals	
"	"		5 Sick Animals admitted	
"	5 June		Rifle Inspection by O.C.	
"	"		5 Sick Animals admitted	

2449 Wt. W14957/M90 750,000 1/16 J.B.C. & A. Forms/C.2118/12.

Army Form C. 2118.

WAR DIARY
or
INTELLIGENCE SUMMARY
(Erase heading not required.)

53RD MOBILE VETERINARY SECTION.

Place	Date	Hour	Summary of Events and Information	Remarks and references to Appendices
Augin	6 June 1917		21 Sick Animals Evacuated to No 3 M.V.S. for Evacuation.	
"	"		Float and Driver 3 Journeys to No 3 M.V.S.	
"	"		Col. Lewis and 2 O. Ranks return from No 3 M.V.S. for duty.	
"	"		13 Sick Animals admitted	
"	7 June		Limbered Wagon to Coal Dump for Fuel.	
"	"		Float and Driver to 3rd M.V.S. with one Sick Animal	
"	"		Float and Driver to XX Cable Section for one Sick Animal	
"	"		2 Sick Animals admitted	
"	8 June		Float and Driver to No 3 M.V.S. with 2 Sick Animals (two journeys)	
"	"		Capt J.C. Boak A.V.C. returns from Leave.	
"	"		5 Sick Animals admitted	
"	9 June		10 Sick Animals Despatched to No 3 M.V.S. to Evacuation.	
"	10 June		Float and Driver proceeds to 2nd R. Marines for 1 Sick Mule.	
"	"		One Sick Animal admitted	

Army Form C. 2118.

WAR DIARY
or
INTELLIGENCE SUMMARY

(Erase heading not required.)

Instructions regarding War Diaries and Intelligence Summaries are contained in F.S. Regs., Part II. and the Staff Manual respectively. Title Pages will be prepared in manuscript.

53RD MOBILE VETERINARY SECTION.

No. ....
Date ....

Place	Date	Hour	Summary of Events and Information	Remarks and references to Appendices
	Augt.	11th June 1917.	O.C. Inspect Saddles. Skeleton Order.	
"	"	"	O.C. " Box Respirators	
"	"	"	No 235. S/Sr. Holden P. a.V.C. proceeds to England on 1 months special Leave.	
"	"	"	O.C. Inspect Rifles	
"	"	"	6 Sick Animals admitted	
"	12th June	"	Shoes and Driver proceed to 2nd Bef Coy R.E. 2 Bn: for one Sick Animal	
"	"	"	" " " " to 3 M.V.S. with 2 Sick Animals (2 Journeys)	
"	"	"	O.C. Visits Unit	
"	"	T/4/040184. D² Collins. A.T. a.S.C. reported for duty from a.S.C. Base Depot Rouen.	
"	"	"	4 Sick Animals admitted	
"	13th June	"	Shoes and Driver proceed to No. 3 Coy. a.S.C. for 1 Sick Animal. Sgt Lewis (?)	
"	"	"	13 Sick Animals moved to No. 3 M.V.S. for Evacuation	
"	"	"	8 Sick Animals admitted	

2449 Wt. W14957/M90 750,000 1/16 J.B.C. & A. Forms/C.2118/12.

Army Form C. 2118.

53RD
MOBILE VETERINARY SECTION.

No.............
Date............

(2)

WAR DIARY
or
INTELLIGENCE SUMMARY
(Erase heading not required.)

Instructions regarding War Diaries and Intelligence Summaries are contained in F. S. Regs., Part II. and the Staff Manual respectively. Title Pages will be prepared in manuscript.

Place	Date	Hour	Summary of Events and Information	Remarks and references to Appendices
Auzin	14 June 1917		O.C. Maps at 63rd (RN) Div Horse Show.	
"	"		4 Sick Animals admitted	
"	15th June		Hoas and Drim proceeds to No 1 Coy 63rd Div no Lism for 1 Sick Animal Ceonio for Chaff.	
"	"		" " "	
"	"		6 Sick Animals admitted.	
"	16th June		O.C. Inspects Section Mens Clothing.	
"	"		Hoas and Driver to No 2 Sig Coy R.E. 2nd Division for 1 Sick Animal	
"	"		" " No 3 M.V.S. with one Sick Animal	
"	"		3 Haws deposited to No.3 M.S.	
"	"		Section Paid by Lt Cooke. (R.A.) at R. Ga. Coy. 63rd (RN) Division	
"	"		18.C. 10459 Pte Burns, G. Mkins for leave 7.30am 16.6.17.	
"	"		15 Sick Animals despatched to No.3 Ch.V.S. for Evacuation	
"	"		O.C. Visits Units	
"	"		5 Sick Animals	

Army Form C. 2118.

WAR DIARY
or
INTELLIGENCE SUMMARY

(Erase heading not required.)

5360 MOBILE VETERINARY SECTION.

Place	Date	Hour	Summary of Events and Information	Remarks and references to Appendices
Aujan	17 June 1917		14 Sick Animals admitted	
"	18 June 1917		16 Sick Animals despatched to N.3 M.V.S. for Evacuation.	
"	"		1 N.C.O. and Driver journeys to N.3 M.V.S. w/c Sick Animals	
"	"		4 Sick Animals admitted	
"	"		O.C. Inspects Rifles, Saddles, and Box Respirators	
"	"		Box Respirator Drill	
"	19 June 1917		Philpot 2nd. T.b. A.V.C. Promoted to A/Sgt. Local Corps Orders No.65 - 15.6.17.	
"	"		12 Sick Animals admitted	
"	20 June		16 Sick Animals admitted	
"	"		O.C. visits Unit	
"	21 June		1 N.C.O. and 3 men return from No.3 M.V.S. for duty.	
"	"		7 Sick Animals admitted	
"	22 June		32 Sick Animals Evacuated to No.13 Base Vety. Hospital 1 N.C.O. & Horse Clerk.	
"	"		1 Cart and Driver one journey to Eerie Railhead & Sick Animals	
			Linden " Gambin " a.D.v.s. 13 Corps visits Section. Seives	
			Lt. Col. Gambin "	
"	"		7 Sick Animals admitted	

2449 Wt. W14957/M90 750,000 1/16 J.B.C. & A. Forms/C.2118/12.

Army Form C. 2118.

53RD MOBILE VETERINARY SECTION.

No.........
Date.........

WAR DIARY
or
INTELLIGENCE SUMMARY

(Erase heading not required.)

Instructions regarding War Diaries and Intelligence Summaries are contained in F. S. Regs., Part II. and the Staff Manual respectively. Title Pages will be prepared in manuscript.

Place	Date	Hour	Summary of Events and Information	Remarks and references to Appendices
Aujon	23 Jan 1917		O.C. Inspect Saddles. Skeleton Order and Rifles	
"	"		Box Respirator Drill	
"	"		O.C. taken to No 2 C.C.S. (Sick)	
"	"		S/S No 2797 Pte Law. E. A.V.C. joined for duty from No 2 B.V.H. Hosp.	
"	"		S/S No 2256 Pte/Sgt Forst proceeds to Indian Vety Hosp proceedings	
"	"		Authority :- Local Corps Ormos No 65. D/15. 6. 17.	
"	"		10 Sick Animals admitted	
"	24 Jan		Capt. G. O'Neill. A.V.C. to Ro Ron Command of Section	
"	"		L/Cpl Clarkson and two others from No 13 B. Vety Hosp.	
"	"		13 Sick Animals admitted	
"	25 Jan		24 Sick Animals Evacuated to No 13 B. Vety Hosp. 1 C.O. & 3 New to Vety. and	
"	"		7 Animals admitted	
"	26 Jan		Gas and Drum Process to 3rd Luce Auth for 1 Can Animal	
"	"		S/Sgt J. C. Short. A.V.C. sent to No 12 Hospital Jun. No 3. C.C.S.	
"	"		14 Sick Animals admitted	

Army Form C. 2118.

WAR DIARY
or
INTELLIGENCE SUMMARY

(Erase heading not required.)

Instructions regarding War Diaries and Intelligence Summaries are contained in F. S. Regs., Part II. and the Staff Manual respectively. Title Pages will be prepared in manuscript.

53RD MOBILE VETERINARY SECTION.

No. .... Date. ....

Place	Date	Hour	Summary of Events and Information	Remarks and references to Appendices
Arjn	27th May 1917.		Driver and 1 Horse. Proceed to No.1 Coy 63rd Train for 1 Sick Animal	
"	"		Rear Part of Section was sent to join to Co.Eg.63 Train	
"	"		27 Sick Animals Evacuated to No.13 O.Vety.Hosp. 1 A.C.O. & 3 Men on leave.	
"	"		24 Sick Animals admitted	
"	28th "		8 Sick Animals admitted.	
"	29th "		1 Horse and a Driver Proceed to 91st Batty 36th Bde R.F.A. 2 Dr for 1 Sick Animal	
"	"		21 Sick Animals Evacuated to No.13 O.Vety.Hosp. 1 A.C.O. & 3 Men on leave	
"	"		and 1 Horse.	
"	"		8 Sick Animals Admitted	
"	30th "		L/Cpl Claxton & 3 Men return from No.13 O. Vety Hosp.	
"	"		3 Sick Animals admitted	

A. O'H... Capt. A.V.C.

O.C. 53rd M.V. Section.

Confidential   53rd M.V.S.

31st July 1917.

War Diary

— of —

53rd Mobile Veterinary Section

— from —

1st July 1917.

— to —

31st July 1917.

Volume No 14.

To.

A.G's Office

3rd Echelon.

P. Roach Capt. A.V.C.
O.C. 53rd M.V.S.

Army Form C. 2118.

WAR DIARY
or
INTELLIGENCE SUMMARY

(Erase heading not required.)

Volume 14.   53rd Mobile Vety Section.

Instructions regarding War Diaries and Intelligence Summaries are contained in F.S. Regs., Part II. and the Staff Manual respectively. Title Pages will be prepared in manuscript.

Place	Date	Hour	Summary of Events and Information	Remarks and references to Appendices
Aubigny	July 1st		D.A.D.V.S. visits Section.	
"	"		O.C. Inspection of Saddles, Box Respirators and Rifles.	
"	"		5 Sick Animals admitted.	
"	July 2nd		Float and Driver to No 3 Coy. 63rd (RN) Divl Train for 1 Sick Animal.	
"	"		15 Sick Animals Evacuated to No 13 Base Vety Hosp. 1 A.C.O. in charge.	
"	"		5 Sick Animals admitted.	
"	July 3rd		L/Cpl Charlton and one man relieving from No 22 Base Vety Hosp.	
"	"		4 Sick Animals admitted.	
"	July 4th		Section Paid by No 4 Coy 63rd (RN) Divl Train.	
"	"		13 Sick Animals admitted.	
"	July 5th		Float & Driver to Boulencourt for Mayo Cripps charge.	
"	"		D.A.D.V.S. visits Section.	
"	"		11 Sick Animals admitted.	

Army Form C. 2118.

WAR DIARY
or
INTELLIGENCE SUMMARY

(Erase heading not required.)

63RD MOBILE VETERINARY SECTION

Place	Date	Hour	Summary of Events and Information	Remarks and references to Appendices
Aughi	July 6th		Horse and Driver Journeys to Lenie Vaillant.	
"	" "		27 Sick Animals Evacuated to No 3 Base Vety Hospital 1 NCO i/c Esc.	
"	" "		O.C. Inspects P.H. Gas Helmets.	
"	" "		11 Sick Animals Admitted	
"	7th		Horse & Driver Proceeds to 139th S.G. Batty R.F.A. 13 Cops for one sick animal.	
"	" "	14/05 15+	Dr Collins, A.S.C. admitted to No 13 Field Ambulance.	
"	" "		12 Sick Animals Evacuated to No 13 B. Vety Hospital. N.C.O. i/c Esc.	
"	" "		11 Sick Animals Admitted	
"	8th		Horse & Driver Proceeds to A/317 Bde 18 F.A. 63(rd) Div. for one Sick animal.	
"	" "		O.C. Inspects Saddles & Rifles.	
"	" "		8 Sick Animals Admitted	
"	9th		Sgt No 2892 Pte Saunders Proceeds to England. 10 Days Leave, from 14.7.17.	
"	" "		OC Visits Units.	
"	" "		Cpl Keen G.L. has returned from No 13 Base Vety Hospital.	
"	" "		4 Sick Animals Admitted	

Army Form C. 2118.

WAR DIARY
or
INTELLIGENCE SUMMARY

(Erase heading not required.)

MOBILE VETERINARY SECTION. 5320

Place	Date	Hour	Summary of Events and Information	Remarks and references to Appendices
Auga.	10th July.		D.D.V.S. Irish Army and A.D.V.S. 13th Corps visit Section and personally inspect Section and Lines, and find when & also action of Lt. Rogers i/c efficiency of Section.	
"	"		T4/050154 Dr Collins I.A.S.C. returns from 13 Corps Rest Station 21. Sick Animal Admitted	
"	11th		T4/050154. Dr Collins I.A.S.C. Admitted 150th Field Ambulance Sick Animals Evacuated to No 13 Base Vety Hospital, 12.00 Noon 1 Sick Animal Admitted	
"	12th		No 2335 Sgt Dalton P.B. A.V.C. returns from 1 months Special leave. D.A.D.V.S. visits Section. 2 Sick Animals Admitted	
"	13th		SE No 2349. L/Cpl Murphy A. proceeds to England 10 days leave. Station Orders & all Sick Animals Saluted at 6.30 in Every Ground until further orders. 3 Sick Animals Admitted	
"	14th		No 570. Sgt East C. A.V.E. reports for duty from No 2 B.V. Hosp. Divisional Commander Inspects Section. D.A.D.V.S. visits Section.	
"	"		(Continued next page)	

WAR DIARY
or
INTELLIGENCE SUMMARY

Army Form C. 2118.

MOBILE VETERINARY SECTION.

Place	Date	Hour	Summary of Events and Information	Remarks and references to Appendices
Auzin	July 14th		O.C. Inspected sick horses. 5 sick animals admitted.	
"	15		A.D.V.S. 13th Corps. & D.A.D.V.S. 63rd (R.N.) Div. General inspection of Section. Lunch. Billets, book work, Latrines. Y/Capt J.C. Brodie reported for duty from A.V.S. Hospital. 3/Capt J.A. O'Neill to B Ech to R.Dn. 119 Coy to B Ech. L/Cpl Keen & 14 sick retiring from 20th Base M.G. Hospital. 9 S.R. Animals admitted.	
"	16		Section Paid. Vent & Driver proceeds to Rly Coy Dept Train to one sick animal. 5 sick animals admitted.	
"	17		D.A.D.V.S. visits Sectn. O.C. inspect Billets. 8 sick animals admitted.	
"	18		No. 2062 L/Cpl Gordon D admitted to 3rd L. Ambulance. 15 sick animals Evacuated to 20th Base Vety Hospital Mce. Nurse. Leat & Driver one journey to Ennin Kailave. 3 sick Animals admitted.	

Army Form C. 2118.

WAR DIARY
or
INTELLIGENCE SUMMARY

(Erase heading not required.)

53RD MOBILE VETERINARY SECTION.

No. ....
Date ....

Instructions regarding War Diaries and Intelligence Summaries are contained in F. S. Regs., Part II. and the Staff Manual respectively. Title Pages will be prepared in manuscript.

Place	Date	Hour	Summary of Events and Information	Remarks and references to Appendices
Musgan	July 19th		3 Lame 9 Driven horses to Rosincourt for Building Material. 9 a.D.V.S. Visit Section. O.C. Inspect Rifles and Box Respirators. 1 Case Diarrh: and 1 mare returned from No.13 Base Vety Hospital. 8 Sick Animals admitted.	
"	20th		O.C. Inspect Billets. 9 Sick Animals Admitted.	
"	21st		13 Sick Animals Evacuated to No.3 Base Vety Hospital and 3 Horses S.S. 102892 Pte Sanders R. returned from 10 days leave. 1 Issue weight Horse and Driver to a body 31/6th R.F.A. In re Sick Animal 7 Sick Animals admitted	
"	22nd		D.A.D.V.S. Visit Section. O.C. Inspect P.to Retunk. 3 Sick Animals Admitted	
"	23rd		20 Sick Animals Evacuated to No.13 Base Vety Hospital M.O. 2 8am 9 Horse and Driver to Berine Boissee S.A. Visit units. SE 10644 Pte Pearland to admitted to 13th Corps Rest Station. L/Cpl Keen returns from No 13 B. Vety Hospital. 16 Sick Animals admitted	

WAR DIARY or INTELLIGENCE SUMMARY

Army Form C. 2118.

53RD MOBILE VETERINARY SECTION

Place	Date	Hour	Summary of Events and Information	Remarks and references to Appendices
August	July 24th		O.C. Visits Units. Float & Driver to Arras.	
"	25th		S.E. No.2062 Sjt Gordon D. transfered to 42 C.C.S. from 3 my Ambulance. 8/S No.2329 Murphy R. returns from 10 days leave. Cpl Claxton & 2 men return from No.22 B.X Hospital. 11 Sick Animals admitted	
"	26th		1st Sick Animals Present to No.13 Base Vety Hospital & 1 Rides 1 P.O. Horse O.C. Visit Units. Float & Driver to C.C.C. to Bridges tested 3 Sick animals admitted.	
"	27th		S.E. No.3063 Cpl Gordon returns from 42 C.C.S. for duty. O.C. Visit units. S.E. No.279. Pte Sempton proceeded to C England 10 days leave. 4 Sick Animals Admitted.	
"	28th		Float & Driver to R.Batty 3) Bn.R.F.A. for 1 Sick Animal O.C. Inspects Buick. O.C. Visit units. 5 Sick Animals Admitted	

Army Form C. 2118.

WAR DIARY
or
INTELLIGENCE SUMMARY

(Erase heading not required.)

53rd MOBILE VETERINARY SECTION.

Place	Date	Hour	Summary of Events and Information	Remarks and references to Appendices
Cnf.	July 29		15. Sick Animals Evacuated to No 3. Base Vety Hospital 1160. mage Shoes and Driver to Ecure Caillard.	
"			AC to Caillard. Nil Sick Animals Admitted.	
"	30.		a. D.V.S. Visits Section. Shoes Driver Proceeds to C.R.E. Borbecus for Building Material. 3. Sick Animals Admitted	
"	31.		O.C. Visits Unit. S8. L/Cpl Pte Wheatland D. returns to duty from 13 Corps Rest Station. 6. Sick Animals Admitted.	

Wood Capt. RA
O.C. 53rd Mobile Veterinary Section

Confidential   Headquarters.
                         A. Branch.
                         31st August 1917.

War Diary

— of —

53rd Mobile Vety Section

— from —

1st August 1917

— to —

31st August 1917

Volume No 15.

To.

The A.G's Office
3rd Echelon.

J. M. Broach Captain
O.C. 53rd M.V.S.

Army Form C. 2118.

WAR DIARY
or
INTELLIGENCE SUMMARY.
(Erase heading not required.)

53RD
MOBILE VETERINARY
SECTION.
No. V. 15.
Date 31.8.17.

Place	Date	Hour	Summary of Events and Information	Remarks and references to Appendices
Augas	1st Aug 1917		7 Sick Animals Evacuated to No 13 Base Vety Hosp. Sick ten horses O.C. to Bonne Bailheul to Supervise Boxing of Sick Animals. That and D.O. to Bonne Called with Sick Animal A.D.V.S. visits Lines. O.C. Inspects P.O. Gas Helmets, & Box Respirators. S.S. No 973 Pte Hart to A.V.C. & A.D.V.S. Office to take over clerical duties 2 Sick Animals Admitted	
"	2nd Aug "		No 1006 Pte Hawkins returns from School of Farriery. O.C. visits Units. Section Paid. Float & D.O. to C.R.E. to Collect Lumber for Horse Standings. 2 Sick Animals Admitted	
"	3rd Aug.		O.C. to St Catherine Inspection of Sick Animals. O.C. Inspects Billets. 1 Sick Animal Admitted	
"	4th Aug.		Float & D.O. to D. Batty 223 Bde R.F.A. for 1 Sick Animal. O.C. Inspection of Rifles. 6 Sick Animals Admitted	

Army Form C. 2118.

WAR DIARY
or
INTELLIGENCE SUMMARY.
(Erase heading not required.)

5380
MOBILE VETERINARY
SECTION.
No. V. 15
Date 31.8.17.

Place	Date	Hour	Summary of Events and Information	Remarks and references to Appendices
Aijin	5th Aug 1917.		No 14/03/026, Dr Smith L reported for duty from A.S.C. Base Depot Havre. Saddlery Inspection by O.C. 13 Sick Animals admitted.	
"	6th Aug		16 Sick Animals Evacuated to No 13 Base Vety Hospital & Kits. 2/P.P.O. Elorth Veterinary. No 4076 Pte Allen L. detailed to 50 C.F. Ambulance, O.C. visits Vaulxen & supervise Burying of Sick Animals. O.C. visits No 4076 Pte to bury Carcass. Hour & Dr to bury Carcass & Jennings. D.A.D.V.S. visits Section. 5 Sick Animals admitted.	
"	7 Aug		R.E. No 25/47 Pte Lane O.C. to VIII Corps Sanitary Section for Course of Instruction. O.C. visits & D.A.D.V.S. visits Section. Hour & Dr & then to R.E. Dump Roclincourt to draw material for horse standings. Rifle Inspection by O.C. 10 Sick Animals admitted. R.E. No 4076 Pte Allen A. to VIII Corps Rest Camp O.	
"	11th Aug		22 Sick Animals Evacuated to No 3 Base Vety Hosp Etaples Havre. O.C. to Bernie Railhead to supervise Burial of Sick Animals. Hour & Dr to Bernie Railhead with Sick Animals, & Carcass to Bernie Farm. No 2 Coy 63rd D.L.I. No Dr attends 2 Pers by train to Jenville the sick on to Wippenhoven. New Clerk No 1 No 13 Base Vety Hosp. 6 Sick Animals admitted.	

A7092. Wt. w17539/M1193, 750,000. 7/17. D. D & I. Ltd. Forms/C2118/14.

Army Form C. 2118.

WAR DIARY
or
INTELLIGENCE SUMMARY.
(Erase heading not required.)

MOBILE VETERINARY SECTION
No. 1/5"
Date 31/7/17

Place	Date	Hour	Summary of Events and Information	Remarks and references to Appendices
Anjou	9 Aug		1 Col teen 9 7 hors returned from No 7. Base Vet Hosp. No 2787 Pte Lingate L returns from 10 days leave. OC inspected Bees of O.C. Widd Unit. O. a D. V. O. visits Section. OU SeeR Animal admitted.	
"	10 Aug		No 1006 Pte Ham. W. proceeded on 10 Days base to France. D. A. D. V. S. visits section. OC visits Units. Horse "D" to 63Fd DAC in chof casting. 6 Sick Animals admitted.	
"	11 Aug		S2. No 2086. Pte Allen A. discharged to VII Corps Rest Camp. Horse "D" to D.R.D. A.S. for stores. OC Inspection of Pipes. OC visits units. 3 Sick Animals admitted.	
"	12 Aug		15 Sick Animals evacuated to No 13 Base Vet Hospital Hd Kean Abage. D. a. D. V. S. visits section. OC visits Roulant to Superior Dorcies of the Armies. DC visit units. Horses "D" to D. Bty 317 Bde R.F.a. for 1 Sick animal " " Gueson Bart. " " " Zundon to Fuel Dump for draw Fuel. 2 Sick Animals admitted.	

Army Form C. 2118.

WAR DIARY
or
INTELLIGENCE SUMMARY.
(Erase heading not required.)

53RD
MOBILE VETERINARY
SECTION
No. V. B.
From 31.8.17.

Place	Date	Hour	Summary of Events and Information	Remarks and references to Appendices
Auf	13 Aug		O.C. Inspects Details. O.C. visits Unit. Inspects 2 P.O. for behalf 1 for Sun. to O.C. Stop. Horse mare returned from 2nd Base Vety Hosp. 3 Sick Animals Admitted (Battlegraph).	
	14 Aug	10.30	Pte. Haget R. returned from A.D.V.S. VIII Corps. D.a.D.V.S. VIII Corps, Section and D.A.A. + Q.M.G. Sick Section. O.C. Inspects Det. 10 Sick Animals Admitted.	
	15 Aug		O.C. Inspects Saddlery. O.C. visits Unit. 2 Sick Animals Admitted.	
	16 Aug		O.C. Inspects Shoe Seloat. D.A.D.V.S. visits Section. Horse Des. proceed to M.E. Park Marquis N. 1 to Sarr Temp. Section Post. O.C. visits Unit. 1 Sick Animal Admitted.	

E.

Army Form C. 2118.

WAR DIARY
or
INTELLIGENCE SUMMARY.
(Erase heading not required.)

Instructions regarding War Diaries and Intelligence Summaries are contained in F.S. Regs., Part II and the Staff Manual respectively. Title pages will be prepared in manuscript.

53RD MOBILE VETERINARY SECTION.
No. V. 15.
Date 31. 8. 17.

Place	Date	Hour	Summary of Events and Information	Remarks and references to Appendices
Auzin	17 Aug		24 Sick Animals Evacuated to No. 13 Base Vety Hospital for Exchange. Ybon, 9 D. to Cerise Railhead to Horses. O.C. to Cerise Railhead to supervise Box Up of Sick Animals. Ybon, & D. to O.C. O.R.D. to proceed to Boves 12" Carriage Exchanges O.C. Visit Unit. D.A.D.V.S. Visit Section. SS. to No. 1036 proceed to England 10 days leave. (10 Days S.) 1 Sick Animal Admitted	
"	18 Aug		O.C. Inspect Bn. t. D.A.D.V.S. Visit Section 4 Sick Animals Admitted	
"	19 Aug		O.C. Visit Unit. 1 C.p.l. Vet. & 2 men Posted to No. 13 B.V. Hosp. Inspection of Saddlery by O.C. 1 Sick Animals Admitted	
"	20 Aug		5 Sick Animals Admitted. [illegible line]	

Army Form C. 2118.

WAR DIARY
or
INTELLIGENCE SUMMARY.
(Erase heading not required.)

53RD MOBILE VETERINARY SECTION

Place	Date	Hour	Summary of Events and Information	Remarks and references to Appendices
Aug.	21.8.17		D.A.D.V.S. visits Section. O.C. visits Unit. O.C. Inspects Billets. Divisional Ammn Coln & D.A.C & Amm Sub Station. 3 sick animals admitted	
	22.8.17		16 sick animals Evacuated to No.3 Base Vet Hosp Via Westoutre Hoyes. From Div. to Locre Railway. O.C. to Locre Railway to supervise loading of sick animals. Ybais D.A.D.V.S. base kept up speed. 4 sick animals admitted.	
	23.8.17		D.A.D.V.S. visits Section. O.C. visits Units. Number returned from H.Q. Coy, 63 Div. train & various A.S.C. reports. Plant returns from D.A.D.V.S. reports. 4 sick animals admitted.	
	24.8.17		10/106 Pte Dain J.D. returns from 10 days leave. O.C. visits units. O.C. Insp. Billets. 1 N.C.O. & man to VIII Corps M.V.S. Detachment Lum Army Attachmt a.g. 28. 10. 179. 22. 8. 17. Remainder Photographed by Richard Chaptn	

A7093. Wt. W.9859/M1293. 750,000. 1/17. D. D. & I. Ltd. Forms/C2118/14.

WAR DIARY
INTELLIGENCE SUMMARY
(Erase heading not required.)

Army Form C. 2118.

53RD MOBILE VETERINARY SECTION.

Place	Date	Hour	Summary of Events and Information	Remarks and references to Appendices
Avesnes	25th Aug		O.C. Daily visit section. OC visit units. Recd. Evac of 1 Sick Horse from No 13 D.V. Hosp. and No.2118.0 Rd. Llanafau to 149 C. Ambulance. Typhaeseal Carnal. 1 Sick Animal admitted.	
"	26th Aug		O.C. Visit unit. OC Inspect saddlery. Do. Do visit section. Do. Do. Evacuated to 24/149 Coy R.E. Fr. 1 Sick Horse. 9 Sick Animals admitted.	
"	27th Aug		A.D.V.S. Visit Section. Evac to Divn S.Q. for 1 Sick Animal. 2 Sick Animals admitted.	
"	28th Aug		A.D.V.S. Visit unit. OC visit units. 32 Sick Animals Evac to A/22 Bde R.F.A. Spli, gartin Bde. 1 Evac to 8 Coys Railhead. 1 Evac to D.V.S. Base. OC Visits cadres of Infantry Batn of Sick Animals. Evac 1 + 59 F.139 to Batty R.9.A. for 1 Sick Animal. Evac to Moroeuil Railhead for Op: O'Niel's Vet. 13 Sick Animals admitted.	

Army Form C. 2118.

WAR DIARY
or
INTELLIGENCE SUMMARY.
(Erase heading not required.)

Instructions regarding War Diaries and Intelligence Summaries are contained in F.S. Regs., Part II. and the Staff Manual respectively. Title pages will be prepared in manuscript.

53RD MOBILE VETERINARY SECTION.
No. V/13
Date 31.8.17

Place	Date	Hour	Summary of Events and Information	Remarks and references to Appendices
Augn	29 Aug		D.a.D.V.S. Visit lectr.	
			A.D.V.S " "	
			OC Inspect Boy Regards of L/Sgt Goo Heaval.	
			#21860 Pte Hickafan b. to 42 Casualty Clearing Sta.	
			9 Sick Animals admitted	
	30 Aug		OC Visit Unit	
			OC Inspect B'mob.	
			to 11036 Pte Davis L. retind from 10 Days Leave.	
			L/Cpl Geo + Shiers retind from No 22 Base Vety Hospital.	
			6 Sick Animals admitted.	
	31 Aug		A.D.V.S. + O.D.V.S. visit section.	
			OC to Leica Cagnier.	
			OC Inspect Rifles, Nature of new German Gas Shell	
			(Calibre 7.7cm) and (10.5 cm) Explained to Men on Parade.	
			9 Precautions to be taken in the event of Shell	
			Explosions in the vicinity of Station. (#49,63 Sgt Fordon B.S. proceed	
			Lector) Raid. 6 Sick Animals admitted. to England 10 Days Leave)	

R.Buah
Captain
OC 53 M.V.S.

Confidential

Headquarters
A. Branch
30th Sept 17.

War Diary

— from —

53rd Mobile Veterinary Section

— from —

1st September 1917

— to —

30th September 1917.

Volume. 16.

To.   The A.G.s Office
      3rd Echelon. Base.

H V Ferrer Capt a Vc.
O.C. 53rd M.V.S.

Army Form C. 2118.

53RD
MOBILE VETERINARY
SECTION.
No...........
Date..........

WAR DIARY
or
INTELLIGENCE SUMMARY.
(Erase heading not required.)

Place	Date	Hour	Summary of Events and Information	Remarks and references to Appendices
Aug.	Sep 1		Horse Driver to Ecurie with Sick Animals. 2 Journeys	
"	"		D.A.D.V.S. Visits Section	
"	"		O.C. Inspect Billets	
"	"		Motor Ambulance of First Army to collect Sick Animals for instruction.	
"	"		5 Sick Animals admitted	
"	Sep 2		O.C. Visits Unit	
"	"		A.A. & Q.M.G. & D.A.V.S. Visits Section	
"	"		Ambulance wagon to Lens Dump.	
"	"		Horse Dr. Sp. 230 & Lens Corps R.E. Marcuil for 1 Sick Animal	
"	"		" to Sados for Stores	
"	"		O.C. Inspect Billets.	
"	"		3 Sick Animals admitted	
"	Sep 3		D.A.D.V.S. & A.D.V.S. Visits Section	
"	"		Horse & Dr. to Petou Bath for 1 Sick Animal	
"	"		24 Sick Animals Evacuated to No 22 Base Vety. Hospital, 1 Horse, 23 Mules, Yser Church	
"	"		In charge	
"	"		O.C. to Lewie Railway to Inspect Boxes of Sick Animals	
"	"		Horse & Dr. to Lewie Railway 3 Journeys from Sick Animals	
"	"		2 Mounted Men A.V.C. to Marcuil to Draw Frozen Fish Lect. Rifles	
"	"		3 Reports Q.S. from D.A.V.S. to Shew same	

Army Form C. 2118.

53RD MOBILE VETERINARY SECTION.

No................
Date................

WAR DIARY
or
INTELLIGENCE SUMMARY.
(Erase heading not required.)

Instructions regarding War Diaries and Intelligence Summaries are contained in F. S. Regs., Part II. and the Staff Manual respectively. Title pages will be prepared in manuscript.

Place	Date	Hour	Summary of Events and Information	Remarks and references to Appendices
Aupen, Sept 4			OC Visit Unit. OC Inspect Beasts. 3 sick animals admitted	
"	" 5th		OC Visit Unit. Inspection of P.B. Ens. Pockets Frees Regimental. 3 sick Animals admitted.	
"	" 6th		OC Visit Unit. Genl Border. OC Inspectors XIII Corps. 2 Sergts Arrived & admitted. 1 Horse. No. 8991 Cpl Evans. OC Inspectors Ground to VI.M.V. Detachment for duty. No 6321 " McCauley " relieved to return to base Horse.	
"	" 7th		Hors. & Drivers to 190th Inf. Bde to exchange for 1 sick Animal. No 632. Gpe McCauley & proceeds to England 10 days Leave. OC Inspect Beasts. O.C Visit Units. Motor Ambulance of First Army proceed 1 sick Animal to Evacuation 2 sick Animals admitted	
"	" 8th		A.D.V.S. Visit Section. OC Visit Unit. Horse & Drivers to 188 Machine Gun Coy to exchange 1 sick Animal. 4 Sick Animals admitted.	

Army Form C. 2118.

WAR DIARY
or
INTELLIGENCE SUMMARY
(Erase heading not required.)

53RD MOBILE VETERINARY SECTION.

No. ....
Date ....

Place	Date	Hour	Summary of Events and Information	Remarks and references to Appendices
Aizin	Sep 9		Removed maps to Fuel Dump. O.C. inspects Billets. O.C. visits Units. Animals sent with 9th & 10th Ambulances of Field Army to evacuate 1 Sick Animal from 1st, 2nd, 63rd (RN) Divisional Sick Lines etc. 1 Sick Animal admitted	
"	Sep 10		Ations & O's to 19th Batt. Divisional Train. A.D.V.S. & D.A.D.V.S. visit Section. D.Rev. & P.M.G. visits. O.C. visits Units Inspect Wagon & Ration Dump for Grew Yangs 3 Sick Animals admitted	
"	Sep 11		D.A.D.V.S. visits Section. Ations & O's to 247th Field Coy R.E. & 1 Sick Animal. O.C. visits Units. O.C. inspects Wagon Line. 3 Sick Animals admitted	
"	Sep 12		Ara & P.M.G. visits Section. O.C. visits units. D.A.D.V.S. visit Section. No.440 Pte/Sergt T.S.P. Lancett R.E. report to duty from No. 13 Base Vety Hospital. SE. No. 953 S/S. Herbert B. Atkins returned to duty from leave in England. May/Sec. Carh. correct from 11th Coy 13 (RN) Batt. Wham reports Complete. 2 Sick Animals admitted.	

WAR DIARY
or
INTELLIGENCE SUMMARY.

(Erase heading not required.)

Army Form C. 2118.

53RD MOBILE VETERINARY SECTION.

Place	Date	Hour	Summary of Events and Information	Remarks and references to Appendices
Auzin	Sept 13		D.A.D.S. & visit Section. O.C visit Line F.	
"	"		O.C. to speak to Missen Bnl.	
"	"		6 Sick Animals admitted.	
"	Sept 14		37 Sick Animals Evacuated to N°1192 Base Vety Hospital. +3 dead.	
"	"		1 Cpl & Carter Yakub.	
"	"		O.C. to Ecurie Railhead to Supervise loading Sick Animals.	
"	"		Hours Dr to Ecurie Railhead with Sick Animals. 3 Journeys.	
"	"		" K 63 (B.H.) Divisional Refilling Point. Over Animal	
"	"		R° 235 Pl/Staff S/P Watson to P Regarde to high Rise to Halt	
"	"		R° 9.03 1 Horse seen by O.C. Proceed to England 10 days Leave	
"	"		D.A.D.V. visit Section. O.C visit Line F.	
"	"		M.O. Ayamhouses. Lieut Ames/ Collect 1 Sick Animal fr	
"	"		Welington. 6 Sick Animals admitted.	
"	Sept 15		O.C visit Unit. D.A.D.V. visit Section.	
"	"		O.C. Inspec.t to Faubery Rifles.	
"	"		4 Sick Animals admitted. 1 Wound Animal admitted	
"	Sept 16		O.C. to 4th Bedfords for opinion as to the Capability of T/x/47546	
"	"		Pte Crawley.T (Col/Sgt Stof.) as Champ Smith.	
"	"		Limber to Tubec Camp. O.C. to Tubec Cashier. Section Paid	

Army Form C. 2118.

53RD MOBILE VETERINARY SECTION.

No..................
Date................

WAR DIARY or INTELLIGENCE SUMMARY.

(Erase heading not required.)

Instructions regarding War Diaries and Intelligence Summaries are contained in F. S. Regs., Part II. and the Staff Manual respectively. Title pages will be prepared in manuscript.

Place	Date	Hour	Summary of Events and Information	Remarks and references to Appendices
Augn.	Oct 1?		A.D.V.S. visits Section. O.C. visits unit. Re Inspect Box Requisition. SPS Scheme. Report on Sick with same.	
"	"		L.A./7566. Re Bowery (Cold Shoer) proved as sheep/shunk after examination by S.O.	
"	"		4 sick animals admitted.	
Augn.	6.8.19.		D.A.D.V.S. visits Section. O.C. visits unit.	
"	"		1/851 Master Ulimo (new ?n/23 Dec Vet Hospital) 3 Ay Ambulance	
"	"		1 foal admitted from (3 Ay Ambulance)	
"	"		4 sick animals admitted	
"	6.9.19.		D.A.D.V.S. visits Section. O.C. visits unit.	
"	"		O.C. Inspects sween tent	
"	4		5 Lt E.S. proceeds to 3rd Field Ambulance for 1 Our Animal	
"	5		R.6231. Pte McCarthy returns from 10 days leave proceeds	
"	"		to E. pt M.V. Detachments for duty	
"	"		3 sick animals admitted.	
"	Sept 25		D.A.D.V.S. + D.V.S. visits section. O.C. visits units.	
"	"		O.C. + Vets Cashin.	
"	"		Staff Sr proceeds to Headquarts 3/75 CCS, I.W.V. for duty	
"	"		R.2362 L/Cpl Anson proceeds to Cala 10 days leave.	
"	"		R.P.G 399 Pte. Wats R.K.I.C. allowed to visit pk duty.	
"	6		3 sick animals admitted.	

Army Form C. 2118.

WAR DIARY
or
INTELLIGENCE SUMMARY.
(Erase heading not required.)

[Stamp: 53RD MOBILE VETERINARY SECTION. No.......... Date..........]

Instructions regarding War Diaries and Intelligence Summaries are contained in F.S. Regs., Part II. and the Staff Manual respectively. Title pages will be prepared in manuscript.

Place	Date	Hour	Summary of Events and Information	Remarks and references to Appendices
Aubigny	Aug 21st		2 Sick Animals forwarded to No 2 Base Vety Hospital including 1	
"	"		1 OR. West Lair in Mange.	
"	"		OC visit Genie Railhead & Sprenis Army & Sick animals	
"	"		thence to Genie Railhead with sick animals. Journey	
"	"		OC visit S.S.O. & D.A.D.V.S.	
"	"		Respirators issued with NC Cartridges	
"	Sept 22nd		OC Inspect West Kent	
"	"		OC Inspect Yeomanry Rifles	
"	Sept 23rd		D.A.D.V.S. & A.D.V.S. visit Section	
"	"		A.D.V.S. O.C. of 1/2 hour M.V.S & of 4th Lowen Division visit Section	
"	"		Prior to Occupation OC visit Units	
"	"		3 Sick Animals admitted	
"	Sept 24th		Section Prepares to Move.	
"	"		OC visits Units.	
"	"		2 Sick Animals admitted	
"	Sept 25th		Section leaves Aubigny 9.22 am en route for Bethencourt	
"	"		Section arrives at Bethencourt 1.0 pm	
"	"		10 Sick Animals handed over to No 10 Corps M.V.S. Clearance Certificate	
"	"		obtained. Billets left clean. No. 953 Pte Burns 4.1. RE Proceeds on	
"	"		OC visits Officer incharge Railhead for arrangements to Proceed. Sick animals admitted	

Army Form C. 2118.

WAR DIARY or INTELLIGENCE SUMMARY.
(Erase heading not required.)

53RD MOBILE VETERINARY SECTION.

No. ....
Date. ....

Place	Date	Hour	Summary of Events and Information	Remarks and references to Appendices
Reninghelst	Sept 26th		O.C. visit units. Total NR. proceeded to Abeele to collect stabling material for fallen return same day. Purcan Commander visits section. Sick near returns from 10 days leave from England.	
"	Sept 27th		O.C. visits section. D.A.D.V.S. visits units. (No. 10692 Pte McMinn A. A.S.C. placed under arrest for neglect of duty. at 10.15 am & 2.15 pm 26.9.17 whilst in charge of sick horses. May chemical carriage taken from stable. (No. 2718) Pte Compton proceed to deg. T. hospital. (Remanded to leave 2/10/17) Sent animal into room to hear 1 mule arriving from D.A.C. Awaiting Inst. F.M.G. top 205. 3 S. & R. Animals admitted.	
"	Sept 28th		No 10692 Pte McMinn A. A.S.C. awarded 21 days F.P. No1. Hearing of A.P.M. 63rd (W) Div. Findings same. Extended F.P. and sent Capt. J.C. Broad A.V.C. proceeds to England on 10 days leave. Mr. Heron A.V.O. taking on. Command of section.	
"	Sept 29th		O.C. visit units. Eshen Raid. 1 R.R. animal admitted. O.C. to Aces Cabin. Ros. Respirator. Inspection by Geo. Sergeant of 63rd (W) Div.	

Army Form C. 2118.

WAR DIARY
or
INTELLIGENCE SUMMARY.
(Erase heading not required.)

53RD MOBILE VETERINARY SECTION.

No............
Date............

Instructions regarding War Diaries and Intelligence Summaries are contained in F. S. Regs., Part II. and the Staff Manual respectively. Title pages will be prepared in manuscript.

Place	Date	Hour	Summary of Events and Information	Remarks and references to Appendices
Rubempré	November 1st 1917		M.V.S. Unit. D.A.D.V.S. 63rd (RN) Division. Year's procedure to D.D.S. 63rd (RN) Div. for Sick Animals. 1 Sick Animal Admitted.	

J. V. Kerr. Captain.
O.C. 53rd M.V. Section.
63 (RN) Division.

Confidential

Headquarters "A"
63rd (RN) Division
31st Oct. 17.

War Diary

— of —

53rd Mobile Veterinary Section.

— from —

1st October 1917.

— to —

31st October 1917.

Volume 7

A.G. Office
3rd Echelon
Base.

P. Broad
Capt. a.V.c.
O.C. 53 M.V.S.

Army Form C. 2118.

WAR DIARY
or
INTELLIGENCE SUMMARY.
(Erase heading not required.)

53RD MOBILE VETERINARY SECTION.

A.

Place	Date	Hour	Summary of Events and Information	Remarks and references to Appendices
Behencourt	1 Oct:		O.C. to Mayincourt to ascertain correct information respecting Mrs.	
			A.a.D.V.S. visits Section.	
			9 Sick Animals Evacuated to No 2 3 V. Coy.	
			N/Sgt. 1 man in charge. I.M. Co. 8.30pm relieves from XIII Corps M.V.O.	
			prior to moving from XIII Corps area.	
"	2 Oct.		D.a.D.V.S. visits Section.	
			N/10 Sick Animals admitted.	
"	3rd Oct.	6.45am.	Section moves from Behencourt, arrives at 3rd Cavy Entraining Station	
		7.30 am.	Train departs from Cavy 10.35am. arrives at Pioncin	
		8.00 pm.	Section arrives at Ham Road 11.00 pm.	
Ham Road	4 Oct.		D.a.D.V.S. visits Section. N/10 Sick Animals admitted.	
"	5 Oct.		S.B. No 193 Pte Preston L. Proceeds to England 10 Days Leave.	
			S.B. M 2063 S/Sgt Endem D. returns from 10 Days Leave.	
			1 Sick Animal admitted	
			S.B. No 25797 Pte Carr E.C. admitted to XIII Corps L. amb.	
"	6th Oct.		5 Sick Animals admitted.	

Army Form C. 2118.

53RD MOBILE VETERINARY SECTION.

No. ....
Date ....

WAR DIARY
or
INTELLIGENCE SUMMARY.
(Erase heading not required.)

Place	Date	Hour	Summary of Events and Information	Remarks and references to Appendices
Cam Corps	7 Oct.		5 Sick Animals Evacuated to N⁰ 4 C⁰s A.V.D. and 2 Sick to D.V.S Visits Station. 3 Sick Animals admitted	
" "	8 Oct.		1 N.C.O, 1 Men Detailed to IV Corps M.V.D. for duty in accordance with D.D.V.S letter Fifth Army. 1 Sick Animal admitted	
" "	9 Oct.		1 Sick Animal admitted.	
" "	10 Oct.		D.A.D.V.S Visits Section. 3 Sick Animals admitted	
" "	11 Oct.		XXXV A.D.V.S. XIII Corps Visits Station. Sgt⁰ Bond J.C relieves from 10 Days Leave. 2 Sick Animals admitted A.F.M. & Sub V.S. arrived. 1 Sick Animal admitted	
" "	12 Oct.		1 Mange Case admitted. St P. 2573. Ptℓ Pool, A. F. Queen, of England 10 Days Leave.	
" "	13 Oct.		13 Sick Animals Evacuated to N⁰ 6 C.o.M. V.D. and 1 Sick to Proealis reports for duty from N⁰ 5 Base Vetℓ Hosp. 1 Sick Animal admitted	

Army Form C. 2118.

53RD MOBILE VETERINARY SECTION.

WAR DIARY or INTELLIGENCE SUMMARY.
(Erase heading not required.)

Place	Date	Hour	Summary of Events and Information	Remarks and references to Appendices
Sam Sok	14 Oct.		Sector Moved to Field Allot. Evacuated By 28M.V.S. 21 Sick Animals admitted	
"	15 Oct.		D.A.D.V.S. visits Section. 3 Privates despatched to No 2 Base Vety Hosp as Class A1. 6 Sick Animals admitted	
"	16 Oct.		19 Sick Animals evacuated to XIV Corps M.V.D. 24 Sick Animals admitted	
"	17 Oct.		A.D.V.S. visits Section. 9 Animals admitted. 1 Animal Died (XVIII Corps)	
"	18 Oct.		Pte McMillan.D. relieved from A.P.M. Supervision of Detention (81 Days.) 5 Animals admitted	
"	19 Oct.		D.A.D.V.S. visits Section. 12 Sick Animals admitted	
"	20 Oct.		Pte McMillan despatched to No 2 Base Vety Hosp as Class A1. 5 Sick Animals admitted. 1 Animal Died	
"	21 Oct.		27 Sick Animals Evacuated to XIV Corps M.V.D. 6 " " admitted	

Army Form C. 2118.

5320
MOBILE VETERINARY SECTION.
No. .... Date ....

WAR DIARY
or
INTELLIGENCE SUMMARY.
(Erase heading not required.)

Instructions regarding War Diaries and Intelligence Summaries are contained in F.S. Regs., Part II. and the Staff Manual respectively. Title pages will be prepared in manuscript.

D.

Place	Date	Hour	Summary of Events and Information	Remarks and references to Appendices
Am Sech	22 Oct.		A.D.V.S. of VIIIth Corps visit section. 3 sick Animals admitted	
"	23 Oct		1 Opr & 1 Man. detailed to Advanced Aid Post. 6 sick Animals admitted. 1 Animal destroyed	
"	24 Oct		Lt. No 273. Pte Mackay returned from 10 Days leave. D.a.D.V.S. visit section. 11 sick Animals admitted	
"	25 Oct		6 sick Animals admitted	
"	26 Oct.		S6 W.D. 6289. Pte Wheeler to proceed to England 10 days leave. 7 sick Animals admitted. 1 Animal destroyed	
"	27 Oct.		7 sick Animal admitted	
"	28th Oct.		A.D.V.S. XVIII Corps visit section. D.a.D.V.S. visit section. 9 sick Animals admitted	
"	29 Oct.		31 sick Animals Evacuated to EV Corps M.V.S. 1 Animal returned to Unit. fit for duty. 2 sick Animals admitted	

Army Form C. 2118.

WAR DIARY
or
INTELLIGENCE SUMMARY.
(Erase heading not required.)

53RD
MOBILE VETERINARY
SECTION.

No.............
Date...........

E.

Place	Date	Hour	Summary of Events and Information	Remarks and references to Appendices
Ham Soch.	30th Oct		36. Sick Animals admitted.	
"	31st Oct		D.A.D.V.S. visits Section.	
			41. Sick Animals admitted.	

H. Broad
Lt. & O.C. M.V.S.
63 (RN) Division

Confidential Headquarters
 "A" Branch.

Vol 17

War Diary

— of —

53rd Mobile Veterinary Section

— from —

1 November 1917

— to —

30th November 1917

Volume 16.

Officer i/c
 a G's Office
 3rd Echelon Base.

1.12.17

J. C. Broad. Captain
O.C. 53rd M.V.S.

Army Form C. 2118.

WAR DIARY
or
INTELLIGENCE SUMMARY.
(Erase heading not required.)

53RD MOBILE VETERINARY SECTION.

No. ....
Date ....

Instructions regarding War Diaries and Intelligence Summaries are contained in F. S. Regs., Part II. and the Staff Manual respectively. Title pages will be prepared in manuscript.

Place	Date	Hour	Summary of Events and Information	Remarks and references to Appendices
Kan Loele	1/Nov/17.		40. Sick Animals admitted. 2 Animals Destroyed. Lt/1+2a/o. Dr Stocking A returns from England 10 Days Leave.	
"	2 Nov.		D. A. D. V. S. Visits Section.	
"	"		20 Sick Animals admitted. 1 Animal Died.	
"	3 Nov.		18 Sick Animals admitted. 1 Animal Died.	
"	"		1 Coy. 93 Men returning XIV Corps A.V.D.1. " Destroyed.	
"	4 Nov.		A. D. V. S. & D. A. D. V. S. 63(7th) Div Visits Section.	
"	"		15 Horses Received by 30th M.V.S.	
"	"		13 Sick Animals admitted.	
"	5th Nov.		A.D.V.S. II Corps. 9 A.D.V.S. XIV Corps Visits Section.	
"	"		1 Animal Died	
"	6th Nov.		D. A. D V. S. 63(7th) Div Visits Section. 1 Animal Destroyed.	
"	"		A.D. V. S. II Corps " "	
"	7 Nov.		127 Sick Animals Evacuated to No 3 Base Vet Hosp.	
"	"		5 Men from 189 Infty Bde detailed for conducting party.	
"	"		190 " " II Corps M.V. Detachment.	
"	"		30 Sick Animals Evacuated to 19 Corps M.V. Detachment.	

Army Form C. 2118.

WAR DIARY
or
INTELLIGENCE SUMMARY.
(Erase heading not required.)

53RD MOBILE VETERINARY SECTION.

Instructions regarding War Diaries and Intelligence Summaries are contained in F. S. Regs., Part II. and the Staff Manual respectively. Title pages will be prepared in manuscript.

B.

Place	Date	Hour	Summary of Events and Information	Remarks and references to Appendices
Hawkhock	8 Nov.		D.A.D.V.S. Visits Section 6 Sick Animals admitted.	
"	9 Nov.		7 Sick Animals admitted. O.C. Visits D.A.D.V.S. Office. 1 Found Animal admitted	
"	10th Nov.		31 Sick Animals admitted D.A.D.V.S. Visits Section	
"	11th Nov.		25 Sick Animals admitted. A.D.V.S. II Corps Visits Section. D.A.D.V.S. & (FM) D.V. Visit Section	
"	12 Nov.		84 Sick Animals Evacuated to No. 13 Base Vety Hosp. 10 Ford Lories despatched to " " "	
"	13th Nov.		20. Sick Animals landed over to No. 32 M.V.S. Section leaves Hawkock 7.15 a.m. arrives in Amrele Area 4.30 p.m.	
Amrele Area	14 Nov.		Section leave Amrele Area 10 oc am D.A.D.V.S. Section Section arrives at Erkelsbrugge 2.00 p.m. Visits	
Erkelsbrugge	15 Nov.		4 Sick Animals admitted.	

Army Form C. 2118.

WAR DIARY
or
INTELLIGENCE SUMMARY.

(Erase heading not required.)

53RD MOBILE VETERINARY SECTION.

Instructions regarding War Diaries and Intelligence Summaries are contained in F. S. Regs., Part II. and the Staff Manual respectively. Title pages will be prepared in manuscript.

Place	Date	Hour	Summary of Events and Information	Remarks and references to Appendices
Earls Staff	16/11/01		1 Sick Animal admitted. Repl. 994. Dpo Carter & 1/2892 Pte Sanders admitted to 149 Field ambulance	
"	17/11.		D.A.D.V.S. visit Section. 1 Sick Animal admitted.	
"	18/11/01		D.A.D.V.S. visit Section. Repl. 30491 Pte Rich land admitted to 13th Casualty Clearing Station. 1 Sick Animal admitted.	
"	19 Nov.		2 Sick Animals admitted.	
"	20th Nov.		9 Sick Animals evacuated to N°20 Res Vety Hosp. including Charger of Brig General Phillips. O.C. of N°20 Base Vety hospital to superintend the evacuation of Brig General Phillips Charger to N°6 B.V.B. Rouen	
"	21/11.		2 Sick Animals admitted. O.C. to take over A/D.A.D.V.S.	
"	22 Nov		O.C. Visit D.A.D.V.S. Office.	
"	23 Nov		1 Sick Animal admitted	
"	24 Nov.		Section Paid. 9 Sick Animals admitted.	

Army Form C. 2118.

WAR DIARY
or
INTELLIGENCE SUMMARY.
(Erase heading not required.)

53RD MOBILE VETERINARY SECTION.

Place	Date	Hour	Summary of Events and Information	Remarks and references to Appendices
Erkelsbrugge	25th Nov.		11 Sick Animals Evacuated to M23 Base Vety Hosp. D.A.D.V.S. Office.	
"	26 Nov		8 Sick Animals admitted Evacuated by Boat to M23 Base Vety Hosp	
"	27th Nov		15 Sick Animals Evacuated to M23 Base Vety Hosp 1 Horse Join dispatched to " " "	
"	28th Nov	3.30pm	Section Moves from Erkelsbrugge. 10. O.C. run. Section arrives at Hondezgie 3.30 pm	
Hondezgie	29th Nov.		D.C. Visit D.A.D.V.S. Office	
"	30th Nov		D.C. Visit D.A.D.V.S. Office.	

J. Roach
Capt A.V.C.
OC 53 M.V.S.

Confidential

63rd (R.N.) Division
"A" Branch
2. 1. 18.

War Diary

of

53rd Mobile Veterinary Section

from

1st December 1917.

to

31st December 1917.

Volume No 19.

Officer i/c
A.G. Office
3rd Echelon.

P. Broad
Capt. AVC
O.C. 53. M. V. S.

Army Form C. 2118.

53RD MOBILE VETERINARY SECTION.

No. ....
Date ....

WAR DIARY
or
INTELLIGENCE SUMMARY.
(Erase heading not required.)

Instructions regarding War Diaries and Intelligence Summaries are contained in F. S. Regs., Part II. and the Staff Manual respectively. Title pages will be prepared in manuscript.

Place	Date	Hour	Summary of Events and Information	Remarks and references to Appendices
HOUTKERQUE	Dec 1		11 sick animals admitted. 2076 Pte Allen proceeded to England on leave. Visited D.A.D.V.S. office. Visited transport lines of 1st Bedfordshire & 1st Shropshire.	
	" 2		Visited transport lines of 1st Royal Fusiliers, 1st KRRC, 1/90 H.L.I. Coys. 1 sick animal admitted. To D.A.D.V.S. office in afternoon.	
	" 3		1 sick animal admitted. Visited transport lines of 189 Brigade. To D.A.D.V.S. office in afternoon.	
	" 4		1 sick animal admitted. 18 sick animals evacuated to 42" M.V.S. To D.A.D.V.S. office in afternoon.	
	" 5		Visited transport lines of 1st Royal Fusiliers, 1st Shropshire, 1st KRRC, 1/90 H.L.I. To D.A.D.V.S. office in afternoon.	
	" 6		To 189 Brigade transport lines. D.A.D.V.S. Brigade from HOUTKERQUE to GODEWAERSVELDE, arriving at 2.15 p.m.	
	" 7		To D.A.D.V.S. in afternoon. To report to him on his return from leave. 5D T/04168 Dr B.L. Nic proceeded to England on leave.	

Army Form C. 2118.

53RD MOBILE VETERINARY SECTION.

No............ Date............

WAR DIARY
or
INTELLIGENCE SUMMARY.
(Erase heading not required.)

Instructions regarding War Diaries and Intelligence Summaries are contained in F.S. Regs., Part II. and the Staff Manual respectively. Title pages will be prepared in manuscript.

Place	Date	Hour	Summary of Events and Information	Remarks and references to Appendices
GODEWAERSVELDE	DEC 8		Inspected all animals of 150' Field Ambulance: visited transport lines of 1/4 K.S.L.I.	
"	9		D.A.D.V.S. visited Section.	
"	10		Section proceeded to Godewaersvelde railhead, at midnight, in readiness to entrain.	
"	11		Section entrained at 2.30 a.m., train leaving railhead at 3.45 a.m. detrained at MIRVAUX(?) at 1.30 p.m. & marched to billets at ROCQUIGNY.	
"	12		A.D.V.S. V" Corps & D.A.D.V.S. visited Section. Visited transport lines of 7" Royal Fusiliers, Nova Batt" & No 3 Coy Divisional Train.	
"	13		Visited lines of Hawke, Nelson, Drake Batt" & 1st, 2nd R.M. Batt" Anson & Howe Batt". 6 sick animals admitted. 1 sick ann evacuated to 663 at Bapaume. Section went from ROCQUIGNY to MANANCOURT, arriving at 12.30 p.m. Pte 4591 Pt Burrage admitted to 150' Field Ambulance. 1 sick animal admitted. Pte 30491 Pt Buckland reported for duty.	
"	14		D.A.D.V.S. visited Section: visited lines of 149' Field Ambulance. 1 sick animal admitted. 984 H/N Clark(?) proceeded on leave to England.	
"	15		D.A.D.V.S. visited Section. 9 sick animals admitted.	

Army Form C. 2118.

53RD MOBILE VETERINARY SECTION

No. ....
Date. ....

WAR DIARY
or
INTELLIGENCE SUMMARY.
(Erase heading not required.)

Instructions regarding War Diaries and Intelligence Summaries are contained in F.S. Regs., Part II. and the Staff Manual respectively. Title pages will be prepared in manuscript.

Place	Date	Hour	Summary of Events and Information	Remarks and references to Appendices
MANANCOURT	Dec 16		Visited lines of Nos. 2, 3 & 4 Coys. Divisional Train. 2 sick animals admitted. 5 sick animals evacuated to 36' Aux. M.V.S.	
	" 17		Section moved to billets at LE MESNIL, arriving at 11.30 a.m.	
LE MESNIL	" 18		D.A.O.V.S. & D.A.D.M.S. visited Section. 4 sick animals admitted.	
	" 19		Visited transport lines of 190 Inf. Brigade at F.M.S. 13 sick animals admitted.	
	" 20		D.A.O.V.S. visited Section. Visited transport lines of 190 Inf. Brigade. 13 sick animals admitted.	
	21		Attended to horses at L.S.L.M. in care of No. 1005 Pte Haw, held at H.Q. of 1st R.M. Bath. at LECHELLE. No 644 Pte Wheatland proceeded to England on leave. 8 sick animals admitted.	
	22		18 sick animals evacuated to No. 3 M.V.S. 5 sick animals admitted. Inders of Court Martial received in case of Pte. Haw. (90 days F.P. No.1) Pte Haw. rejoined own 18-4-PM	
	23		Visited transport lines of 190 Inf. Brigade. 13 sick animals admitted. Found recurrent at 9.15 pm. Sick by D.A.O.V.S. Scrap by wounds, & instruction to take ? on duties.	
	24		Visited D.A.O.V.S. office to take over duties of D.A.O.V.S. temporarily, D.A.O.V.S. having died of wounds last night. 7 sick animals evacuated to No 3 M.V.S. 1 sick animal admitted.	

Army Form C. 2118.

53RD MOBILE VETERINARY SECTION.

No. ....
Date ....

WAR DIARY
or
INTELLIGENCE SUMMARY.
(Erase heading not required.)

Instructions regarding War Diaries and Intelligence Summaries are contained in F. S. Regs., Part II. and the Staff Manual respectively. Title pages will be prepared in manuscript.

Place	Date	Hour	Summary of Events and Information	Remarks and references to Appendices
LE MESNIL	Dec 25		Visited lines of No 3 Coy Divisional Train. Capt Taylor AVC took over duties of DADVS. No 87415 Pr Moore reported for duty from No 7 Base Vy Hospital. 5 men sent to No 3 MVS a. wooding party.	
	26		Visited transport lines of 148 Field Ambulance. 9 sick animals admitted.	
	27		Visited transport lines of 190 Inf Brigade also 301 R Coumulation Coy 128 Labour Coy RE. Nº 20 P. Hoyt admitted to 150 Field Ambulance.	
	28		Area + Adv. Ord Commandant visited Section. Visited lines of No 3 Coy Divisional Train. 11 sick animals evacuated.	
	29		Visited transport lines of 190 Inf Brigade. 79 04515 Pr Barber 252. returned from leave. 9 sick animals admitted.	
	30		Visited DADVS office, to report to DADVS (Lyn Winterton RVC). 2349 SP Smith Murphy AVC MC admitted to 148 Field Ambulance. 5 sick animals admitted	
	31		11 sick animals admitted. Inspected all animals in Section for contagious diseases	

Broad
Capt. AVC.

Confidential

53rd Mobile Veterinary Section
63rd (RN) Division

War Diary
of
53rd Mobile Veterinary Section

from

January 1st 1918

to

January 31st 1918

Volume 20

To

The A.G.'s Office
3rd Echelon
Base

J. Broad Capt A.V.C.
O.C.
53rd Mobile Veterinary Section

Army Form C. 2118.

MOBILE VETERINARY SECTION
53rd
No..........
Date..........

WAR DIARY
or
INTELLIGENCE SUMMARY.
(Erase heading not required.)

Instructions regarding War Diaries and Intelligence Summaries are contained in F. S. Regs., Part II. and the Staff Manual respectively. Title pages will be prepared in manuscript.

Place	Date	Hour	Summary of Events and Information	Remarks and references to Appendices
LE MESNIL	1918 JAN 1.		DADVS visited Section. 1 sick animal admitted.	
	" 2		Visited transport lines of 190 Inf. Brigade. 20 O.Rs. & 4 pl. Slavin returned from leave to England.	
	" 3		3 sick animals admitted.	
			Visited animals of 126 Labour Coy & 148 Field Ambulance. 21 sick animals admitted.	
	" 4		Visited DADVS office: 8 sick animals admitted. 2 animals returned to unit.	
	" 5		Visited animals of No 3 Coy Divisional Train & 128 Labour Coy R.E. 19 sick animals evacuated.	
			26 sick animals admitted. 2 animals returned to unit.	
	" 6		Inspected animals of 19 Pioneer Park A.S.C. 11 sick animals admitted. 2 animals returned to units. Visited two teams of 307 Road Construction Co.	
	" 7		Visited transport lines of 190 Inf. Brigade. 8 sick animals admitted. 18 sick animals evacuated.	
	" 8		Lt. Col. Wheatland returned from leave to England. 5 sick animals admitted. 5 animals returned to unit. Visited transport lines of No 3 Coy Divisional Train & 148 F.A. R.A.M.C.	
	" 9		DADVS visited Section. Visited T-Boat V.E.C.S. 5 sick animals admitted. 14 sick animals evacuated. 2 animals returned to units.	
	" 10		Visited lines of 148 Field Ambulance & No 3 Coy Div. Train. 10 sick animals admitted.	

Army Form C. 2118.

53RD MOBILE VETERINARY SECTION

No............
Date............

WAR DIARY
or
INTELLIGENCE SUMMARY.
(Erase heading not required.)

Instructions regarding War Diaries and Intelligence Summaries are contained in F. S. Regs., Part II. and the Staff Manual respectively. Title pages will be prepared in manuscript.

Place	Date	Hour	Summary of Events and Information	Remarks and references to Appendices
LE MESNIL	1915 JAN.11		Visited Horse lines of 128 Labour Co. 307 Road Construction Co. & 19 Reserve Park. & D.A.D.V.S. Office.	
	12		1 Sgt Clement 6 proceeded on 10 days leave to Boulogne. 2 found unfit & sent to 190 M.V.S. 15 sick animals admitted.	
	13		Inspected animals of 19 Reserve Park and D.A.D.V.S. 1 sick animal admitted. 1 animal destroyed.	
	14		Visited lines of 1/6 3 Co. Divisional Train. 7 animals returned to units. 8 sick animals admitted.	
	15		Visited transport lines of 190 Inf. Brigade. 4 animals returned to units. 9 sick animals admitted.	
	16		Visited lines of 148 Field Ambulance & 188 Labour Co. 1 animal returned to unit. 13 sick animals admitted.	
	17		Medical Board assembled at 148 Field Ambulance to classify M.V.S. men of Section. 3 animals returned to units. 12 sick animals admitted.	
	18		Visited lines of No 3 Co. Divisional Train; and 19 Reserve Park. 1 animal returned to unit. 10 sick animals admitted.	
			Visited lines of 128 Labour Co & 307 Road Construction Co. & D.A.D.V.S. Office and weekly return. 5 animals returned to units. 6 sick animals admitted. 23 animals evacuated.	

Army Form C. 2118.

MOBILE VETERINARY SECTION.
5380
No..........
Date..........

WAR DIARY
or
INTELLIGENCE SUMMARY.
(Erase heading not required.)

Instructions regarding War Diaries and Intelligence Summaries are contained in F. S. Regs., Part II. and the Staff Manual respectively. Title pages will be prepared in manuscript.

Place	Date	Hour	Summary of Events and Information	Remarks and references to Appendices
LE MESNIL	1918 Jan 19		Inspected all animals of 148th Field Ambulance and D.A.D.V.S. 13 sick animals admitted. 17 sick animals evacuated.	
	20		Visited Transport lines of 190 Inf. Brigade. 9 animals returned to units. 5 sick animals admitted.	
	21		Visited lines of No. 3 Co. Divisional Train & 188 Vet'n Co. R.E. 2 animals returned to unit. 1 sick animal admitted.	
	22		D.A.D.V.S. visited Section. 6 animals returned to units. 23 sick animals admitted.	
	23		Proceeded METZ, to inspect animals of 16 Sqdn R.F.C., but did not find them. Visited transport lines of 190 Inf Brigade at BEAUVINCOURT and found to have one horse & mule of 128 O.B.M., 80 R.E. on mange had broken out on one horse. 18 sick animals admitted. One Dr Assistant moved Section for duty from 48 C.C.S.	
	24		Visited animals of 15 Squadron R.F.C. 188 Vet'n Co. 148 Field Ambulance. 30 sick animals evacuated. 18 sick animals admitted.	
	25		D.A.D.V.S. visited Section. To D.A.D.V.S. office at HAPINCOURT with early return suspected of Mange. 14 animals returned to unit. 20 sick animals admitted.	
	26		To D.A.D.V.S. office & return. Visited animals of 148 F'd Ambulance. 1 animal returned to unit. 13 sick animals admitted.	

WAR DIARY

53RD MOBILE VETERINARY SECTION.

Place	Date	Hour	Summary of Events and Information	Remarks and references to Appendices
LE MESNIL	1918 JAN 27		Fatigue party (1 NCO + 8 men) reported from 188° Inf Brigade for duty with Section for the day. 1 animal returned to unit. 10 sick animals admitted.	
	28		DADVS visited Section. Visited transport lines of 190° Inf Brigade. 8 sick animals admitted. Fatigue party from 188° Inf Brigade reported for daily duty, cleaning up camp.	
	29		2°do A/Cpl Lauriste returned from leave in France. Lieut Veterinary charge of animals of 77° Army Brigade, RFA, to V.O.R. proceeding on leave to England. 32 sick animals evacuated. 23 sick animals admitted. 5 animals returned to units.	
	30		Visited animals of 149 V.P Ambulance, H.Hoursh (Heurer) Barr, 9 & 10/86 Divisional Train. 15 sick animals admitted.	
	31		Visited lines of 148 V.P. Ambulance, + 188 Coln Co.RE. AOHS-DADS visited Section. 11 sick animals admitted. 45 sick animals evacuated.	

R. Brook
Capt AVC
O.C. 53" Mobile Veterinary Section
63 (2nd) Division

Confidential　　　　　　　　　　　53rd Mobile Veterinary Section
　　　　　　　　　　　　　　　　　　　　March 1st 1918

War Diary
of
53rd Mobile Veterinary Section
from
February 1st 1918
to
February 28th 1918

Volume 21.

To A.G's Office　　　　　　　　　　J. Broad Capt AVC
3rd Echelon　　　　　　　　　　　　　O.C.
　　　　　　　　　　　　　　　　53rd Mob. Vet. Section

Army Form C. 2118.

WAR DIARY
or
INTELLIGENCE SUMMARY.

(Erase heading not required.)

53RD MOBILE VETERINARY SECTION.

No. ....
Date. ....

Instructions regarding War Diaries and Intelligence Summaries are contained in F. S. Regs., Part II. and the Staff Manual respectively. Title pages will be prepared in manuscript.

Place	Date	Hour	Summary of Events and Information	Remarks and references to Appendices
LE MESNIL	FEB 1918			
	1		Visited office of D.A.D.V.S. Lt Saunsbury proceeded to England on leave. 10 sick animals admitted.	
"	2		D.D.V.S. Third Army. A.D.V.S. V Corps. D.A.D.V.S. inspected Section. 1 sick animal admitted. 1 animal returned to unit for duty.	
"	3		15 sick animals admitted. 10 sick animals evacuated. 3 animals returned to unit for duty.	
"	4		Inspection of Section by D.V.S. accompanied by D.D.V.S. Third Army. A.D.V.S. V Corps. and D.A.D.V.S. Visited transport lines of D/77 Army Brigade R.F.A. to inspect animals. 8 sick animals admitted. 1 animal returned to unit for duty.	
"	5		Inspected animals of 223 M.G. Coy. & 146 Fd Ambulance. 22 sick animals admitted. 1 animal destroyed & 1 returned to unit for duty.	
"	6		Visited lines of 128 Siege By R.E. C/77 Army Brigade R.F.A. and Fort By 68 (D) Div Amm Park. In company with D.A.D.V.S. inspected all animals of 190 Infy Brigade. 7 sick animals admitted.	

Army Form C. 2118.

53RD MOBILE VETERINARY SECTION.

No.................
Date...............

WAR DIARY
or
INTELLIGENCE SUMMARY.
(Erase heading not required.)

Instructions regarding War Diaries and Intelligence Summaries are contained in F.S. Regs., Part II. and the Staff Manual respectively. Title pages will be prepared in manuscript.

Place	Date	Hour	Summary of Events and Information	Remarks and references to Appendices
LE MESNIL	1918 FEB 7		Visited transport lines of 147 (A.T.) Coy. R.E. 1 animal returned to unit for duty. DADVS inspected Section horses & men's kits.	
	8		Visited office of DADVS. Visited waggon lines of N/77 Army Brigade, R.F.A. 2 sick animals admitted; 9 sick animals evacuated. 3 animals returned to units for duty.	
	9		Proceeded to transport lines of 190 Inf. Brigade with 1 man to carry out thorough disinfection of water troughs, as a case of contagious stomatitis was suspected to have been watered there. 7 sick animals admitted. 2 animals returned to units for duty.	
	10		Visited office of DADVS. Inspected all animals of R.H. by Decauville train. 3 animals returned to units for duty. Stocks back.	
	11		Visited waggon lines of A/77 Army Brigade, R.F.A. Proceeded to NEUVILLE to inspect billets of 19 Div. M.V.S. which is being relieved by this Section shortly. 2 sick animals admitted. 13 animals returned to units for duty.	
	12		DADVS inspected all animals in M.V.S. 8 Wheelers of Arc reported for duty on return from leave. 6 sick animals admitted. 13 sick animals evacuated. 3 animals returned to units for duty.	

Army Form C. 2118.

WAR DIARY
or
INTELLIGENCE SUMMARY.

(Erase heading not required.)

53RD MOBILE VETERINARY SECTION.
No..........
Date..........

Instructions regarding War Diaries and Intelligence Summaries are contained in F.S. Regs., Part II. and the Staff Manual respectively. Title pages will be prepared in manuscript.

Place	Date 1918	Hour	Summary of Events and Information	Remarks and references to Appendices
LE MESNIL	Feb 13		Visited transport lines of 148 Fd Ambulance, 1Ay(AT)/9 R.A., 128 Labouring Pe. 29 animals returned to units for duty. 1 N.C.O. sent to NEUVILLE as advance party. To take over stores etc. from 19' Div M.V.S.	
	14		Section arrived at NEUVILLE. 1 sick animal admitted. 10 sick animals evacuated. 2 animals returned to units for duty. Inspected remounts of 77' Army Brigade R.F.A.	
NEUVILLE	15		V.O. ½ of 77' Army Brigade R.F.A. reported back from leave. DADVS visited Section. 3 sick animals admitted.	
	16		DADVS visited Section. Inspected Lieut. K. 13 sick animals evacuated. 4 sick animals admitted. Q' Page. Q' Miller reported for duty from 133 Hospital Name. Q' Barber despatched to reports	
	17		DADVS visited Section. Inspected sick animals.	
	18		V.O. ½ 3rd Army HQ for duty. Visited transport lines of 190 Inf' Brigade. 316 Road Construction Co + 4 Reme R.E. 7 sick animals evacuated. DADVS visited Section.	
	19		Visited transport lines of 148 Fd Ambulance + th Nicols Coney Bn at METZ. DADVS proceeded to T Corps H.Q. to take up duties of A.D.V.S. (proceeding on leave).	

Army Form C. 2118.

WAR DIARY
or
INTELLIGENCE SUMMARY.
(Erase heading not required.)

53RD MOBILE VETERINARY SECTION.

Place	Date	Hour	Summary of Events and Information	Remarks and references to Appendices
NEUVILLE	1918 Feb 19		Assumed duties of D.A.D.V.S. Inspected Horses of D.H.Q. C.R.A. & C.R.E.	
"	20		Visited transport lines of 148 Fd Ambulance at METZ; also 1st Wilts Rifles and 63 (2v) Divisional Signal Coy. 1 animal returned to unit for duty.	
NEUVI	21		Visited transport lines of 4 Bedfordshire, 7 Royal West Kents, 7 Royal Fusiliers & 14 Worcs 14 (Pioneer) Batt. Called to Hammersmith Wood to see horse of 7 East Kents which had to be destroyed. 7 sick animals admitted.	
	22		D.A.D.V.S. office for weekly returns. 8. Others AVC sent to No 2 Veterinary Hospital for duty, being surplus to establishment of Section. 7 sick animals evacuated.	
	23		To office of A.D.V.S. Visited lines of No 1 Coy Divisional Train. 5 sick animals admitted. 1 animal returned to unit for duty.	
	24		Visited transport lines of 190 Inf Brigade. 28 remounts arrived at Section to await distribution. 7 sick animals admitted.	
	25		Visited stables of D.H.Q. C.R.A. & C.R.E. 1 sick animal admitted.	
	26		Visited lines of 19 Reserve Park A.S.C. & 316 Road Construction Co R.E. 5 sick horses admitted; 6 sick animals evacuated. 10 animals returned to units for [duty].	

Army Form C. 2118.

5330
MOBILE VETERINARY SECTION.

WAR DIARY
or
INTELLIGENCE SUMMARY.

Place	Date	Hour	Summary of Events and Information	Remarks and references to Appendices
NEUVILLE	1918 FEB 27		To D.A.D.V.S. office re putting animals of Division through Corps Horse Ops. 5 sick animals admitted. 8 sick animals evacuated.	
"	28		To DADVS office. O.C. Horses proceeds to England on leave. Cooks Swn of 2nd Bgde. Divisional train. 1 sick animal admitted.	

J Dodd
Cpl A.V.C.

Army Form C. 2118.

WAR DIARY
or
INTELLIGENCE SUMMARY.
(Erase heading not required.)

53RD MOBILE VETERINARY SECTION.

Place	Date	Hour	Summary of Events and Information	Remarks and references to Appendices
NEUVILLE	1918 Mch 1		Visited animals of 190 Inf. Brigade. 3 sick animals admitted: 1 animal returned to unit for duty; 1 animal found.	
	2		2 sick animals admitted.	
	3		Visited animals of Signal Coy. + D.H.Q.	
	4		Visited animals of 148 Field Ambulance + 306 Road Construction Coy. 4 sick animals admitted: 7 sick animals evacuated: 3 animals returned to units for duty.	
	5		Visited animals of 190 Inf. Brigade: 1 sick animal admitted. 1 animal returned to unit for duty.	
	6		Visited animals of 14 Worcester (Pioneer) Batt., + of D.H.Q. 6 sick animals admitted.	
	7		Visited 14 Reserve Park, ASC.	
	8		Capt Few A.V.C. joined Section, as actg O.C. 1 sick animal admitted. 1 animal returned to unit.	
	9		Proceeded on leave to England for 14 days. Capt Few A.V.C. assumed command of Section. 2 animals returned to units for duty.	
	10		4 sick animals admitted.	
	11		2 sick animals admitted.	
			11 sick animals evacuated: 7 sick animals admitted.	
	12		D.A.D.V.S. visited Section. 3 sick animals admitted: 3 sick animals evacuated. 1 returned to unit.	

Army Form C. 2118.

WAR DIARY
or
INTELLIGENCE SUMMARY.
(Erase heading not required.)

53RD MOBILE VETERINARY SECTION.

Instructions regarding War Diaries and Intelligence Summaries are contained in F. S. Regs., Part II. and the Staff Manual respectively. Title pages will be prepared in manuscript.

Place	Date	Hour	Summary of Events and Information	Remarks and references to Appendices
NEUVILLE	1918 Mch 13		D.A.D.V.S. visited Section. 9 sick animals admitted; 3 sick animals evacuated. 2 animals sent to units.	
	14		D.A.D.V.S. visited Section; 3 sick animals evacuated. 2 animals returned to units for duty.	
	15		D.A.D.V.S. visited Section. 3 sick animals admitted; 2 sick animals evacuated. 2 animals returned to units for duty. 1 animal sent to unit.	
	16		D.A.D.V.S. visited Section. 4 sick animals admitted. 4 found animals admitted, suffering from gas.	
	17		D.A.D.V.S. visited Section. 1 sick animal admitted. 2 animals returned to units.	
	18		D.A.D.V.S. visited Section. 5 sick animals admitted. 1 found animal admitted. 5 sick animals evacuated.	
	19		D.A.D.V.S. visited Section. 1 sick animal admitted.	
	20		D.A.D.V.S. visited Section. 1 sick animal admitted.	
	21		D.A.D.V.S. visited Section. 11 sick animals admitted. 4 sick animals evacuated. 9 found animals admitted.	
	22		Section left NEUVILLE at 10.30 am. arrived LECHELLE [signature] 5 A.V.C. brindles given Section for duty from 14th Vet. Hospital.	
LECHELLE	23		Section left LECHELLE at 12.30 am. arrived LESBOEUFS 6.30 am. Left LESBOEUFS at 11.30 am. arrived at BAZENTIN LE PETIT at 3.0 p.m.	

Army Form C. 2118.

53RD MOBILE VETERINARY SECTION.

No................
Date................

WAR DIARY
or
INTELLIGENCE SUMMARY.
(Erase heading not required.)

Instructions regarding War Diaries and Intelligence Summaries are contained in F. S. Regs., Part II. and the Staff Manual respectively. Title pages will be prepared in manuscript.

Place	Date	Hour	Summary of Events and Information	Remarks and references to Appendices
BAZENTIN LE PETIT	1918 Mch 24		Section left BAZENTIN LE PETIT at 9.30 a.m; arrived at DERNANCOURT at 12.30 p.m.	
DERNANCOURT	25		Section left DERNANCOURT at 10.30 a.m; arrived at GOUZINCOURT at 2.30 p.m; left GOUZINCOURT at 7.30 p.m; arrived at LEALVILLERS at 11.0 p.m. 2 animals destroyed.	
LEALVILLERS	26		Section stood to all day, ready to move, according to instructions.	
	27		Section left LEALVILLERS at 3.0 p.m; arrived PUCHEVILLERS at 6.30 p.m. 3 animals destroyed.	
PUCHEVILLERS	28		Routine as usual.	
	29		Section left PUCHEVILLERS at 10.30 a.m; arrived at PERNOIS at 2.30 p.m. 2 animals destroyed.	
PERNOIS	30		Routine as usual.	
	31		16 sick animals evacuated from CANAPLES Station. Daily routine as usual.	

R. Roach
Capt AVC.
O.C. 53rd Mobile Veterinary Section.

<u>Confidential</u>　　　　　　　　Headquarters.

　　　　　　　　　　　　　　　　　　　　53ᵈ Mobile Veterinary Section

　　　　　　　　　　　　　　　　　　　　May 1ˢᵗ 1918

<u>War Diary</u>

of

<u>53ᵈ Mobile Veterinary Section</u>

from

April 1ˢᵗ 1918

to

April 30 1918

<u>Volume 23</u>

To

The A.G's Office

3ᵈ Echelon

　　　　　　　　　　　　　　　　　P. Broad

　　　　　　　　　　　　　　　　　　Capt AVC

　　　　　　　　　　O.C.

　　　　　　　　　　　　　　　53 Mobile Veterinary Section

Army Form C. 2118.

5380
MOBILE VETERINARY SECTION.

No. ....
Date ....

WAR DIARY
or
INTELLIGENCE SUMMARY.
(Erase heading not required.)

Instructions regarding War Diaries and Intelligence Summaries are contained in F. S. Regs., Part II. and the Staff Manual respectively. Title pages will be prepared in manuscript.

Place	Date	Hour	Summary of Events and Information	Remarks and references to Appendices
PERNOIS	April 1		D.A.D.V.S. visited Section. 12 sick animals admitted. Three privates (Category A) despatched to No 2 Base Vet Hospital.	
"	2		Three privates (Category A) despatched to No 2 Base Vet Hospital. 14 sick animals admitted.	
"	3		T/A/Capt McCarthy reverts to permanent grade for drunkenness. 8/0 Clansbey awarded 7 days C.C. & forfeits 7 days pay for drunkenness. 2 sick animals evacuated to T Corps V.E.C. Section left PERNOIS at 3.10 pm - arrived at PUCHEVILLERS at 7.0 pm.	
PUCHEVILLERS	4		D.A.D.V.S. visited Section. Section moved into billets in PUCHEVILLERS. 2 sick animals admitted. 4 found animals admitted.	
"	5		D.A.D.V.S. visited Section. 4 sick animals admitted.	
"	6		Visited transport lines of 188 Inf Brigade, 63 M.G. Coy. with D.A.D.V.S. 4 sick animals admitted. 7 animals returned to units.	
"	7		2 sick animals admitted. Section left PUCHEVILLERS at 4.10 pm - arrived at TOUTENCOURT at 6.0 pm.	
TOUTENCOURT	8		2 sick animals admitted. D.A.D.V.S. & D.A.Q.M.G. visited Section.	

Army Form C. 2118.

MOBILE VETERINARY SECTION.
No...............
Date...............

WAR DIARY
or
INTELLIGENCE SUMMARY.
(Erase heading not required.)

Place	Date	Hour	Summary of Events and Information	Remarks and references to Appendices
	APRIL			
TOUTENCOURT	9		D.A.D.V.S. visited Section. 3 sick animals admitted. 2 animals returned to units. 1 animal destroyed.	
"	10		1 sick animal admitted. 1 animal returned to unit. 5 sick animals evacuated to "V" C.V.E.S. One private joined Section for duty.	
"	11		D.A.D.V.S. visited Section. 2 sick animals admitted.	
"	12		Visited transport lines of 190. Inf. Brigade, & examined all animals. 3 sick animals admitted.	
"	13		Visited transport lines of 14th Worcs. River Batt. 3 sick animals admitted.	
"	14		Visited transport lines of 190 Inf. Brigade. D.A.D.V.S. (Maj Dunlop MC AVC) visited Section for Sen Hum. on taking over appointment of D.A.D.V.S. 63 (RN) Divison. from Maj. Quekett M.C. 2 sick animals admitted. 1 found animal cast shod. 1 animal returned to unit.	
"	15		4 sick animals admitted. 1 animal returned to unit. 1 animal cast to animals reformed Section (Category 3) bet down supplies to establishment	
"	16		D.A.D.V.S. visited Section. Corporal Anson proceeded with D.A.D.V.S. to LEALVILLERS to attend mare belonging to French civilian. 10 sick animals evacuated. 7 sick animals admitted. 1 animal destroyed.	

Army Form C. 2118.

MOBILE VETERINARY SECTION.
No..........
Date..........

WAR DIARY
or
INTELLIGENCE SUMMARY.
(Erase heading not required.)

Instructions regarding War Diaries and Intelligence Summaries are contained in F. S. Regs., Part II. and the Staff Manual respectively. Title pages will be prepared in manuscript.

3

Place	Date	Hour	Summary of Events and Information	Remarks and references to Appendices
TOUTENCOURT	APRIL 17		Visited transport lines of 190 Inf Brigade & 4 Worcests (Diary/Batt). 8 sick animals admitted. 7 found animals admitted. 1 animal evacuated to D.V.E.S. by float. 3 hides sent to T.C.V.E.S.	
"	18		D.A.D.V.S. visited section. 6 privates dispatched to No 2 Base Vet Hospital, as supplies to establishment. 10 sick animals admitted.	
"	19		Visited office of D.A.D.V.S. 21 sick animals evacuated, including 1 by float, & 1 hide. 10 sick animals admitted.	
"	20		Visited transport lines of 190 Inf Brigade; 4 sick animals admitted. 14 animals returned to units.	
"	21		7 sick animals admitted. 14 sick animals evacuated to T.C.V.E.S. also 1 hide.	
"	22		D.A.D.V.S. visited section. Attended at No 3 Gp 63 Div train as member of a Board of Examiners for Shoeing Smiths, from 10 a.m. to 5 p.m.	
"	23		Visited transport lines of 190 Inf Brigade of TRAINS. 2 sick animals admitted. 13 sick animals evacuated.	

Army Form C. 2118.

WAR DIARY or INTELLIGENCE SUMMARY.
(Erase heading not required.)

53rd MOBILE VETERINARY SECTION.

No. ....
Date ....

Place	Date	Hour	Summary of Events and Information	Remarks and references to Appendices
TOUTENCOURT	APRIL 24		Attended at 10 a.m. 63 (R.N.) Div Hdqrs, as president of Board of Survey on Army Cwlts. 5 sick animals admitted.	
	25		Visited units of 190' Inf Brigade with DADVS. ADVS visited section.	
	26		Visited units of 190' Inf Brigade with DADVS. Pte Harvey awarded 21 days FP № 2 for sleeping whilst on night guard. 3 sick animals admitted.	
	27		Visited office of DADVS. 9 sick animals admitted.	
	28		17 sick animals evacuated to No 5 V.C.V.E.S (one animal by float) to sick animals admitted	
	29		Visited horse lines of 63' M.G. Bath with DADVS. 4 sick animals admitted. 8 animals evacuated by float to V.C.V.E.S. visited French Army Horse at Puchevillers. 8 sick animals admitted. 1 animal evacuated by float to V.C.V.E.S.	
	30		Visited horse Q. Puelles belonging to French Army. Visited transport lines of in Scottish 18 sick animals evacuated to V.C.V.E.S. evacuated 1 by float. 3 sick animals admitted	

Broad Capt AVC
O.C. 53' Mobile Veterinary Section

Confidential

53' Mob. Vety. Section
63' (R.N.) Division.
2' June. '18

War Diary

of

O.C. 53' Mob. Vety Section

from

1' May. 1918.

to

31' May. 1918.

The C.G.o. Office
3' Echelon.

Broad Captain. A.V.C.
O. C.   53' Mob. Vety. Section

Army Form C. 2118.

53RD
MOBILE VETERINARY SECTION.
No. V24
Date. ....

WAR DIARY
or
INTELLIGENCE SUMMARY.
(Erase heading not required.)

Instructions regarding War Diaries and Intelligence Summaries are contained in F. S. Regs., Part II. and the Staff Manual respectively. Title pages will be prepared in manuscript.

Place	Date	Hour	Summary of Events and Information	Remarks and references to Appendices
TOUTENCOURT	1918 May 1		Obsvd detachment of 14" Reserve Bde. and of 20 Reserve Bde. and inspected all horses	
	2		9 sick animals admitted. 2 sick animals evacuated. 5 animals returned to units.	
	3		Visited 1 on line of C. Royal Irish Lancers, & Detachment 1st Attchd. Rifle B. & K. & Own Hssrs. also OC and GO CB de Chevaux. ADVS & DADVS visited Section. 6 sick animals admitted. 1 animal evacuated by float.	
	4		Attended conference of VOs at DADVS office. 2 sick animals admitted by float. 1 animal returned to unit	
	5		12 sick animals evacuated to No. Corps Vet. S. 3 sick animals admitted.	
	6		2 sick animals evacuated by motor float. 5 sick animals admitted. Visited Lines of 14 Reserve Reserve Bde. & No. Corps H.A. Signal Co.	
	7		Visited lines of OC & OC Cable Section. Inspected all animals. 1 visit and 2 animals admitted. 1 animal returned to unit	
	8		DADVS visited Section. Visited detachment of 14 Reserve Bde. & 20 Reserve Bde. 2 sick animals admitted. 1 animal returned to unit. Visited Reinforcement Lines Y.M. Royal Artillery & Reinforcement & Attchd. Rifle Bde. for Sy. B.H.A. 3 sick animals evacuated. 1 animal admitted.	

Army Form C. 2118.

53RD MOBILE VETERINARY SECTION.
No. ....
Date ....

WAR DIARY
or
INTELLIGENCE SUMMARY.

B

(Erase heading not required.)

Instructions regarding War Diaries and Intelligence Summaries are contained in F. S. Regs., Part II. and the Staff Manual respectively. Title pages will be prepared in manuscript.

Place	Date	Hour	Summary of Events and Information	Remarks and references to Appendices
TOOTENCOURT	1918 May 9		Visited lines of 247, 248, 249 Field Coys RE with DADVS. 28 animals admitted	
"	10		Visited detachments of 14 & 20 Res Pks	
"	11		Attended conference of VOs at DADVS office. 21 animals evacuated. 1 animal destroyed	
"	11		Visited place in neighbourhood with DADVS, with a view to starting Convalescent Horse Camp	
"	11		Visited lines of 188 Inf Brigade. 6 animals admitted animals ran to her. 23 animals evacuated to T Coys VES.	
"	12		Visited lines of OC. CO Coll Station T Coys HA Cavalry and detachments of 14 & 20 Res Pks	
"	12		21 animals admitted for foreign mud. 8 sick animals admitted	
"	13		4 sick animals admitted. 10 sick animals evacuated to T Coys VES.	
"	14		Visited lines of 1 Royal Irishes & Bn Jorkshires & 2 190 Inf Bn 190. 2 found animals admitted	
"	15		Visited lines of 1st Miss Rifles & 63 MG Batt. 21 animals killed and 2 Cheveral Res Bty	
"	16		4 surplus AVC OR despatched to 2 CDH Hospital	
"	16		Visited lines of detachments of 14 & 20 Horse Parks. OO. CO Coll Station & T Coys MG Cavan	
"	16		21 animals admitted for Rat Camp	
"	17		Attended conference of VOs at DADVS office. sick horses animals of CRE. 6 animals evacuated to T Coys VES.	

Army Form C. 2118.

53RD
MOBILE VETERINARY
SECTION.

No. W.D. V.24
Date................

WAR DIARY
or
INTELLIGENCE SUMMARY.
(Erase heading not required.)

Instructions regarding War Diaries and Intelligence Summaries are contained in F.S. Regs., Part II. and the Staff Manual respectively. Title pages will be prepared in manuscript.

Place	Date	Hour	Summary of Events and Information	Remarks and references to Appendices
TOUTENCOURT	1918 May 18		Visited Animals of CRE & MG Bde HQ. 8 sick animals admitted.	
"	19		24 animals admitted for Rest Camp. 2 sick animals admitted. Made for of Rest Camp &	
"	20		complete arrangements for accommodation for men &c. 3 sick animals admitted. Inspected Rest Camp.	
"	21		Ordered transport down of Y Depot Transits H. Reorganisation of Labour Pl. & Co. 2/Bn K-20	
"	22		Inspected Rest Camps. 2 animals admitted. 12 animals evacuated to T. Corps V.E.S.	
"	23		Visited G.O.C. Horse Lines. Inspected Rest Camp.	
"	24		Visited lines of detachments of K-20 Reserve Bde. T Capt H.A. Gilpin O.O & O.C. Subs Station.	
"	25		8 sick animals evacuated to T Corps V.E.S. & Sub Units animals.	
"	26		Attended Conference of VOs & DADVS offrs to sick animals ascertain route Rest Camp.	
"	27		5 sick animals admitted. Inspected Rest Camp with DADVS	
"	28		Visited & orders of Recipients, Red Cross been taken by org. Inspected Rest Camp. 1 sick animal	
"	29		admitted.	
"	30		3 sick animals admitted. 8 sick animals evacuated to T. Corps V.E.S.	

Army Form C. 2118.

53RD MOBILE VETERINARY SECTION.
No. ....
Date ....

WAR DIARY
or
INTELLIGENCE SUMMARY.
(Erase heading not required.)

D

Instructions regarding War Diaries and Intelligence Summaries are contained in F. S. Regs., Part II. and the Staff Manual respectively. Title pages will be prepared in manuscript.

Place	Date	Hour	Summary of Events and Information	Remarks and references to Appendices
TOUTENCOURT	1918 May 28		Visited Transport lines of 1/1 Royal Scots & 1/1 Bedfordshire & 1/Aust 7th Toronto Queen Bn.	
			18 sick animals admitted. 8 sick animals evacuated via Gy Hosp.	
	29		38 animals Mange R cases from Rd Transp. Cases none 1/1 Aust's 13 are animals injured shell fire or bullet. 20 sick animals evacuated via Gy psd.	
	30		Orders received to find section to TOUTENCOURT O32.d.99 this VS in emergency.	
			Noble felling. 16 sick animals evacuated to Capt V.E.S. Order Rd Corps.	
	31		Attendis conference of VOs of DAOVS office. 22 animals returned to units from Rd Corps.	
			9 sick animals admitted. Visited animals of 153 Vickers Bn.	

Wood
RAVC
OC 53 Mobile Veterinary Section

Confidential

Headquarters

53ʳᵈ Mobile Veterinary Section

June 30ᵗʰ 1918

War Diary
of
53ʳᵈ Mobile Veterinary Section

from

June 1ˢᵗ 1918

to

June 30ᵗʰ 1918

Volume 25

To

The A.G's Office
3ʳᵈ Echelon.

J. Broad. Capt AVC
O.C.
53ʳᵈ Mobile Veterinary Section

Army Form C. 2118.

WAR DIARY
or
INTELLIGENCE SUMMARY.
(Erase heading not required.)

53RD MOBILE VETERINARY SECTION.

Instructions regarding War Diaries and Intelligence Summaries are contained in F.S. Regs., Part II. and the Staff Manual respectively. Title pages will be prepared in manuscript.

Place	Date	Hour	Summary of Events and Information	Remarks and references to Appendices
TOUTENCOURT	1918 JUNE 1		No 440 Staff/Corpl Laurerile E. despatched to No 2u Veterinary Hospital (Authority Office Y AVC Base Records letter 18/925/18. 1 sick animal evacuated to V Corps V.E.S. by float 10 sick animals admitted.	
	2		Section routine 2 sick animals admitted.	
	3		2 sick animals admitted. 1 sick transport lives of Artists Rifles and 10 Worcesters Section lines by Divisional Bar Office.	
	4		Visited transport lines of V Corps HA Signals OO + CO Both Sections. 1 sick animal admitted. 3 animals returned to units. 12 sick animals evacuated to V Corps V.E.S. 1 by float.	
	5		Visited transport lines of 4/4 + 20 Army Pavilion &ton Cos 9 sick animals admitted Visited transport lines of 190 Infy Brigade and 14 Division 10 sick animals admitted. 2 by float from Hatonville. 1 animal died	
	6		1 sick animal admitted by float from Lidwille. 9 sick animals admitted. Conference of OC AVC of DADVS office O Heavies Brigad Examination for Strong Cocks at 12 o'cl+ Divisional Road. SE 8961 Pt/Corpl Veure C.S. admitted to 150 ft Ambulance suffering from	
	7		injury hopefin resulting for hicks by horse.	

Army Form C. 2118.

53RD
MOBILE VETERINARY
SECTION.

No............
Date............

WAR DIARY
or
INTELLIGENCE SUMMARY.
(Erase heading not required.)

Instructions regarding War Diaries and Intelligence Summaries are contained in F. S. Regs., Part II. and the Staff Manual respectively. Title pages will be prepared in manuscript.

Place	Date	Hour	Summary of Events and Information	Remarks and references to Appendices
TOUTENCOURT	1918 JUNE 8.		Visited transport lines of 190 Inf. Brigade. 5 sick animals admitted. 17 sick animals returned to unit including 2 by float. 7/392244 Dr Smith A. and Trooper Gr. discharged. are gone for duty from A.S.C. Base Depot, Havre.	
	9		Visited office of D.A.D.V.S. 1 sick horse destroyed.	
	10		2 sick animals admitted.	
	11		2 sick animals evacuated by float to Corps V.E.S. D.A.D.V.S. visited section. 3 sick animals admitted. Visited transport lines of 63 M.G. Batt⁰. 248. 249 Field Co RE.	
	12		7 sick animals admitted including one by float. Visited transport lines of 247 St. By R.E.	
	13		15 sick animals evacuated to Corps V.E.S. including one by float. 4 sick animals admitted.	
	14		Visited transport lines of 248 Field By RE. 4 sick animals admitted. 1 animal evacuated by motor float to M.V.S. Visited transport lines of 63 M.G. Batt⁰, 249 St. Co RE. R/Head animals admitted. Conference of VC's at D.A.D.V.S. office. 4527 S/Sgt Beal S.F. reports for duty from No 2 Veterinary Hospital.	
	15		Visited transport lines of 249 Ft Co RE. 2 sick animals returned to unit animal admitted.	

Army Form C. 2118.

53RD MOBILE VETERINARY SECTION.

No............ Date............

WAR DIARY or INTELLIGENCE SUMMARY.

(Erase heading not required.)

Instructions regarding War Diaries and Intelligence Summaries are contained in F. S. Regs., Part II. and the Staff Manual respectively. Title pages will be prepared in manuscript.

Place	Date	Hour	Summary of Events and Information	Remarks and references to Appendices
TOUTENCOURT	1918 JUNE 16		Visited V Corps V.E.S. 8 370 P/A/Bays Cav 6.F. Inoculated to R.2 Veterinary Hospital.	
			No. 732244 Dr Church was having severe euphoria established. Despatched to A/C Base Depot.	
	17		Heavy 2 hours relieved to ruits. 4 sick animals admitted.	
			Visited transport lines of 247 bg RS and 42 1 Bay Lahore Bg. 1 animal admitting & evacuated to V Corps V.E.S. by first. 1 sick animal destroyed. 3 sick animals admitted.	
	18		8 sick animals admitted. 19 sick animals evacuated to V Corps V.E.S. including those of R.A.L. (Heat Exhaustion from 49 M.V.S.) 1 sick animal died 1 gassed animal admitted.	
	19		Visited transport lines of 63 M.G. Bn.	
			Inspected all animals of 63 M.G. Bn with D.A.D.V.S. 8 sick animals admitted. Arrangements for evacuation by first to V Corps V.E.S.	
	20		D.A.D.V.S. visited Station. 14 sick animals admitted including one by first. Other transport lines of 247, 249 Sd L.R.F.	
	21		Conference of V.Os of D.A.D.V.S office. 18 sick animals evacuated to V Corps V.E.S. including one by first. 8 sick animals admitted.	
	22		Visited transport lines of R/Y Field C.R.E. 2 sick animals admitted.	

D. D. & L., London, E.C.
Wt. W1771/M2031 750,000 5/17 Sch. 52 Forms/C2118/14
(A5001)

Army Form C. 2118.

WAR DIARY
or
INTELLIGENCE SUMMARY.
(Erase heading not required.)

Instructions regarding War Diaries and Intelligence Summaries are contained in F. S. Regs., Part II. and the Staff Manual respectively. Title pages will be prepared in manuscript.

[Stamp: 53RD MOBILE VETERINARY SECTION. No......... Date.........]

Place	Date	Hour	Summary of Events and Information	Remarks and references to Appendices
TOUTENCOURT	1918 JUNE 23		Visited grazing field & inspected condition of stable and harbour. DADVS & DAQMG visited section.	
	24		Section routine, received ch. for bulletproof walls. 9 sick animals admitted, including one by road.	
	25		Visited lines of 4 companies of Chinese labour. 3 sick animals admitted. 2 sick animals evacuated to V Corps V.E.S. including one by road.	
	26		DADVS visited Section. 20 T/SHIRES Dn Chinaman were prepared & despatched to England. 1 sick animal admitted, 1 by road.	
	27		Visited lines of Chinese Labour Companies (4) at Hy R.E. Dn Pierre Park & Vet Colon &c 3 sick animals admitted. 15 sick animals evacuated en route to V Corps V.E.S. including one by road.	
	28		Conference of VOs at DADVS office. 7 sick animals admitted including one by road. 1202 Pte/Pany 3 AVC reported for duty fm No 2 Veterinary Hospital.	
	29		Visited DADVS office. 5 sick animals admitted. 12 & Corps VES en-route on by road.	
	30		Section routine. 6 sick animals admitted. 1 animal returned to unit.	

H. Brody
Capt AVC
O.C. 53 Mobile Veterinary Section

Army Form C. 2118.

63

5380 MOBILE VETERINARY SECTION.
No ....
Date ....

Vol 2

WAR DIARY
or
INTELLIGENCE SUMMARY.
(Erase heading not required.)

Instructions regarding War Diaries and Intelligence Summaries are contained in F. S. Regs., Part II. and the Staff Manual respectively. Title pages will be prepared in manuscript.

Place	Date	Hour	Summary of Events and Information	Remarks and references to Appendices
TOUTENCOURT	1918 JULY 1		4 sick animals admitted. 1 sick animal evacuated to V Corps V.E.S. by road. 1 found animal admitted.	
	2		Visited horse lines of 401 Coy. Divisional Train & 150 (R.N.) Field Ambulance. 12 sick animals evacuated. 1 found animal admitted.	
	3		Visited D.A.D.V.S. office. 2 sick animals admitted.	
	4		Visited # horse lines of 4 companies of 63 Divisional Train. 700 Labour Coy. & 147 AT Coy R.E.	
	5		D.A.D.V.S. visited Section. 8 sick animals admitted. To conference of V.O's at D.A.D.V.S. office. 6 sick animals admitted. 4 veterinary wallets Mark III, returned to No.1 Advanced Depot Veterinary Stores, by authority of D.V.S. Circular memo 245 Q 296/16 24/5/68 T. HARVEY special 14 days special leave to England.	
	6		Visited horse lines of 481 Coy. 63 Divisional Train. 4 sick animals admitted. Rations & grazing found in perfect condition.	
	7		Visited D.A.D.V.S. office. 17 sick animals evacuated. 1 animal returned to unit.	
	8		Visited horse lines of No.1 Mon. Coy. 63 Divisional Train. 1 sick animal admitted.	

D. D. & L., London, E.C.
Wt. W1771/M2031 750,000 5/17 Sch. 52 Forms/C2118/14
(A801)

Army Form C. 2118.

5380
MOBILE VETERINARY SECTION.
No. ....
Date ....

WAR DIARY
or
INTELLIGENCE SUMMARY.

(Erase heading not required.)

Instructions regarding War Diaries and Intelligence Summaries are contained in F. S. Regs., Part II. and the Staff Manual respectively. Title pages will be prepared in manuscript.

Place	Date 1916	Hour	Summary of Events and Information	Remarks and references to Appendices
TOUTENCOURT	July 9		3 sick animals admitted.	
	10		Visited Horse lines of 2cd + 3cd Cy. 63 Divisional Train. 13 sick animals admitted. 1 joint animal admitted.	
	11		24 sick animals evacuated to No 7 Corps V.E.S., including 1 by float. 17 sick animals admitted. Visited Horse lines of 147 AT Cy R.E. + 700 Labour Cy. 1 animal returned to unit.	
	12		To Enquire of V.O. of DADVS Office. 1 sick animal destroyed. 5 sick animals admitted, including 1 by float.	
	13		Doctor review. 12 sick animals evacuated to V Corps V.E.S., including 1 by float. 3 sick animals admitted.	
	14		9 sick animals admitted. No 7151 R.S. gifsorony G. A.S.C. turned over in dog box to England.	
	15		DADVS asked Doctor. 4 sick animals admitted. Visited 147 AT Cy. R.E.	
	16		Visited 4 Coys of 63 Divisional Train. 4 sick animals admitted.	

D. D. & L., London, E.C.
Wt. W1771/M2031 750,000 5/17 Sch. 52 Forms/C2118/14
(A5001)

Army Form C. 2118.

WAR DIARY
or
INTELLIGENCE SUMMARY.
(Erase heading not required.)

53RD MOBILE VETERINARY SECTION.
No. ....
Date. ....

Place	Date	Hour	Summary of Events and Information	Remarks and references to Appendices
TOUTENCOURT	1918 JULY 17		ADVS & Capt [?] visited Section; noted Horse lines of 150 Field Ambulance. 8 sick animals admitted	
	18		DADVS visited Section. 15 sick animals evacuated to T.B.P.&V.E.S. 1 sick animal admitted. No 35/905 ffmule TAYLOR T. xferd for duty from 2o.R. Dow Weaning Hospital	
	19		To Cy forces of VOs of DADVS office. Visited Horse lines of 150 Field Ambulance. 63 Machine Gun Battalion & Hot Coy 63 Divisional Train. 6 sick animals admitted.	
	20		S/Sgt 2347 ffmule MURPHY A.W. posted to 2o.R.Dow Weaning Hospital for duty. 16 sick animals admitted	
	21		To DADVS office. Visited Horse lines of 2o.P.Coy. 63 Divisional Train. 18 sick animals evacuated to T.B.P.&V.E.S. 3 sick animals admitted. Pte Nurse C. HARVEY T. Leave from six days Special Leave to England	
	22		Section routine. 5 sick animals admitted	
	23		Visited Horse lines of 150 Field Ambulance & P.S.2o.Coy. 63 Divisional Train. 4 sick animals admitted	

Army Form C. 2118.

53RD MOBILE VETERINARY SECTION.
No.................
Date...............

WAR DIARY or INTELLIGENCE SUMMARY.

(Erase heading not required.)

Instructions regarding War Diaries and Intelligence Summaries are contained in F.S. Regs., Part II. and the Staff Manual respectively. Title pages will be prepared in manuscript.

Place	Date	Hour	Summary of Events and Information	Remarks and references to Appendices
TOUTENCOURT	1918 JULY 24		DADVS visited Section. Visited Hqrs Lines of Com. 1 & 2 of 63 Division & staff.	
	25		4 Hy AT Bn. RE. 2 sick animals admitted. 1 by float.	
			Visited 700 Labour Coy. 8 sick animals admitted including 1 Off. Horse 10 wr animals evacuated to V Corps V.E.S.	
	26		Co Conference of VOs at DADVS Office. 2 sick animals admitted.	
	27		Section routine. 8 sick animals admitted. one by float. four out of admitted	
			2 animals returned to unit	
	28		SF193 Qr JOHNSTON in proceeded to England on 10 days special leave. 3 sick animals admitted, one by float. Closed transport Guns of 63 Machine Gun Bn. DADVS early Section and gave orders for section to move on Bg. A. SARTON. 16 sick animals sent to	
			49 MVS	
	29		Section left camp at 9.30 am arriving at destination at SARTON at 1.15 pm DADVS visited Section	
	30		ADVS (T/Col) + DADVS visited Section. 6 sick animals admitted	
			Visited transport lines of 188 Inft. Brigade. Nos. 2 + 3 of 63 Div. Am. 63 M.G.B.Hs.	
	31		2 sick animals admitted. 1 found animal admitted.	

H. Brook Cpt AVC
O.C. 53 Mobile Veterinary Section

Confidential   53rd Mobile Veterinary Section

                                              Aug. 31st 1918

War Diary

of

53rd Mobile Veterinary Section

from

August 1st 1918

to

August 31st 1918

VOLUME 27.

To.

The A.G.'s Office
3rd Echelon

J.C. Broad Capt A.V.C.
O.C.
53rd Mobile Veterinary Section.

Army Form C. 2118.

53RD MOBILE VETERINARY SECTION.

No........ Date........

WAR DIARY
or
INTELLIGENCE SUMMARY.
(Erase heading not required.)

A

Instructions regarding War Diaries and Intelligence Summaries are contained in F. S. Regs., Part II. and the Staff Manual respectively. Title pages will be prepared in manuscript.

Place	Date	Hour	Summary of Events and Information	Remarks and references to Appendices
SARTON	Aug 1 1918		Visited transport lines of 249 Field Coy RE. Visited 1/24 Ambulance. 8 sick animals evacuated to IV Corp VES. 1 sick animal admitted.	
	2		Conference of VOs at DADVS office. Section relieved.	
	3		2 found animals admitted. DADVS visited Section.	
	4		Moved Section from Sarton to RAINCHEVAL.	
RAINCHEVAL	5		Visited DADVS office at BEAUDUSSNE. Moved Section to Irish huts in Raincheval. Pressed camp being reserved for RCA.	
	6		DADVS visited Section. 2 sick animals admitted.	
	7		Visited two of the Divisional Hair companies and 750 Field Ambulance.	
	8		Orders received to prepare for immediate move. 7 sick animals handed over to 33 M.V.S. 2 sick animals admitted. Moved Section to ARQUEVES to work with No.1 Cav Divisional train.	
ARQUEVES	9		Moved off at 0.15. Arrived at CONTAY at 3.20 am. Visited DADVS office at BAVELINCOURT. Visited transport lines of 53 M.G. Batt" Auxr Batt" Act by Cav train.	
CONTAY	10		8 sick animals admitted. 6 sick animals handed over to 23 M.V.S. Order part by Cav train.	

Army Form C. 2118.

WAR DIARY
or
INTELLIGENCE SUMMARY. B
(Erase heading not required.)

Instructions regarding War Diaries and Intelligence Summaries are contained in F. S. Regs., Part II. and the Staff Manual respectively. Title pages will be prepared in manuscript.

5380
MOBILE VETERINARY SECTION.
No............
Date............

Place	Date	Hour	Summary of Events and Information	Remarks and references to Appendices
CONTAY	Aug 11. 1918		Visited transport lines of 150 Fd Ambulance	
"	12		DADVS visited Section. Visited No 2 & 3 Coy Divisional Train & 149 Fd Ambulance. 7 sick animals admitted	
"	13		6 sick animals admitted. 6 sick animals evacuated to III Corps V.E.S. No. 1126 Pte Davies S. proceded to England on 14 days leave	
"	14		Moved Section from CONTAY to ESBARTS at 8.0 am arriving at 9.30 am DADVS visited Section	
ESBARTS	15		1 sick animal admitted.	
"			Moved Section from ESBARTS to SARTON arriving at 5.30 pm	
SARTON	16		Conference of V.Os at DADVS Office at PAS. Visited lines of No 3 Coy Divisional Train	
"	17		Moved Section to FAMECHON.	
FAMECHON	18		ADVS V Corps visited Section. 11 Sick animals admitted. DADVS visited Section	
"	19		Moved Section to PAS, and there received orders to proceed forthwith to COUIN, and /or No 1 Coy Divisional Train arrived at COUIN at 10.30 pm. 7 sick animals evacuated to IV Corps V.E.S. 14 sick animals admitted.	

Army Form C.2118.

63RD MOBILE VETERINARY SECTION.

No. ....
Date ....

WAR DIARY
or
INTELLIGENCE SUMMARY.

(Erase heading not required.)

Instructions regarding War Diaries and Intelligence Summaries are contained in F. S. Regs., Part II. and the Staff Manual respectively. Title pages will be prepared in manuscript.

Place	Date	Hour	Summary of Events and Information	Remarks and references to Appendices
COUIN	Aug 20 1918		Visited DADVS office at PAS. Received orders to establish an advanced collecting post at FONQUEVILLERS. Went there to choose site. 12 sick animals admitted from Div Artillery, for treatment. 4 sick animals evacuated, 1 by float. 3 sick animals admitted.	
	21		Advance post established at site 150 yds W of FONQUEVILLERS at 1.80pm (1 NCO + 4 men). ADVS IV Corps visited Section.	
	22		Visited advanced collecting post & moved it ½ mile further west to avoid hostile shell fire. 9 sick animals admitted, including 2 by float from advance post. 2 wounded animals shot. Visited transport lines of 150th & 149th Fd Ambulances.	
	23		Conference of VOs at DADVS office visited advance post. ADVS IV Corps visited Section. 7 sick animals admitted. 1 sick animal destroyed. DADVS visited Section.	
	24		17 sick animals evacuated to IV Corps V.E.S. 10 sick animals admitted. Visited advance post.	
	25		13 sick animals evacuated (1 by float) to IV Corps V.E.S. Moved Section to HANNESCAMPS, leaving 3 float cases at COUIN in charge of 1 NCO + 2 men.	
HANNESCAMPS	26		Established advanced collecting post at BUCQUOY, (1 NCO + 3 men). Visited party at COUIN and cleared all cases by float to IV Corps post at PAS. 17 sick animals admitted.	

Army Form

53RD MOBILE VETERINARY SECTION.
No ....
Date ....

WAR DIARY
or
INTELLIGENCE SUMMARY.
(Erase heading not required.)

D

Instructions regarding War Diaries and Intelligence Summaries are contained in F. S. Regs., Part II. and the Staff Manual respectively. Title pages will be prepared in manuscript.

Place	Date	Hour	Summary of Events and Information	Remarks and references to Appendices
HANNESCAMPS	Aug 27 '1918		Visited advanced post. 12 sick animals admitted. 26 sick animals evacuated.	
	28		Visited advanced post. 23 sick animals admitted. 10 sick animals evacuated.	
	29		Moved advanced post to ACHIET-LE-PETIT. To DNO. with DADVS to see animals admitted. 18 sick animals evacuated. 1 sick animal destroyed.	
	30		Visited advanced post. 3 sick animals admitted. 1 sick animal destroyed. 13 sick animals evacuated to IV Corps VES Pol in BAS.	
	31		Moved advanced post 3/4 mile W. of given location owing to hostile shell fire. 1 sick animal evacuated by flat. Orders received to move Section on 1st prox.	

R Broad
Capt AVC
OC 53° Mobile Veterinary Section
63 (RN) Division

Army Form C. 2118.

53RD MOBILE VETERINARY SECTION.

No. ....
Date ....

WAR DIARY
or
INTELLIGENCE SUMMARY.
(Erase heading not required.)

A

Instructions regarding War Diaries and Intelligence Summaries are contained in F. S. Regs., Part II. and the Staff Manual respectively. Title pages will be prepared in manuscript.

Place	Date	Hour	Summary of Events and Information	Remarks and references to Appendices
SARTON	Aug 1 1918		Visited transport lines of 2/9 field Cy R.E. and 2/2nd Australian S.H.A Company.	
	2		8 sick animals evacuated to IV Corps V.E.S. 1 sick animal admitted.	
	3		Conference of O.Os. of DADVS office visited orders routine	
	4		2 sick animals admitted. DADVS visited Section.	
			3 sick Section for Orders to proceed	
BRUIN HAYNE	5		Visited DADVS office at Beauquesne. Moved Section to H.Q. Guards Divisional R. concentration area for R.S.M.	
	6		DADVS visited Section. 2 sick animals admitted.	
	7		Moved into H.Q. Churches train transport and 60 Field Ambulances.	
	8		Orders received to prepare for immediate move. 7 sick animals handed on to 22 M.V.S. 2 sick animals admitted. Moved Section to ARQUEVES & met off H.Q. by Divisional train.	
ARQUEVES	9		Moved off at 0.15. Arrived at CONTAY at 3.20 am. Under DADVS office and DAVE in charge Usual Routine. 9 63 M.G. Battn. Anim Battn H.Q. Coy train.	
CONTAY	10		8 sick animals admitted. 0 sick animals handed on to 23 M.V.S. Cooks & w/Coy Coy train.	

Army Form C. 2118.

WAR DIARY
or
INTELLIGENCE SUMMARY.
(Erase heading not required.)

53RD MOBILE VETERINARY SECTION.
No. ....
Date ....

Instructions regarding War Diaries and Intelligence Summaries are contained in F. S. Regs., Part II. and the Staff Manual respectively. Title pages will be prepared in manuscript.

Place	Date	Hour	Summary of Events and Information	Remarks and references to Appendices
CONTAY	Aug 11. 1916		Visited transport lines of 150 ft Ambulance.	
	12		DADVS arrived. Orders issued. 1/5 2 & 3 Coy evacuated. Took over of 1st Division.	
			9 sick animals admitted.	
	13		8 sick animals admitted. 6 sick animals evacuated to II Cav VFS + one P. Dep't	
			proceeded to Belgium on 14 days leave.	
	14		Moved Section from CONTAY to ESBARTS at 8.0 am, arriving at 9.30 am. DADVS asked Orders	
			1 sick animal admitted.	
ESBARTS	15		Moved Section from ESBARTS to SARTON, arriving at 5.30 pm.	
SARTON	18		Inspected VO's of DADVS office at Pas. Visited lines of 2 & 3 Cav Divisions team.	
FIENVILLERS			Moved Section to FIENVILLERS.	
			ADVs & typewriter Orders. 11 Cav animals evacuated. DADVS visited Section	
	19		Moved Section to PAS and then received orders to proceed forthwith to COUIN, and for	
			A.1 Coy. evacuated train arrived at COUIN at 10.30pm. 7 sick animals admitted.	
			16 sick animals evacuated to IV Corps VFS.	

WAR DIARY or INTELLIGENCE SUMMARY

Army Form C. 2118.

53RD MOBILE VETERINARY SECTION.

No..................
Date................

(Erase heading not required.)

Place	Date	Hour	Summary of Events and Information	Remarks and references to Appendices
COUIN	Aug 20/1918		Visit D.A.D.V.S. Office at P.M. Heard astote to establish an advanced collecting post at FONQUEVILLERS. Sent two N. Cliver side 12 sick animals admitted the W. Ridley in Railway. 2 sick animals evacuated 1 by Rail. 3 Sick animals a night 2.	
	21		Animal post established Set 158.105 N. of FONQUEVILLERS 1 officer N.C.O's & camp.	
	22		ADVS + O.C. visit Section. Ensured advanced collecting post Went to Ju xra further east and side post at B Country advanced, advancing 2 by Rail. One evacuated. 2 recovered, returned and Hospital Set Q 150 107 S. Gaubretenne	
	23		Reports of SO LI DADVS office. Orders received Adv. nov. R.C.P. north Octoa for an 11th Admitted 1 sick animal destroyed. D.D.V.S. visit Section 10 sick animals evacuated to 10 Corps V.S. 10 sick animal admitted.	
	24		..... section fire	
	25		13 sick animals received by Rail to 10 Corps V.S. Upon Orders to move can 20 party 3 post less at BUNN and any 5 mess dinner.	
HENNESCAMP FG	26		Established advanced collecting post at BUCQUOY (1000 x 3 miles). Other Party of C.C.V.S. and came at noon by Rail to IV Corps post at P.M. 17 sick animals admitted.	

A7032. Wt. W.1285.9/M1293. 750,000. 1/17. D. D & I. Ltd. Forms/C2118/14.

Army Form C. 2118.

WAR DIARY
or
INTELLIGENCE SUMMARY.

(Erase heading not required.)

53RD MOBILE VETERINARY SECTION.

No. ....
Date ....

Instructions regarding War Diaries and Intelligence Summaries are contained in F. S. Regs., Part II. and the Staff Manual respectively. Title pages will be prepared in manuscript.

Place	Date	Hour	Summary of Events and Information	Remarks and references to Appendices
DINNESCAMPS	Aug 27 1918		Under Collection post. 12 sick animals admitted. 25 sick animals evacuated.	
	28.		Under Collection post. 23 sick animals below M.D. 10 sick animals evacuated.	
	29.		Under collection post. To render assistance 1 sick animals destroyed.	
	30.		Under collection post. 3 sick animals admitted. 1 sick animal destroyed. 13 sick animals evacuated to IV Corps V.F.S. post at Pas.	
	31.		Unit advanced post to within W. of proud harbour through Achiet Le Grand & Bihucourt. Unit open ready to receive Sick at 6 p.m.	

[signature]
Capt AVC
OC 53 Mobile Veterinary Section
63 (RN) Division.

CONFIDENTIAL   53rd. MOBILE VETERINARY SECTION
                                63rd (R.N.) DIVISION

WAR DIARY

of

O.C. 53rd MOBILE VETERINARY SECTION

FROM

1st SEPT. 1918

to

30th SEPT. 1918

. . . .

VOLUME 28.

To -:   A.G.'s OFFICE
            3rd ECHELON.

                                        P.W.Brood
                                            Capt. A.V.C.
                                    O.C.
                                53rd MOBILE VETERINARY SECTION

Army Form C. 2118.

WAR DIARY
or
INTELLIGENCE SUMMARY.
(Erase heading not required.)

Instructions regarding War Diaries and Intelligence Summaries are contained in F.S. Regs., Part II. and the Staff Manual respectively. Title pages will be prepared in manuscript.

53rd MOBILE VETERINARY SECTION.
No.............
Date............

A

Place	Date	Hour	Summary of Events and Information	Remarks and references to Appendices
HANNESCAMPS	Sept 1st 1918.		On receipt of instructions to move Section, the advanced collecting post was called in. Section left Hannescamps at 12.45 pm arriving at Blaireville at 2.45 pm. DADVS visited Section.	
BLAIREVILLE	2		An advanced collecting post established by 10.15 am at point 3½ mile SE of Mercatel. A.D.V.S. XVII Corps visited Section. 20 sick animals admitted, chiefly foot wounds.	
	3		Moved advanced collecting post to site ½ mile west of FONTAINE LES CROISELLES. 11 sick animals admitted; 24 sick animals evacuated. 1 sick animal destroyed.	
	4		Moved Section to HENIN, arriving 3.30 pm. 6 sick animals admitted. 11 sick animals evacuated.	
HENIN	5		Moved Section to site ½ mile W of FONTAINE LES CROISELLES: established an advanced collecting post at HENDECOURT. 3 sick animals admitted. 8 sick animals evacuated.	
FONTAINE LES CROISELLES	6		Conference of V.O's at DADVS office. Visited transport lines of 2 & 3 rd Cay. Div. Fran. 16 sick animals admitted. 3 captured animals admitted.	
	7		Advanced collecting post called in at 6.0 pm. 24 sick animals evacuated. 2 sick animals destroyed. 12 sick animals admitted.	

Army Form C. 2118.

WAR DIARY
or
INTELLIGENCE SUMMARY.

(Erase heading not required.)

B

53RD
MOBILE VETERINARY
SECTION.

No............
Date............

Instructions regarding War Diaries and Intelligence Summaries are contained in F. S. Regs., Part II. and the Staff Manual respectively. Title pages will be prepared in manuscript.

Place	Date	Hour	Summary of Events and Information	Remarks and references to Appendices
FONTAINES LES CROISELLES	Sept 8th 1918		Moved section to BELLACOURT, arriving at 2.30 p.m.	
BELLACOURT	9th		Visited office of DADVS at BAVINCOURT. 13 sick animals admitted	
	10		DADVS proceeded on 14 days leave to U.K.; proceeded to DHQ to assume duties of DADVS. 5 sick animals evacuated. 2 animals returned to units. 3 found & 2 captured animals admitted.	
	11		Visited transport lines of 249 Bde Field Coy R.E. 188 Sig Brigade & 189 Brigade. 7 sick animals admitted; 4 captured animals admitted; 1 animal returned to unit.	
	12		Visited transport lines of 190 Inf Brigade, 247 Field Coy R.E. & X H Coy Div Train. 1 sick animal admitted. 2 horses returned to unit.	
	13		Conference of VO at DADVS office. Visited transport lines of 9 Royal Coy and inspected animals of DHQ. 9 sick animals evacuated, including one by float. 1 sick animal admitted.	
	14		Visited transport lines of 4 Bedfordshire & Royal Scots. 2 sick animals admitted.	

Army Form C. 2118.

53RD
MOBILE VETERINARY
SECTION.
No..........
Date..........

WAR DIARY
or
INTELLIGENCE SUMMARY.
(Erase heading not required.)

Instructions regarding War Diaries and Intelligence Summaries are contained in F. S. Regs., Part II. and the Staff Manual respectively. Title pages will be prepared in manuscript.

Place	Date	Hour	Summary of Events and Information	Remarks and references to Appendices
BELLACOURT	Sept 15 1918		Visited transport lines of Signal Coy and Anzac Bat: 4 found animals admitted.	
	16		6 sick animals evacuated. 4 captured animals issued to units	
BOYELLES	17		Moved section to BOYELLES, arriving at R.O. midday	
	18		ADVS XVII Corps visited Section. 1 sick animal admitted. Received section from D.H.Q.	
	19		3 sick animals admitted. Proceeded to D.H.Q. & inspected horses of 17 Tyndos Bat & 76 labour Coy & D.H.Q. 150 Field Ambulance Signal Coy. 3 captured animals issued to units	
	20		Conference of VOs at DADVS office. Visited Section to N.E. of Boyelles. 8 legr.Roe. Visited Vet. Coy Div. train & D.H.Q. 8 found animals issued to units. 1 sick animal admitted.	
BOYELLES - ST LEGER Rd	21		Visited transport lines of Signal Coy, 249 Field Coy RE & D.H.Q. 5 sick animals evacuated, and one destroyed. 2 sick animals admitted.	
	22		Inspected remounts at S.M. Section, D.A.C. 2 sick animals admitted.	

Army Form C. 2118.

WAR DIARY
or
INTELLIGENCE SUMMARY.
(Erase heading not required.)

Instructions regarding War Diaries and Intelligence Summaries are contained in F. S. Regs., Part II. and the Staff Manual respectively. Title pages will be prepared in manuscript.

D

MOBILE VETERINARY SECTION.
No.................
Date..............

Place	Date	Hour	Summary of Events and Information	Remarks and references to Appendices
BOYELLES–ST LEGER Rd	Sept 23rd 1918		Inspected remounts at SAA Section DAC. 5 sick animals evacuated, including one foot case. 4 sick animals admitted.	
	24		Visited lines of M.G. Batt., 169 Inf Brigade, 2,3, 4 Coy Div Train, 249 Field Coy. 4 sick animals admitted.	
	25		Visited Div Reinforcement Camp to see sick horse. 3 sick animals evacuated, including one by float. 1 sick animal sick.	
	26		Sector routine. to D.H.Q. to arrange move of Section. 3 sick animals admitted	
	27		Section left camp at 9.0 am among at site nr LONGATTE at 11.45am. Advanced collecting post established on NOREUIL–QUÉANT road about 1 kilometre west of QUÉANT. 5 sick animals admitted	
LONGATTE	28		lines of SAA Section DAC. to Div D.H.Q. 5 sick animals admitted Moved Section from LONGATTE to site about 1½ miles SW of MŒUVRES, arriving at 2.5 pm. Called in advanced collecting post. 6 sick animals evacuated to 6 Coy KVES at VAULX–VRAUCOURT. visited lines of 2, 3 Coy Div Train.	
MŒUVRES	29		A.A. r D.M.C. 63 Div. visited Section. Moved Section to site by Sugar factory on Bapaume–Cambrai Road, 1 mile W of ANNEUX, arriving at R.O. noon.	

(A8091) D. D. & L., London, E.C. Wt. W1771/M2031 750,000 5/17 Sch. 52 Forms/C2. 12/14

Army Form C. 2118.

53RD
MOBILE VETERINARY
SECTION.
No.
Date.

WAR DIARY
or
INTELLIGENCE SUMMARY.
(Erase heading not required.)

Instructions regarding War Diaries and Intelligence Summaries are contained in F. S. Regs., Part II. and the Staff Manual respectively. Title pages will be prepared in manuscript.

Place	Date	Hour	Summary of Events and Information	Remarks and references to Appendices
SUGAR FACTORY.	1918 Sept. 30		20 sick animals evacuated. 1 sick animal destroyed. Useless Burn of SAA Section. 63 (RN) DAC. 37 sick animals admitted.	

R.Brook Capt AVC.
O.C. 53' Mobile Veterinary Section

Army Form C. 2118.

WAR DIARY
or
INTELLIGENCE SUMMARY.
(Erase heading not required.)

63RD MOBILE VETERINARY SECTION

Place	Date	Hour	Summary of Events and Information	Remarks and references to Appendices
SUGAR FACTORY (NEAR GRAINCOURT)	October 1 1918		33 sick animals evacuated to XVII Corps V.E.S, including one by horse float. 3 sick animals destroyed. 2 animals evacuated by motor ambulance. 37 sick animals admitted.	
"	2		27 sick animals evacuated, including one by horse float. 2 animals evacuated by motor ambulance. 16 sick animals admitted.	
	3		13 sick animals evacuated, including one by horse float. 2 sick animals evacuated by motor float. 1 sick animal destroyed. 10 sick animals admitted. A.D.V.S. XVII Corps visited Section	
	4		1 sick animal evacuated by horse float. 3 sick animals destroyed. 30 sick animals admitted. Major J.J. DUNLOP. M.C. (D.A.D.V.S. 63 (RN) Division) returned from leave. Conference of V.Os. at D.A.D.V.S. office.	
	5		34 sick animals evacuated to XVII Corps V.E.S, including one by horse float. 8 sick animals admitted. Visited lines of 1st 2, 3 & 4 Bcys. 63 Divisional Train.	
	6		11 sick animals admitted. 1 sick animal destroyed. Visited lines of S.A.A. Sect. 63 (RN) D.A.C.	

Army Form C. 2118.

WAR DIARY
or
INTELLIGENCE SUMMARY.

(Erase heading not required.)

53RD MOBILE VETERINARY SECTION.

Instructions regarding War Diaries and Intelligence Summaries are contained in F. S. Regs., Part II. and the Staff Manual respectively. Title pages will be prepared in manuscript.

Place	Date	Hour	Summary of Events and Information	Remarks and references to Appendices
SUGAR FACTORY (NEAR GRAINCOURT)	October 7' 1918		Inspected animals of No R.S. Corps Divisional Train with D.A.D.V.S. 11 sick animals evacuated to XVII Corps V.E.S, including one by horse float. 1 sick animal destroyed.	
"	8		4 sick animals evacuated by motor ambulance. 21 sick animals admitted.	
"	9		19 sick animals evacuated, including one by horse float. 15 sick animals admitted.	
"	10		6 sick animals admitted. 12 sick animals evacuated to XVII V.E.S. 5 sick animals handed over to 57 Div M.V.S. Moved Section from present location to MORCHIES arriving at 7.0 pm	
MORCHIES	11		8 sick animals evacuated to XVII V.E.S. 1 animal admitted.	
BAILLEULMONT	12		Moved Section to BAILLEULMONT arriving at 4.45 pm.	
ROELLECOURT	13		Moved Section to ROELLECOURT arriving at 3.30 pm	
"	14		D.A.D.V.S. visited Section. Section routine: visited transport lines of 186 Inf Brigade.	
			Visited transport lines of 63 M.G. Batt: 249 Field Co. R.E.	

Army Form C. 2118.

WAR DIARY
or
INTELLIGENCE SUMMARY

(Erase heading not required.)

53RD MOBILE VETERINARY SECTION.

Place	Date	Hour	Summary of Events and Information	Remarks and references to Appendices
ROELLECOURT	1918 OCT 14		9 sick animals admitted. Visited W Collecting Post at FAVECOURT.	
	15		6 sick animals evacuated to W Collecting Post. 5 sick animals admitted	
			Visited 146 Fd Ambulance horse lines	
	16		Visited 130 Fd Ambulance horse lines, and 63 M.G. Batt.	
	18		No 452" P/A/Sgt. Kent proceeded to U.K. 14 days leave. No. T/t. 057225 P/t Miller F.	
			proceeded to U.K. 14 days leave. 3 sick animals admitted	
	19		Capt. J. E. Broad. V.C. proceeded to U.K. 14 days leave.	
			Lieut. J. Finlayson takes over duties of above officer	
			Officer visits Artists Bn of gds at 188 B.H.Q.	

Army Form C. 2118.

WAR DIARY
or
INTELLIGENCE SUMMARY

(Erase heading not required.)

D

Instructions regarding War Diaries and Intelligence Summaries are contained in F. S. Regs., Part II. and the Staff Manual respectively. Title pages will be prepared in manuscript.

5380
MOBILE VETERINARY SECTION.

Place	Date	Hour	Summary of Events and Information	Remarks and references to Appendices
ROELLECOURT.	10/18 20.		O/c visits Artist Batt.	
	21		10 sick animals evacuated to N°2 V.E.P. D.A.D. V.S. visits Section	
			O/c visits Drake Hooden Hawke Batt. 7 sick animals admitted	
	22		Section departs from ROELLECOURT. 9-30 AM	
BERLENCOURT.	22.	3 PM	D.A.D.V.S. visits Section	
	23		Went to RAMECOURT for 188 B.M. charger O/c visits 189 B.H.Q Drake Hood Batt	
			+ N° 3 Co. Train.	
	24		D.A.D.V.S visits Section O/c visits S.A.A. Section 188 B.H.Q. Anson.	
			R. Marine & R. Irish Batt. 3 sick animals admitted	
	25		O/c to D.A.D.V.S. office conference of V.Os	

Army Form C. 2118.

MOBILE VETERINARY SECTION. 5380

WAR DIARY
or
INTELLIGENCE SUMMARY.
(Erase heading not required.)

E

Instructions regarding War Diaries and Intelligence Summaries are contained in F.S. Regs., Part II. and the Staff Manual respectively. Title pages will be prepared in manuscript.

Place	Date	Hour	Summary of Events and Information	Remarks and references to Appendices
BERLENCOURT	25		O/c visits S.A.A. Section 190 B.H.Q. Fusiliers Bedfords & Artists Batt.	
	26		N°.4 Co. Div. Train & 247 Field Co. R.E.	
			D.A.D.V.S. visits section O/c visits R. Irish Batt. 249 Fld. Co. R.E.	
	27		S.A.A. Section	
		N° 12.02	Pte Harvey S.J. proceeded to U.K. 14 days leave. 74/24970 Driver Stocking proceeded to U.K. 14 days leave O/c visited 182 B.H.Q. Anzac.	
	28		6 Animals evacuated to N°.2 V.E.P. O/c visits 190 B.H.Q. Fusiliers Bedfords & Artists Batt. N°.4 Co. Div. Train 247 Fld. Co. R.E. 1 Sick animal admitted	
	29		D.A.D.V.S. visits section accompanied by the D.A.D.V.S. O/c visits R. Irish & Hood Batt. 189 B.H.Q. 249 Fld. Co. R.E.	

Army Form C. 2118.

63RD
MOBILE VETERINARY
SECTION.

WAR DIARY
or
INTELLIGENCE SUMMARY.
(Erase heading not required.)

F

Place	Date	Hour	Summary of Events and Information	Remarks and references to Appendices
BERLENCOURT	30		O/c visits 190 B.H.Q. Fusiliers Bedfords & Actiols Batt. No 3. Coo. Div. Train D.A.D.V.S. visits section. Total do 188 B.H. Q for sick animals. 15 sick animals admitted	
	31		O/c visits S.A.A. Section & 14th Worcestershire Regt. J. Finlayson Lieut. A.V.C. for O/c 63 M.V.S.	

CONFIDENTIAL   53rd MOBILE VETERINARY SECTION

                                                    30/11/18

WAR DIARY
of
53rd MOBILE VETERINARY SECTION
from
NOV. 1st. 1918
to
NOV. 30th 1918

VOLUME 30

To :-

　　The A.G's Office

　　　　3rd Echelon

                                              Capt. A.V.C.

                              O.C.

                          53rd MOBILE VETERINARY SECTION

Army Form C. 2118.

WAR DIARY
or
INTELLIGENCE SUMMARY.
(Erase heading not required.)

63RD MOBILE VETERINARY SECTION.

Place	Date	Hour	Summary of Events and Information	Remarks and references to Appendices
BERLENCOURT	Nov 1st 1918		Section leaves BERLENCOURT at 8.15 a.m. and arrives at CARRENCY at 17.45.	
			14 sick animals evacuated by rail from TINQUES.	
CARRENCY	2"		Section left CARRENCY at 9.0, & arrived at COURCELLES at 16.45. DADVS visited Section.	
COURCELLES	3"		3 sick animals admitted.	
"	4"		4 sick animals evacuated to XXII Corps V.E.S. 2 sick animals admitted. DADVS visited Section.	
"	5		Section left COURCELLES at 8.15, & arrived at THIANT at 19.00. 1 sick animal evacuated to XXII Corps V.E.S.	
THIANT	6		3 sick animals admitted. DADVS visited Section.	
"	7		Established an advanced collecting post at SAULTAIN, with 1 NCO & 2 men. 8 sick animals admitted, including one by hoof from VERCHAIN.	
"	8		2 sick animals admitted. O.C. returned to Section from leave to England.	
"	9		16 sick animals evacuated to No. 4/47 V.S. Section left THIANT at 14.30, & arrived at SAULTAIN at 17.15. Pte Cheese 6.8 reported for duty, from No. 2 O.C.H. Hospital.	
SAULTAIN	10		Section left SAULTAIN at 8.15, & arrived at ANGRE at 12.15.	

Army Form C. 2118.

WAR DIARY
or
INTELLIGENCE SUMMARY.
(Erase heading not required.)

53RD MOBILE VETERINARY SECTION.

Place	Date 1918	Hour	Summary of Events and Information	Remarks and references to Appendices
ANGRE	Nov. 11		Section left ANGRE at 8.45, & arrived at BLAUGIES at 12.30. 3 sick animals left with Mayor at ANGRE, with H.R. form 2.B.	
BLAUGIES	12		Section left BLAUGIES at 9.30 & arrived at HARVENET at 13.30.	
HARVENET	13		1 sick animal admitted.	
"	14		19 sick animals admitted, including one by float. D.A.D.V.S. visited Section.	
"	15		1 sick animal admitted by float.	
"	16		7 sick animals admitted, and 8 Bavarian horses which had been left without orders.	
"	17		19 sick animals admitted. Asked transport lorry of 63rd Divisional Train & 249th Field Cy. R.E.	
"	18		25 sick animals evacuated to XXII Corps V.E.S., including one by float. 6 men from 63rd Divisional Employment Coy. report for duty. 18 sick animals admitted. D.A.D.V.S. visited Section.	
"	19		11 sick animals admitted. ADVS XXII Corps, & DADVS visited Section. Evacuation party returned from V.E.S.	

Army Form C. 2118.

WAR DIARY
or
INTELLIGENCE SUMMARY.

(Erase heading not required.)

53RD MOBILE VETERINARY SECTION.

Place	Date	Hour	Summary of Events and Information	Remarks and references to Appendices
HARVENGT	1916			
"	20		62 sick animals admitted. 30 sick animals evacuated to XXII Corps V.E.S.	
"	21		1 sick animal admitted, by float. Visited transport lines J.63 M.E. Batt.	
"	22		1 sick animal admitted. 31 sick animals evacuated to XXII Corps V.E.S. vehicles one by float. Visited transport lines J.150 Field Ambulance & 63 Divisional Train	
"	23		22 sick animals admitted. D.A.D.V.S. visited Section.	
"	24		39 sick animals evacuated to XXII Corps V.E.S. 8 sick animals admitted. 2 horses lent to civilian farmer for use on land.	
"	25		20 sick animals admitted. 8 men sent for duty from 25th Regt R.F.A. to accompany sick down to V.E.S. 2 horses lent to civilian farmer.	
"			9 animals returned to units	
"	26		1 sick animal destroyed admitted.	
"	27		1 sick animal admitted.	
"	28		Section left HARVENGT at 8.30, arrived at ANGRE at 15.30; roads very congested with troops and transport. 3 sick animals handed over to 58 D.V. M.V.S. at HARVENGT.	

Army Form C. 2118.

WAR DIARY
or
INTELLIGENCE SUMMARY.

(Erase heading not required.)

53RD MOBILE VETERINARY SECTION.

Place	Date	Hour	Summary of Events and Information	Remarks and references to Appendices
ANGRE	1918			
	Nov 29		30 sick animals evacuated to XXII Corps V.E.S. with 2 N.C.Os & 8 men from R.F.A. to accompany them. D.A.D.V.S. visited Section.	
	30		36 sick animals admitted. 2 horses collected from civilians at TAISNIERES, on instructions from D.A.D.V. 63 (RV) Division	

Howard Capt AVC
O/c 53' Mobile Veterinary Section

CONFIDENTIAL   53rd MOBILE VETERINARY SECTION

                                                    December 31st 1918

                         WAR DIARY
                             of
                  53rd MOBILE VETERINARY SECTION
                            from
                        Dec. 1st 1918
                             to
                       Dec. 31st 1918

                          VOLUME 31

To -:   The A.G's Office
             3rd Echelon

                                              Capt. R.A.V.C.
                                      O.C. 53rd Mobile Veterinary Section

Army Form C. 2118.

WAR DIARY or INTELLIGENCE SUMMARY.

(Erase heading not required.)

53RD MOBILE VETERINARY SECTION.

Place	Date	Hour	Summary of Events and Information	Remarks and references to Appendices
ANGRE 1918 DEC.	1		42 sick animals evacuated to 22° V.E.S. 10 sick animals admitted, one by float	
"	2		visited waggon lines of 223° Brigade RFA	
"	3		2 sick animals admitted. Visited waggon lines of 223° Brigade RFA. D.A.D.V.S. visited Section. 3 sick animals admitted: No 1985 Pte Baker V.+ proceeded on 14 days leave to England.	
"	4		4 sick animals admitted: visited lines of 223° Brigade R.F.A. Ösika Batt Section/Check	
"	5		visited Batt Section at Conde, and 63 Labour Coy, & 75° Funnelling Coy, 3 sick animals admitted	
"	6		Conference of V.O.s at D.A.D.V.S. office: 5 found animals admitted. 2 sick animals admitted	
"	7		6 animals collected from inhabitants by authority of D.A.P.M. 63° (A.N) Division. 6 sick animals admitted. D.A.D.V.S. visited Section. visited lines of 223° Brigade RFA.	
"	8		30 sick animals evacuated to 22° V.E.S. 2 sick animals admitted.	
"	9		D.A.D.V.S. visited Section: visited lines of 223° Brigade RFA: 8 sick animals admitted.	

Army Form C. 2118.

53RD MOBILE VETERINARY SECTION.

WAR DIARY or INTELLIGENCE SUMMARY.

(Erase heading not required.)

Instructions regarding War Diaries and Intelligence Summaries are contained in F.S. Regs., Part II. and the Staff Manual respectively. Title pages will be prepared in manuscript.

Place	Date	Hour	Summary of Events and Information	Remarks and references to Appendices
ANGRE	1918 DEC 10		3 animals collected from civilians by authority of D.A.D.V.S. without sick horse; 16 sick animals admitted, one by float.	
	11		Visited 80", 136" Labour Coy. at Erucke & Quievrechain and 176" Tunnelling Coy. Veterinary attendance to 2 cows & horse belonging to civilians. 10 sick animals of 223 Brigade R.F.A. 8 sick animals admitted.	
	12		36 sick animals evacuated to 22" V.E.S. including one by float. 3 sick from admitted.	
	13		Conference of V.Os. at D.A.D.V.S. office.	
	14		1 animal collected from civilian, authority of D.A.D.V.S. Veterinary attendance given to civilians horse and cows; 10 sick animals of 223 Brigade R.F.A. Lecture and office routine.	
	15		Visited two of 223 Brigade R.F.A. 10 sick animals of 246 Field by R.E. with D.A.D.V.S. 8 sick animals admitted.	
	16		1 sick horse admitted by float. Lecture office routine.	
	17		Visited 80", 136" Labour Coy., 176" Tunnelling Coy. 13 sick animals evacuated to 22" V.E.S. including 1 float case. 8 sick animals admitted.	

Army Form C. 2118.

53RD MOBILE VETERINARY SECTION.

WAR DIARY
or
INTELLIGENCE SUMMARY.
(Erase heading not required.)

Place	Date	Hour	Summary of Events and Information	Remarks and references to Appendices
ANGRE	1918 Dec 18		Section & office routine; 2 sick animals admitted.	
"	19		Conference of V.Os at DADVS office; visited lines of 223 Brigade RFA. 3 sick animals admitted.	
"	20		7th ADVS 8th Corps, & DADVS. visited Section; 3 animals collected from inhabitants admitted; 3 sick animals admitted.	
"	21		Moved Section from present standings to factory on road to ANGREAU, where more suitable accommodation was available. Pte Baker returned from leave.	
"	22		Visited lines of 223 Brigade RFA.	
"	23		Attended parade of animals from 223 Brigade RFA, by DDVS 1st Army, for casting; 4 animals evacuated to 22 V.E.S. Visited lines of animals under charge of Agricultural Officer at Quievrechain; 17 sick animals admitted.	
"	24		21 sick animals evacuated to 22 V.E.S; 2 sick animals admitted.	
"	25		Section routine: visited lines of Depot Coy at Rosin, to attend to sick mule.	
"	26		Conference of V.Os at DADVS. office; visited lines of 223 Brigade RFA.	

Army Form C. 2118.

53RD MOBILE VETERINARY SECTION.

WAR DIARY or INTELLIGENCE SUMMARY.

(Erase heading not required.)

Instructions regarding War Diaries and Intelligence Summaries are contained in F. S. Regs., Part II. and the Staff Manual respectively. Title pages will be prepared in manuscript.

Place	Date	Hour	Summary of Events and Information	Remarks and references to Appendices
ANGRE	1918 DEC. 27		Section and office routine: found men billets for men of Section near present lines.	
	28		46 animals admitted for casting authority D.D.V.S. 1st Army	
	29		45 animals evacuated to 22 V.E.S. for casting rate. 18 sick animals admitted. Visited lines of 223 Brigade R.F.A. 2 sick animals admitted.	
	30		7 sick animals admitted. Office Section routine	
	31		Visited Section of 223 Brigade R.F.A. at ONNEZIES. 9 sick animals admitted. Assistance was given daily to Belgian civilians in the way of loan of horse harness and driver for farming & general carting work - also veterinary attendance to sick animals where asked for.	

R. Broad
Capt. R.A.V.C.
O.C. 53rd Mobile Veterinary Section.

CONFIDENTIAL   53rd Mobile Veterinary Sectin
-----------   ---------------------------

                                            January 31st 1919

                    WAR DIARY
                        of
            53rd MOBILE VETERINARY SECTION
                       from
                 January 1st 1919
                        to
                 January 31st 1919

                     VOLUME 32

To -:
        The A.G's office
                3rd Echelon

                                        (signed)
                                            Capt. R.A.V.C
                            O.C. 53rd MOB. VET. SECTION.

Army Form C. 2118.

53RD MOBILE VETERINARY SECTION.

WAR DIARY
or
INTELLIGENCE SUMMARY.

(Erase heading not required.)

Instructions regarding War Diaries and Intelligence Summaries are contained in F. S. Regs., Part II. and the Staff Manual respectively. Title pages will be prepared in manuscript.

Place	Date	Hour	Summary of Events and Information	Remarks and references to Appendices
ANGRE	Jan 1 1919		D.A.D.V.S. visited Section. 1 sick animal admitted. Attended veterinary board for classifying horses of Division	
"	2		Attended veterinary board.	
"	3		Attended veterinary board. 5 sick animals admitted. 70 animals evacuated to 22" V.E.S.	
"	4		Attended veterinary board. 3 sick animals admitted.	
"	5		Attended veterinary board. 3 sick animals admitted.	
"	6		Attended veterinary board. 6 sick animals admitted.	
"	7		Attended veterinary board. 2 sick animals admitted.	
"	8		Attended veterinary board. 8 sick animals admitted. D.A.D.V.S. visited Section.	
"	9		Attended veterinary board. 2 sick animals admitted.	
"	10		Attended veterinary board. 2 sick animals admitted. (1 by flea)	
"	11		Attended veterinary board. 3 sick animals admitted.	
"	12		Attended veterinary board. 6 found animals + 2 sick animals admitted. (1 by flea)	

Army Form C. 2118.

WAR DIARY
or
INTELLIGENCE SUMMARY.

(Erase heading not required.)

53RD MOBILE VETERINARY SECTION.

Instructions regarding War Diaries and Intelligence Summaries are contained in F. S. Regs., Part II. and the Staff Manual respectively. Title pages will be prepared in manuscript.

Place	Date	Hour	Summary of Events and Information	Remarks and references to Appendices
ANGRE	Jan. 13. 1919		Attended veterinary board.	
	14		Attended veterinary board. 7 sick animals admitted	
	15		Attended veterinary board. 1 sick animal admitted	
	16		No SE 5119 Sergt TAPLIN. J.W. R.A.V.C. reported for duty from No 2 Veterinary Hospital	
	17		Attended veterinary board. 3 animals admitted	
	18		Attended veterinary board. 3 animals admitted	
	19		Attended veterinary board. 3 animals admitted	
	20		29 sick animals evacuated to 22 V.E.S. Used nuts for wallen testing	
	21		SE 9153 Sergt HERBERT. T.B.W. despatched to No 2 Veterinary Hospital. Used nuts for wallen testing	
	22		Used nuts for wallen testing. 4 sick animals admitted	
	23		One Horse & 8 hides evacuated to R2 V.E.S. by flat. Used nuts. 4 animals admitted	
	24		D.A.D.V.S. A.side Section. Used nuts. 3 sick animals admitted	

Army Form C. 2118.

WAR DIARY
or
INTELLIGENCE SUMMARY

(Erase heading not required.)

53RD MOBILE VETERINARY SECTION.

Place	Date	Hour	Summary of Events and Information	Remarks and references to Appendices
ANGRE	Jan 25		14 sick animals evacuated to 22" V.E.S. 1 animal admitted; visited units.	
	26		Section routine. 2 sick animals admitted.	
	27		3 sick animals admitted.	
	28		Visited parade of Y class animals prior to despatch to concentration camps with D.A.D.V.S.	
	29		One private despatched to Horse Concentration Camp for duty. Visited units & inspected Y class animals. 4 sick animals admitted.	
	30		Conference of V.Os at D.A.D.V.S office. Visited units.	
	31		25 sick animals admitted; Section routine.	

T. R. Wood
Capt R.A.V.C.

O.C. 53rd Mobile Veterinary Section.

CONFIDENTIAL   53rd MOBILE VETERINARY SECTION

                                       February 28th 1919

WAR DIARY

of

53rd MOBILE VETERINARY SECTION

from

FEBRUARY 1st 1919

to

FEBRUARY 28th 1919

VOLUME 33

To -: The A.G's office
           3rd Echelon

                                       Capt. R.A.V.C.

                                       O/C 53rd Mobile Veterinary Section

Army Form C. 2118.

63RD
MOBILE VETERINARY
SECTION.

No..................
Date.................

WAR DIARY
or
INTELLIGENCE SUMMARY.

(Erase heading not required.)

A

Instructions regarding War Diaries and Intelligence Summaries are contained in F. S. Regs., Part II. and the Staff Manual respectively. Title pages will be prepared in manuscript.

Place	Date	Hour	Summary of Events and Information	Remarks and references to Appendices
ANGRE	1919			
Feb	1		Visited waggon lines of A.B. C/223 Brigade RFA. Visited DADVS office. 29 sick animals evacuated to 22' V.F.S.	
"	2		Visited D/223 Brigade RFA. 4 n more evacuated to 18' V.F.S. 7 sick animals admitted.	
"	3		Visited lines of 201 Coy Divisional Train, and to 2 Section 10 Army Auxiliary Horse Coy.	
"	4		Visited waggon lines of A 18/223 Brigade RFA. 4 sick animals admitted.	
"	5		DADVS visited Section. Visited Nos 1,3 + 4 Coys Divisional Train, 9 1/223 Bgde RFA. 2 sick animals admitted. 1 sick horse died (skinned & buried).	
"	6		Conference of V.Os. at DADVS office. 3 sick animals admitted. Inspection of demobilization of Qr Wheeler W. RAVC as from Jan. 21" received visited Details at Quevrain re sale of D Group horses.	

Army Form C. 2118.

53RD MOBILE VETERINARY SECTION.
No..........
Date..........

WAR DIARY or INTELLIGENCE SUMMARY.
(Erase heading not required.)

Instructions regarding War Diaries and Intelligence Summaries are contained in F.S. Regs., Part II. and the Staff Manual respectively. Title pages will be prepared in manuscript.

B

Place	Date	Hour	Summary of Events and Information	Remarks and references to Appendices
ANGRE	1919			
Feb	7		Pte Clausbury returned from 14 days leave to U.K. 2 horses sold to bitcher al Quievrain. Visited No 1 Coy Divisional Train and inspected 21 horses prior to transfer	
"	8		15 sick animals evacuated to 22° V.E.S.	
"	9		Visited B battery, 223 Brigade RFA wagon lines	
"	10		Visited wagon lines of A & C batteries 223 Brigade RFA. 1 D horse sold to bitcher at Norin.	
"	11		S.2503 Qr. Hetcher RM reports for duty from 3rd Coy Divisional Train. 3 D animals sold to bitcher at Hame. 2 D animals sold to bitcher at Quievrain. Visited lines of Nos 3 & 4 Coy Divisional Train Personnel Board visited Section to classify horses. 20 sick animals admitted	
"	12		Visited lines of No 1 Coy Divisional Train, 9 LB 2 Ocken 10° Army Auxiliary Horse Co. Qr Steadman & A.S.C. despatches to Divisional Train for demobilization. 12 sick animals evacuated to 22° V.E.S. 5 sick animals admitted	

Army Form C. 2118.

53RD
MOBILE VETERINARY SECTION.

No ....
Date ....

WAR DIARY
or
INTELLIGENCE SUMMARY.
(Erase heading not required.)

Instructions regarding War Diaries and Intelligence Summaries are contained in F. S. Regs., Part II. and the Staff Manual respectively. Title pages will be prepared in manuscript.

Place	Date	Hour	Summary of Events and Information	Remarks and references to Appendices
ANGRE	1919			
	13		Conference of VOs at DADVS office. Office routine.	
	14		Visited waggon lines of Y223 Brigade RFA. 5 sick animals admitted.	
	15		Visited waggon lines of A,B/223 Brigade RFA. 16 sick animals evacuated to 22° V.E.S. 2 animals collected from sickness sent in by DAPH	
	16		Visited waggon lines of C,D/223 Brigade RFA. 2 animals admitted. Pte Jordan A.E. returned from 14 days leave to UK	
	17		Tested all remaining animals of 223 Brigade RFA with mallein, also animals of 89°, 7/8 Lettern Coy., at Quievrain. 1 sick animal admitted. Inspected all animals mallened yesterday. 2 D horses sent to belote at Quievrain. 9 sick animals admitted.	
	18		Office + Section routine. 2 sick animals admitted. Visited waggon lines of D/223 Bgd 274	
	19		Conference of VOs at DADVS office. 9 sick animals admitted.	
	20		One horse collected from Elouges & Hon. Mallened remaining horses of 2, 3 + 4 Coys.	
	21		Severe at rain at Quievrain. 3 sick animals admitted.	

Army Form C. 2118.

53RD
MOBILE VETERINARY
SECTION.

No............
Date............

WAR DIARY
or
INTELLIGENCE SUMMARY.
(Erase heading not required.)

Instructions regarding War Diaries and Intelligence Summaries are contained in F. S. Regs., Part II. and the Staff Manual respectively. Title pages will be prepared in manuscript.

Place	Date	Hour	Summary of Events and Information	Remarks and references to Appendices
ANGRE	1919 Feb 22		Inspected all horse in allotment yesterday. Asked lines 9 & 2 Col 10 "Army Reinforcement Non Coy" 14 sick animals evacuated to 22 V.E.S.	
	23		2 animals collected from Personnel Staging Camp at of Earle 1 sick animal admitted. Asked 13.C/223 Brigade RFA	
	24		To DADVS. office to D animals sent to batches. 1 sink evacuated to 22 V.E.S. by road. 4 sick animals admitted.	
	25		2 mules sent to batches at Quiévrain. Inspected Y Group horse at Authregnies for to despatch to Base Remount Depot. 4 Mares (Y Group) sent from Section. 2 sick animals admitted.	
	26		To DADVS. office. 1 sick horse evacuated to 22 V.E.S. by Road. 1 sick animal admitted.	
	27		Dr Jackson W. returned from 10 days leave to UK. 2 sick animals admitted.	
	28		Asked Remount railhead to inspect 2 Group animals prior to entrainment to Cherbourg Hospital at Rouen. To DADVS. office. 8 sick animals admitted.	

Brood
Capt. RAV
O/C 53rd Mobile Veterinary Section.

Confidential   53rd Mobile Veterinary Setion

                                                 March 31st 1919

WAR DIARY

of

53rd MOBILE VETERINARY SECTION

from

MARCH 1st 1919

to

MARCH 31st 1919

VOLUME 34

To -: The A.G's Office
        3rd Echelon

                                          [signature]
                                                Capt. R.A.V.C

                                          O.C.
                                          53rd Mobile veterinary Section

Army Form C. 2118.

53RD
MOBILE VETERINARY
SECTION.

WAR DIARY
or
INTELLIGENCE SUMMARY.
(Erase heading not required.)

A

Instructions regarding War Diaries and Intelligence Summaries are contained in F. S. Regs., Part II. and the Staff Manual respectively. Title pages will be prepared in manuscript.

Place	Date 1919	Hour	Summary of Events and Information	Remarks and references to Appendices
ANGRE	Mch 1		Inspected 100 horses at Audregnies, prior to despatch to Rouen Remount Depot. Visited lines of A/223 Bde RFA. 17 sick animals evacuated to 22. V.E.S.	
"	2		To DADVS office re sale of horses.	
"	3		Held sale of 93 Z horses and mules by Public Auction at DOUR. 3 sick animals admitted.	
"	4		Visited lines of B/223 Bde RFA. 6 sick animals admitted.	
"	5		Inspected Group of horses at Augre, prior to despatch to Rouen Remount Depot. DADVS ordered section not further of demobilization of SE 1985D. Q. SPENCER E. to join 7/2/19 returns from Base Records office. 27 sick animals admitted.	
"	6		Visited butcher at Quievrain, re sale of 3 animals for butchery. 29 sick animals evacuated to 22 V.E.S. 4 sick animals admitted. Conference of VOs at DADVS office.	
"	7		To DADVS office. 7 sick animals admitted.	
"	8		9 sick animals evacuated to 22. V.E.S. 7 sick animals admitted.	
"	9		Visited lines of Devotional Men. 715 Salon Cy. at Quievrain. 2 sick animals admitted.	
"	10		Held sale of 93 Z horses and mules by Public Auction at DOUR.	
"	11		Inspected 400 horses & mules at Augre, prior to despatch to Rouen Remount Depot. 30 sick animals admitted.	
"	12		11 sick animals evacuated to 22 V.E.S. 2 sick animals admitted. To butcher at Quievrain re sale of animals for butchery. To No 1 Cy 63 Div. Train. Visit to St Ghislain to get billets for section.	
"	13		To butcher at Quievrain. To DADVS office.	
"	14		Inspected 23 R.P. horses at Quievrain, prior to despatch R.P. Base, and group of Z animals in Neuron at Quievrain. SE 6317 Q. CHEESE CT. despatched to 18 V.E.S. for duty. 3 sick animals admitted.	
"	15		Moved Section from Angre to St Ghislain.	

Army Form C. 2118.

53RD MOBILE VETERINARY SECTION.

WAR DIARY or INTELLIGENCE SUMMARY.

(Erase heading not required.)

Instructions regarding War Diaries and Intelligence Summaries are contained in F.S. Regs., Part II. and the Staff Manual respectively. Title pages will be prepared in manuscript.

Place	Date 1919	Hour	Summary of Events and Information	Remarks and references to Appendices
ST. GHISLAIN	Mch 16		Visited 317 Bde RFA at Tasmuel. 23 sick animals admitted. DADVS visited Section	
	17		28 sick animals evacuated to 22 V.E.S. 6 sick animals admitted.	
	18		To Mons to inspect civilian's stable. return by Army lorry. 3 X Rates of Section transferred to 7th Army Bde RFA	
	19		31 sick animals admitted	
	20		To 68 DAC. R23 Bgn, 317 Bde RFA 9 sick animals admitted	
	21		38 sick animals evacuated to 22 V.F.S. 5 sick animals admitted. Conference of VOs at DADVs Office	
	22		2 sick animals admitted	
	23		2 sick animals admitted	
	24		Visited 10 Army Auxiliary Horse Co. at Quievrain	
	25		Suspects & mules at Mons prior to despatch to 22 V.E.S. 5 sick animals admitted	
			To V.E.S. 22 at Mons. ADVS 22 Corps to try to obtain Oats Carts; none available. T2/116970 Dr STOCKING A. despatched to 63 Div. Train for demobilization. 4 sick animals admitted.	
	26		Held Pde of 1445 Z animals by Public Auctn at ST GHISLAIN. 4 sick animals admitted.	
	27		4 Z Rates of Section despatched to 22 V.E.S. Suspected Gurf of 2 horses prior to despatch to 22 V.E.S. 1 sick animal admitted. Conference of VOs at DADVs Office	
	28		8 sick animals evacuated to 22 V.E.S. To Boot to at Quievrain re sale of Horses for Civilies. 1 sick animal admitted	
	29		To Personal Shoeing Comp at St Saulve. 1 sick animal admitted	
	30		—	
	31		DADVS proceeded on short leave to Paris. Sgt am charge of DADVs duties. following men dispatched to Convalescent Camps at Valenciennes for demobilization:- SE 1202 Pte HARVEY S. SE 11026 Pte DAVIES S. and SE 9055 S/Sgt TAYLOR.	

J. B. Broad. Capt RAVC
O/c 53 MOBILE VETERINARY SECTION

Duplicate

Volume No. _____

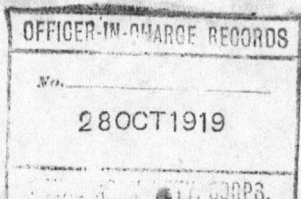
OFFICER-IN-CHARGE RECORDS
No. _____
28 OCT 1919

EGYPTIAN EXPEDITIONARY FORCE.

WAR DIARY

Unit 53rd mobile veterinary section

From 1-4-19   To 30-4-19

53 M.V.S.

Army Form C. 2118.

WAR DIARY
or
INTELLIGENCE SUMMARY.

(Erase heading not required.)

Army Form C. 2118.

April 1919.

No. _____

28 OCT 1919

ROYAL ARMY VETY. CORPS.

Place	Date	Hour	Summary of Events and Information	Remarks and references to Appendices
Shafts	April 1.		Admitted 2 sick animals from 247 Coy. R.A.S.C. M.T.S.	
Alexandria	2.		Evacuated do to 26 Vety: Hosp: Mec. M.T.S.	
	3.		No entry. M.T.S.	
			do. M.T.S.	
	4.		Admitted 5 sick animals 1 from 91 M.P. 53rd Divn. 1 + 39 Bty 26y Bde R.F.A. 1 from A/266 Bde R.F.A. + 1 from A/966 Bde R.F.A. T/02136 Pte Senior J. SE/11160 Pte Youlook E. H.O.Ro. posted to Base Depot. Kantara. T/02136 Pte Senior J. SE/26627 Pte Paveon W. M.T.S. SE/23227 Pte Gano C.T. + SE/26627 Pte Paveon W. M.T.S.	
	5.		Evacuated 5 sick animals to 26 Vety Hosp: Mec. M.T.S.	
	6.		No entry. M.T.S.	
	7.		Admitted 2 sick animals 1 from 265 Bde R.F.A. + 1 from 266 Bde R.F.A. M.T.S.	
	8.		No entry M.T.S.	
	9.		do. M.T.S.	
	10.		Admitted 4 sick animals 1 from C/303 Bde R.F.A. 1 from B/266 Bde R.F.A. 1 from B/266 Bde 1 from 4/ Res Fl from 53rd D.A.C. M.T.S	

Army Form C. 2118.

WAR DIARY
or
INTELLIGENCE SUMMARY.
(Erase heading not required.)

Instructions regarding War Diaries and Intelligence Summaries are contained in F. S. Regs., Part II, and the Staff Manual respectively. Title pages will be prepared in manuscript.

Place	Date	Hour	Summary of Events and Information	Remarks and references to Appendices
Chatby	April 11.		No entry. WKJ.	
	12.		Admitted 2 sick animals from C/267 Bde R.F.A. WKJ.	
	13.		No entry. WKJ.	
	14.		Admitted 3 sick animals 2 from 265 Bde R.F.A. 1 from 60th Div R.F.A. Details S.E./1868. Pte Crompton A.T. Admitted to Hospital WKJ.	
	15.		No entry WKJ.	
	16.		do WKJ.	
	17.		do. WKJ.	
	18.		Admitted 3 sick animals 1 from 249 Coy. R.C.A. 86. 2 from 519 Coy. R.C.A.S.B. Evacuated 13. sick animals to 26 Vety. Hosp. Mecc. WKJ.	
	19.		Admitted 7 sick animals 3 from 53rd D.A.C. 1 from 516 R.W.T. 1 from C/265 Bde. R.F.A. 2 from 4th Aust. Light Horse Bde. WKJ.	
	20.		Admitted 3 sick animals from 265 Bde R.F.A. Evacuated 7. do to 26 Vety. Hosp. Mecc. WKJ.	

A 5834 Wt. W4973/M687 750,000 8/16 D. D. & L. Ltd. Forms/C.2118/13.

Army Form C. 2118.

WAR DIARY
or
INTELLIGENCE SUMMARY.
(Erase heading not required.)

Instructions regarding War Diaries and Intelligence Summaries are contained in F. S. Regs., Part II. and the Staff Manual respectively. Title pages will be prepared in manuscript.

Place	Date April	Hour	Summary of Events and Information	Remarks and references to Appendices
Chatby.	21.		Admitted 2 Sick Animals from 267 Bde R.F.A. NWS.	
Alexandria	22.		Admitted 6 do. 1 from F.A. Anzac Mounted Divn. 4 from 2nd Lig. Horse Anzac Mounted Divn. 4 from 5th L.H. Anzac Divn. NWS.	
	23.		Evacuated 10 Sick Animals to 26 Vety. Hospital Mex. NWS.	
	24.		No entry. NWS.	
	25.		Admitted 4 Sick Animals 2 17th Ind. Inf. 1 from 2nd Cavl. L.H.F.A. 1. from 2nd Anzac M.L. Squad. NWS.	
	26.		Admitted one Sick Animal from H.C. Coy R.A.S.C. Evacuated 5 to 6 26 Vety Hospl Mex NWS.	
	27.		No entry. NWS.	
	28.		Admitted 3 Sick Animals 2 from A/267. Bde R.F.A. 1 from 1st Coy. Cop. N.W.S.	
	29.		No entry. NWS.	1-5-19
	30.		Evacuated 3 Sick Animals to 26 Vety. Hosp. Mex. NWS.	

W.A. Wacy Capt. R.A.V.C.
O.C. 53rd Mobile Vety. Section

63RD DIVISION

63RD (RN) DIVL TRAIN
MAY 1916 - APR 1919

761 to 764 Companies ASC

RN Div Train/vol 1

Confidential

War Diary

of

Royal Naval Divisional Train.

May 1916.

Army Form C. 2118.

WAR DIARY
or
INTELLIGENCE SUMMARY. Royal Naval Divisional Train

(Erase heading not required.)

Instructions regarding War Diaries and Intelligence Summaries are contained in F. S. Regs., Part II. and the Staff Manual respectively. Title pages will be prepared in manuscript.

Place	Date	Hour	Summary of Events and Information	Remarks and references to Appendices
Abbeville	18/5/16		Lt. G.J. Shallcross R.S.C. reported his arrival from 1st B.H.T.D. to take up the duties of Adjutant to the Divisional Train.	
"	22/5/16		Lt. Col. A.R. Liddell arrived from 55th Divisional A.S.C. Train to assume command of the Divisional Train.	
"	23/5/16		No. 3 Coy commanded by Capt. C.S. Chapman arrived at Abbeville from Muroilles.	
"	24/5/16		No. 3 Coy refitted at A.H.T.D. and marched to their billets at POUHTIERS.	
"	"		No. 2 Coy commanded by Capt. J. Strong arrived from Muroilles.	
"	25/5/16		No. 2 Coy refitted at A.H.T.D. and marched to their billets at WIRY-AU-MONT.	
"	"		No. 4 Coy commanded by Capt. A.E. Balfour and Hq. Coy commanded by Capt. O. Sholin arrived from Muroilles.	
"	26/5/16		No. 4 Coy refitted at A.H.T.D. and proceeded to their billets at BETTINCOURT.	
"	29/5/16		Baggage Section of Hq. Coy fitted out and marched to HALLENCOURT.	
"	29/5/16		Supply Section of H.Q. Coy fitted out and marched to HALLENCOURT. Train H.Qs. established at the same village.	
Hallencourt.	30/5/16		Capt. C.S. Murray took over command of No. 2 Coy and Capt. F.H. Tivey of No. 4 Coy.	

A. R. Liddell Lieut. Colonel
Cmdg. R.N. Divisional Train

RN Div Train Vol 2

Confidential

War Diary

of

R. N Divisional Train.

From 1st June, 1916.   To. 30th June. 1916.

Army Form C. 2118.

WAR DIARY
or
INTELLIGENCE SUMMARY.
(Erase heading not required.)

Instructions regarding War Diaries and Intelligence Summaries are contained in F. S. Regs., Part II. and the Staff Manual respectively. Title pages will be prepared in manuscript.

Place	Date	Hour	Summary of Events and Information	Remarks and references to Appendices
Hallencourt	1/6/16		Divisional Train commenced Advance Move from Abbeville.	
"	2/6/16		2nd Field Ambulance completed up to Establishment.	
"	3/6/16		1st Line Transport of 3 Brigade H.Q. and of D.H.Q. completed up to Establishment.	
"	5/6/16		1st Field Ambulance completed up to Establishment with the exception of 1 M.O. (Class 1).	
"	6/6/16		3rd Field Ambulance completed up to Establishment with the exception of 1 M.O. (Class 1), Capt S Sorry.	
"	7/6/16		No. 4 Coy prepared to move off to the 1st Army Area. Lt A.R. Ridington + 2 S/Lt Purcell joined yes.	
"	8/6/16		No. 4 Coy entrained at Abbeville for 1st Army Area.	
"	9/6/16		No. 3 Coy prepared to move off to the 1st Army Area.	
"	10/6/16		No. 3 Coy entrained at Abbeville for 1st Army Area.	
"	11/6/16		Hqrs + Hqrs Coy Trains left Hallencourt and bivouaced at the Forage Abbeville.	
Abbeville	12/6/16		Hqrs + Hqrs Coy Train left Abbeville by 3 Trains for 1st Army Area. The C.O., S.S.O., and Adjutant proceeding by Motor. 1st Train Hqrs and part of Hqrs Coy arrived at HOUVELIN 8-30 p.m.	
Houvelin	13/6/16		Remainder of Hqrs Coy arrived HOUVELIN 6-30 a.m. Train Hqrs, Hqrs Coy, No. 3 and 4 Coys are now billeted at HOUVELIN. No. 2 Coy remaining at WIRY-AU-MONT. Major F. Holmes R.M. proceed on leave. Capt E.C. Shewsman A.S.C.	

WAR DIARY or INTELLIGENCE SUMMARY

Army Form C. 2118.

(Erase heading not required.)

Instructions regarding War Diaries and Intelligence Summaries are contained in F.S. Regs, Part II. and the Staff Manual respectively. Title pages will be prepared in manuscript.

Place	Date	Hour	Summary of Events and Information	Remarks and references to Appendices
Houvelin	13/6/16		T/Capt. C.G. Murray R.M. appointed S.S.O. vice Major F. Holmes R.M.	
"	15/6/16		No. 4 Coy moved to billets in BRUAY	T/Capt. C.G. Murray proceeded on leave.
"	16/6/16		No. 4 Coy moved into billets at MAGNICOURT from BRUAY while Train Hqrs. H.Q. Coy and No. 3 Coy moved into billets at MAGNICOURT from HOUVELIN.	
Magnicourt.	18/6/16		The Divisional Train commenced administering to the Division. Refilling point being situated on the HOUVELIN - LA COMTE ROAD (Ref: Sheet 36 B O 23 d - 24 a.c.)	
"	19/6/16		No. 2 Company arrived at MAGNICOURT from HALLENCOURT. The whole Divisional Train is now billeted in MAGNICOURT. T/Capt. J. Corry arrived from leave.	
"	20/6/16		T/Capt. J. Corry R.M. proceeded to 1st Base H.T. Depot as being supernumerary to establishment.	
"	20/6/16		T/Lieut. R V Muller R.M. was placed on the sick list.	
"	21/6/16		T/Lieut. R V Muller R.M. was sent to the 2nd Field Ambulance for treatment.	T/Capt. C.G. Murray R.M. returned from leave.
"	25/6/16		T/Lt R.V. Muller R.M. returned from hospital.	
"	24/6/16		T/Lt W.R. Livingston (attached No 4 Coy) posted to No 4 Coy from 19/6/16 inclusive.	
"			T/Lt E.T. Wilkins proceeded to England on leave.	
"	29/6/16		T/Major F. Holmes R.M. returned from leave and posted to Hqrs. Coy.	

Army Form C. 2118.

WAR DIARY
or
INTELLIGENCE SUMMARY.
(Erase heading not required.)

Place	Date	Hour	Summary of Events and Information	Remarks and references to Appendices
Happencourt	24/6/16		T/Lt. R.V. Austin attached to 1st Hood Bn. (1st Line Transport)	
"	30/6/16		T/Major F Holmes R.M. took over command of H.Q. Coy from T/Capt. C.O.F. Martin D.S.C., R.M.	

A Riddell
Lt. Col. A.S.C.
Commdg R.N. Divisional Train.

30/6/16

63/ July

63 Div Train Vol 3

Confidential

War Diary

of

63rd (R.N) Divisional Train.

From 1st July 1916 to 31st July 1916.

Volume 2

John Mulholland
Lt & Adjt
for
Lt Col Comdg
31/7/16   63rd Divl Train

Army Form C. 2118.

WAR DIARY
or
INTELLIGENCE SUMMARY.
(Erase heading not required.)

Instructions regarding War Diaries and Intelligence Summaries are contained in F.S. Regs., Part II. and the Staff Manual respectively. Title pages will be prepared in manuscript.

Place	Date	Hour	Summary of Events and Information	Remarks and references to Appendices
Magnicourt	1-7-16		A draft of 93 Other Ranks arrived from RND Base Depot. Lieut. J. Marrow RM appointed O.C. Salvage Coy.	
"	3-7-16		Lieut. E.T. Williams returned off Leave from England	
"	7-7-16		Lieut. A.L. Rogers R.M. reported his arrival from the Hood Batt. and is posted to No. 2 Company	
"	8-7-16		Capt. L.M. Murdoch R.M. proceeded on Leave to England	
"	9-7-16		4 Bgds of Artillery arrived. In consequence of this Refilling point had to be extended	
"	10-7-16		3rd Bgde Dumps being changed to O.18.c.7.2	
"	11-7-16		2nd Horse & 1st Divn. Transport was attached to No.2 Coy, pending its departure to the Base. 2nd Hood & 1st S.L. Transport together with the Train transport allotted to 3rd Bgde H.Q.'s and to the 2nd Hood Bn. left under Sub. Lt. Morkey for the A.H.T.D. ABBEVILLE. Baggage & Supply Section of No.2 Coy proceeded to bivouac at BARLIN.	
"	13/7/16		S.S.M. W.H. Fuller A.S.C. reported his arrival from 8th Divn. Train and was posted to No.3 Coy.	
"	14/7/16		G.O. Train inspected 3rd Field Ambulance.	
"	16-7-16		H.Q.s of No.2 Coy and the whole of No. 3 Coy moved to Bivouac at BARLIN.	
"	16.7.16		Capt. L.M. Murdoch RM returned off leave from England	
"	17.7.16		Train Hqs moved to billets in BARLIN. No.2 Coy moved to Annonues & BARLIN. Refilling point for the 3 Bgdes changed to K.26.a.7.5. (Sheet 36 B)	

WAR DIARY
or
INTELLIGENCE SUMMARY.
(Erase heading not required.)

Army Form C. 2118.

Place	Date	Hour	Summary of Events and Information	Remarks and references to Appendices
BARLIN	18.7.16		HQ Coy detachment moved to bivouacs at BARLIN.	
"	19.7.16		HQ Coy two detachment moved to bivouacs at CAMBLAIN CHATELAIN.	
BARLIN.	20.7.16		T/Capt A.E. Balfour RM assumed Command of No. 2 Coy vice T/Capt C.G. Murray RM. T/Lt O.H. Sayer transferred from Headquarters who is placed on the sick list.	
			No. 4 Coy to No. 2 Coy. HQs of HQ Coy moved to bivouacs at BARLIN leaving detachment at CAMBLAIN CHATELAIN. Refilling Point for 315th and 316th Bgdes RFA at T10.d 3.5 (Sheet 36 B). Lieut Ellis and Sub Lieut Carnell and Baird attached to Field Ambulances for instruction from Infantry Battalions.	
"	22.7.16		T/Capt C.G. Murray admitted to Field Ambulance. O.C. Train inspected 2nd F. Amb.	
"	25.7.16		Detachment of HQ Coy under Lt. Burrell RM moved to bivouacs at BARLIN. Refilling point for the whole Division now at K.26.a. 2.10 (Sheet 36 B)	
※	26.7.16		C.O. Train inspected 1st Field Ambulance. Lieut Ellis and Sub Lt Carnell and Baird rejoined their respective Battalions.	
"	27.7.16		D.D.S.+ T. 1st Army inspected Divisional Train.	
"	30.7.16		T/Major F. Holmes placed on sick list. DDR and DDVS 1st Army inspected Divisional Train.	
※	29.7.16		T/Lt W.M. Primrose RM wounded, but remained on duty.	

A.R.Russell
Lt. Col. ASC
Comg 63rd (RN) Divl. Train
31/7/16

63/Train Vol 4

CONFIDENTIAL.

WAR DIARY
of
63rd (R.N) DIVISIONAL TRAIN.

VOLUME 3.

From 1st August, 1916. to 31st August, 1916.

A R Liddell
Lieut. Col. A.S.C.
Commdg. 63rd (R.N) Divnl Train.

Army Form C. 2118.

WAR DIARY
or
INTELLIGENCE SUMMARY.
(Erase heading not required.)

Instructions regarding War Diaries and Intelligence Summaries are contained in F. S. Regs., Part II. and the Staff Manual respectively. Title pages will be prepared in manuscript.

Place	Date	Hour	Summary of Events and Information	Remarks and references to Appendices
BARLIN	1/5/16	—	T/Lt R.V. Mullen, R.M., returned to duty from Hood Batt. and is posted to No 2 Company.	
"	"	—	C.O. train inspected 1st line transport of 7th Batt. Royal Fusiliers.	
"	2/5/16	—	190th Cycle group refilled direct from Barlin Railway Station.	
"	"	"	From the trucks on to the train wagons.	
"	"	"	T/Lieut R.V. Mullen transferred to No 3 Company.	
"	5/5/16	—	Provisional troops group refilled direct from Railway Station Barlin.	
"	"	—	J.M. Gill Greggainis arrives from Auxiliary.	
"	7/14/89	4.55 P.M.	H.T. Coy 1st Army Corps is posted to No 2 Coy.	
"	"	—	C.O. train inspected 4th Brigade 1st Line Transport.	
"	6/5/16	—	T/Major J. Hinds R.M. is struck off the riot list.	
"	"	—	C.O. train interviewed M. Le Commandant 89th Batt. 1st Reg. d'Art. Apied	
"	"	"	with regard to their rations.	
"	7/5/16	1	T/Lieut A.L. Sugar, R.M., from being attached to No 2 Coy is posted to No 2 Company.	
"	8/5/16	"	189th Cycle group refilled direct from Railway Station Barlin.	

Army Form C. 2118.

WAR DIARY
or
INTELLIGENCE SUMMARY.
(Erase heading not required.)

Instructions regarding War Diaries and Intelligence Summaries are contained in F. S. Regs., Part II. and the Staff Manual respectively. Title pages will be prepared in manuscript.

Place	Date	Hour	Summary of Events and Information	Remarks and references to Appendices
BARLIN	9/8/16	—	T/Capt. A.E. Balfour proceeded on 3 days leave to Paris	
"	"	—	C.O. Train inspected 1st Line Transport of Horse Batt. & Brake Batt.	
"	"	—	T/Lieut Mulligan transferred from 3 Coy to 4 Coy	
"	"	—	T/Capt. H.V. Scott-Willcox RM transferred from 3 Coy to H Coy	
"	10/8/16	—	T/Lieut E.T. Perkins placed on Sick List.	
"	11/8/16	—	C.O. Train inspected 1st Line Transport of 2nd R.M. Battalion. T/Capt. A.E. Balfour returned from Paris.	
"	13/8/16	—	Notification received that T/Capt. C.E. Murray RM struck off the strength from 30.7.16 T/Lieut E.T. Mellerson RM struck off Sick List.	
"	14/8/16	—	C.O. Train inspected 1st Line Transport of Hawke Battalion.	
"	15.9.16	—	T/Lieut F.G. McPherson RM reports for duty from 1st Base H.T. Depot and is posted to HQ. Company.	
"	15.8.16	—	Sentence on No 1941 Gunner W. Goodwin "B" Batty 315th Byde RFA attached HQS Company promulgated.	
"	16.8.16	—	T/Lieut H.E. Cook RM reported for duty from 1st BHTD	
"	19.8.16	—	T/Capt H.V. Scott Willcox sent to 188th B.Byde depot to be attached to a French Mortar Batty for course.	
"	20.8.16	—	G.O.C. Train inspected 1st Line transport of 1st R.M. Batln and Heavy Batty T/Lieut V. King RM placed on Sick List.	

T2134. Wt. W708—776. 500000. 4/15. Sir J. C. & S.

Army Form C. 2118.

WAR DIARY
or
INTELLIGENCE SUMMARY.
(Erase heading not required.)

Instructions regarding War Diaries and Intelligence Summaries are contained in F.S. Regs., Part II. and the Staff Manual respectively. Title pages will be prepared in manuscript.

Place	Date	Hour	Summary of Events and Information	Remarks and references to Appendices
BARLIN	22/8/16		S/4/075258 Sergt J.G Campbell, A.S.C. reported from No. 6. Field Supply Depot for a fortnights test as to his qualifications for horse transport work.	
"	"		Lieut. W.E Cook, R.M., No. 3 Coy. transferred to No 2 Coy.	
"	"		Lieut J. King, R.M. is struck off the sick list.	
"	23/8/16		C.O. Train inspected 1st Line transport Howe Batt.	
"	"		C.O. Train inspected 1st Line transport Anson Batt.	
"	24/8/16		2253 Private R.M. Knight, H.A.C. Batt. examined by the C.O Train as to his suitability for commission in the A.S.C.	
"	25/8/16		C.O. Train inspected 1st line transport 10th Royal Dublin Fusiliers	
"	26/8/16		Lt. Cook R.M. was sent in charge of 5 G.S. wagons to proceed to Aux Rouleaux (mafsy. Sheet 36B R22 S) The convoy arrived there about B.20 pm and the drivers prepared to feed the horses, while the drivers were so occupied the convoy was shelled and the horses took fright. 3 Wagons were damaged 1 of which was put out of action. 2 Horses were injured apparently by shells. Elliott was able to proceed with 4 wagons and brought back the empty Gen Service from "Rouleaux house" Lieut J.A Middleton placed on Sick List.	
	28.8.16			

Army Form C. 2118.

WAR DIARY
or
INTELLIGENCE SUMMARY.
(Erase heading not required.)

Instructions regarding War Diaries and Intelligence Summaries are contained in F. S. Regs., Part II. and the Staff Manual respectively. Title pages will be prepared in manuscript.

Place	Date	Hour	Summary of Events and Information	Remarks and references to Appendices
BARLIN.	29.8.16		Private P. Doherty. RM. Private A. McFfeiden RM and Private 63 Rhodes RM tried by F.G.C.M.	
	30.8.16		Sentences Promulgated. No 3 Coy. 34th Divisional are attached to 63rd Div. Train.	
	31.8.16		111th RFA 34th Division were fed from Ruitland	

A. R. Russell
Lieut Col. ASC.
Commdg 63rd (RN) Divnl Train

CONFIDENTIAL

WAR   DIARY

of

63rd (R.N) DIVISIONAL TRAIN

From 1st September, 1916   To   30th September, 1916.

(VOLUME 4)

A R Liddell
Lieut. Col. A.S.C.
Commdg, 63rd (R.N) Divnl. Train.

Army Form C. 2118.

WAR DIARY
or
INTELLIGENCE SUMMARY.
(Erase heading not required.)

63rd (RN) Divisional Train

Place	Date	Hour	Summary of Events and Information	Remarks and references to Appendices
BARLIN.	19.9.16		Train Headquarters moved to billets at BRUAY. Headquarters Company, Divisional Train moved to billets at DIVION. No 2 Company, Divisional Train moved to billets at Fmé de Labriche. No 3 Company, Divisional Troops changed to OURTON - DIEVAL Road (I. 34. c. 6.8. Sheet 36B) Refilling Point for Divisional Troops changed to OURTON - DIEVAL Road (I. 34. a. 6.3. Sheet 36.B) Refilling Point for 188th Bgde Group changed to HERMIN. T/Serj. W.R.E. Unthank returned off leave. Refilling Point for 189 Bgde Group changed to	
"	20.9.16		T/Capt. C.L Chapman RM granted leave to England.	
BRUAY.	21.9.16		Train HQ's moved to billets at OURTON. No 4 Company moved to billets at LA THIEULOYE. No 2 Company moved to billets at OURTON. 190th Bde Refilling Point changed to La Thieuloye - Monchy Breton Road (Map Ref: O.25.c Sheet 36B)	
OURTON.	24.9.16		T/Lieut L reported for duty from 19 Base H.T. Depot and is posted to No 2 Coy. 6th Potter RN	
"	"		T/Lieut M.J Balfour-Murphy RM transferred to No 3 Coy.	
"	29.9.16		All baggage wagons & baggage section horses (with exception of those allotted to D.A.C.) were sent out to train refresher units. In view of the Divnl Pont. March on 30/9/16	
"	30.9.16		T/Lieut. R.V. Muller RM. proceeded to A.S.C. Base Depot Havre	

A.P.
Lt. Col. a.S.C.
Commdg 63rd (RN) Divnl Train

Army Form C. 2118.

63rd (R.N.) Divisional Train

WAR DIARY
or
INTELLIGENCE SUMMARY.
(Erase heading not required.)

Instructions regarding War Diaries and Intelligence Summaries are contained in F.S. Regs., Part II. and the Staff Manual respectively. Title pages will be prepared in manuscript.

Place	Date	Hour	Summary of Events and Information	Remarks and references to Appendices
BARLIN	4/9/16	-	T/Lieut L.A. Middleton is struck off the sick list	
"	"	-	C.O. Train inspected 1st Line Transport H.A.C. Batt.	
"	5/9/16	-	C.O. Train inspected 1st Line Transport 14th Worcester (Pioneer) Batt.	
"	8/9/16	-	C.O. Train inspected 1st Line Transport of 189th Machine Gun Company. C.O.C. Division	
"	"	"	inspected Headquarters Company.	
"	10/9/16	-	The 9 supplies complete turnover (supplies through 1 composite Brigade R.F.A being adjusted) returned to A.H.T.D. under T/Lieut G.F. Killick R.N.	
"	"	-	T/Major F. Holmes proceeded to England for temporary duty with the Admiralty	
"	9/9/16	-	T/Surgeon W.R.E. Murdoch proceeded on special leave to England	
"	12/9/16	-	S.M. (W.O. Class 1) J.J. Ashton transferred to 3rd Field Ambulance	
"	"	-	C.O. Train inspected 1st Line Transport of 190th Bgde M.G. Coy	
"	16/9/16	"	Sub Lieut Bradfield, Davidson and Andrews attached for instruction from Infantry Battalions.	
"	16/9/16		Sub Lieut Bradfield, Davidson and Andrews rejoined their respective Battalions.	
"	19/9/16		No 4 Company, Divisional Train moved to billets in OURTON.	
"	"		Refilling Point of 190th Cycle Coy transferred to OURTON - DIEVAL Road (I 34 a. 6.3 Sheet 36B)	

Vol 6

CONFIDENTIAL.

WAR   DIARY

of

63rd (R.N) Divisional Train.

VOLUME 5

From 1st October, 1916 to 31st October, 1916.

Lieut. Col. A.S.C.
Commdg, 63rd (R.N) Divnl. Train.

Army Form C. 2118.

WAR DIARY
or
INTELLIGENCE SUMMARY.
(Erase heading not required.)

63rd (R.N.) Divisional Train

Place	Date	Hour	Summary of Events and Information	Remarks and references to Appendices
OURTON.	1.10.16	-	T/Capt C.L. Chapman returned off leave. T/Lieut. V. King proceeded to England on leave. T/Lieut A.E. Dugan R.N. proceeded to Abbancourt H.T. Depot for a course of instruction in H.T. duties.	
"	"	-	All Baggage wagons sent out to Units.	
"	2.10.16	-	Train HQs, HQs Company, Nos. 3 & 4 Companies moved to REBREUVIETTE. No. 2 Coy moved to PETIT-BOURET see CHAMP.	
"	3.10.16	-	Supply section wagons allotted to dismounted units delivered ⅔ portion of the supplies to these units in the old area, and then, together with the baggage wagons, met at a rendezvous arranged by O.s.C Companies. HQs Company marched together with its Supply Section to REBREUVIETTE, delivering the supplies in the REBREUVIETTE area. The Brigade Companies Supply Section wagons had to deliver the remainder of the supplies in the REBREUVIETTE area. Owing to the congestion of roads the supply sections did not arrive at their respective destinations until about 8pm, when the Divisional Train had to refill again for the next day's delivery. Refilling was completed about 2.30 am on the 4th inst.	
REBREUVIETTE	4.10.16		The Divisional Train moved to CROSS-ROADS. (Maps Ref: O.1 Central Sheet 57D)	

Army Form C. 2118.

WAR DIARY
or
INTELLIGENCE SUMMARY.
(Erase heading not required.)

63rd (RN) Divisional Train.

Instructions regarding War Diaries and Intelligence Summaries are contained in F. S. Regs., Part II. and the Staff Manual respectively. Title pages will be prepared in manuscript.

Place	Date	Hour	Summary of Events and Information	Remarks and references to Appendices
Acheux ville	9/10/16		Leaving camp at 6 a.m. During the congestion of roads and steep hills, the Supply Section wagons were not able to deliver until, in some cases, by 12 noon on the 5th inst. All the transframes with the exception of No. 2 Company, stayed the night on the road, the MGs of No. 2 Company reaching camp about 8 pm on the 4th inst.	
O.I. CENTRAL	5.10.16		Refilling point was on the VARENNES - HEDAUVILLE ROAD, and supplies were issued that afternoon to the units, the Supply Section wagons returning to camp at O.I. Central that day.	
"	10.10.16		T/Capt. H.V. Scott-Willett R.M. posted to 2nd Batn Royal Marines as a Totient provisionally but remained with the Divisional Train pending over command of MS Coy.	
"	13.10.16		T/Major F. Holmes R.M. returned for duty with Divisional Train, having completed his duty at the Admiralty. T/Lieut. V. King RM returned from leave.	
"	14/10/16		T/Major F. Holmes RM took over command of MS Coy from T/Capt H.V. Scott Willett RM. T/Lieut. N.E. Goth RM. transferred from No.2 Company to M.S. Company.	
"	16.10.16		T/Capt. H.V. Scott Willett RM. left to join 2nd RM Battalion. T/Lieut. G.L. Burrell RM. having been accepted as an Observer on probation in Royal Flying Corps, & left to join RFC.	

Army Form C. 2118.

WAR DIARY
or
INTELLIGENCE SUMMARY.
(Erase heading not required.)

63rd (RN) Divisional Train

Instructions regarding War Diaries and Intelligence Summaries are contained in F. S. Regs., Part II. and the Staff Manual respectively. Title pages will be prepared in manuscript.

Place	Date	Hour	Summary of Events and Information	Remarks and references to Appendices
O.I Central	16.10.16		Railhead changed to ACHEUX. Time of loading 10. a.m.	
O.I CENTRAL	16.10.16		7/Capt L.H. Murdoch. RM transferred from No 4 Company to Headquarters Company.	
			7/Lieut E.T. Willis RM transferred from Headquarters Company to No 4 Company.	
"	17.10.16		7/Lieut H. Lawrence, RM reported from ASC Base Depot and so posted to No 4 Company	
"	18.10.16		Railhead changed to BELLE EGLISE. Time of loading 10. am	
"	20.10.16		15 G.S. wagons (9 from No 3 Coy and 6 from No 4 Coy) detached to HEDAUVILLE under command of Lieut H.F. Kellwick. RM.	
"	25.10.16		7/Lieut E.T. Milking transferred from Royal Marines to Army Service Corps from 5.9.16 Left for A.S.C. Base Depot (I.H.T. and S). 7/Capt F.W. Tooby RM admitted to 2nd Field Ambl. Sick.	
"	"		7/Lieut A.L. Bugors RM.g returned from A.H.T.D., ABBEVILLE having completed course of instruction	
"	"		7/Lieut W.R. Lidington R.M. took over command of No 4 Company from 7/Capt F.W. Tooby R.M.	
"	27.10.16		The 6 Baggage Section Wagons of No 4 Coy with the detachment at HEDAUVILLE returned to No. 4 Company. 2 Baggage Section wagons from No 2 Coy joined the detachment	

A R Lincoln
Lieut Col. ASC
Commdg. 63rd (RN) Divnl. Train

Vol 7

ROYAL NAVAL
DIVISIONAL TRAIN.
No..............
Date... 1/12/16

War Diary
63rd (RN) Divl Train

Volume VI

John Mulholland
Lieut & Adjt
for Lt Col Commdg
63rd (RN) Divl Train

Army Form C. 2118.

WAR DIARY
or
INTELLIGENCE SUMMARY.
(Erase heading not required.)

63rd (RN) Divisional Train

Place	Date	Hour	Summary of Events and Information	Remarks and references to Appendices
O.I. Central	2.11.16		2/Lieut A.L. Dugan RM transferred from Requisitioning No 2 Company to Transport Subaltern No 4 Company.	
			2/Lieut A. Lawrence, R.M. transferred from Transport Subaltern No 4 Company to Requisitioning Officer No 4 Company. 2/Lieut A.L. Dugan, R.M. admitted to 2nd Field Ambulance sick. 2/Lieut M/ Balfour-Murphy R.M. two detached to the 1st Army Purchase Board. G.O.C, 63rd (RN) Division	
			inspected the camp of the Divisional Train	
	4/11/16		Refilling Point for the 188th Bgde Group changed to O.I. Central	
	5/11/16		Refilling Point for the 188th Bgde Group changed to old place, VARENNES - HEDAUVILLE road	
	9/11/16		2/Lieut A. Lawrence, R.M. attached to No 2 by as Supply Officer	
	11/11/16		2/Lieut P. Allaro proceeded to England on leave	
	9/11/16		Refilling point for the 190th Bgde changed to O.I. Central	
	11/11/16		Refilling point for the 190th Bgde changed to old place, VARENNES - HEDAUVILLE road	
	12/11/16		2/Lieut A.L. Dugan RM returned from 2nd Field Ambulance. 2/Major F.W. Nobly RM struck off the strength (Auth:- 63rd Divnl. Routine Order No. 1037 dated 11/11/16.)	

T2134. Wt. W708-776. 500000. 4/15. Sir J.C. & S.

WAR DIARY or INTELLIGENCE SUMMARY

Army Form C. 2118.

Place	Date	Hour	Summary of Events and Information	Remarks and references to Appendices
O.I Central	13.11.16		Drawing time at Railhead changed from 10 a.m. to 9 a.m.	
"	14.11.16		No. 2 Company moved to BEAUVAL. Refilling Point for 188 Bde Group changed to ARQUEVES. Refilling Point for 189 Bde Group changed to O.I Central (Sheet 57D). Refilling Point for 190th Bde Group was on the VARENNES - HEDAUVILLE Road.	
"	15.11.16		Train HQrs moved to DOULLENS. No. 2 Company moved to BERNAVILLE. No. 3 Company moved to GEZAINCOURT. No. 4 Company moved to BEAUVAL. Refilling Point for 188th Bde Group changed to BEAUVAL. Refilling Point for 189th & 190th Bde Groups was at ARQUEVES. 7th Bn. V. King R.R. M.G. Coy attached to 3 Company.	
DOULLENS.	19.11.16		Train HQrs moved to BERNAVILLE. No. 3 Coy moved to FIENVILLERS. No. 4 Coy moved to FERME - LE - QUESNEL. Refilling Point for 188th Bde Group changed to Pool E in BERNAVILLE. Refilling Point for 189 Bde Group changed to GEZAINCOURT. Refilling Point for 190th Bde changed to BERNAVAL Thiend R.V. Muller R.M. reported from A.S.C. Base Depot and posted to No.4 Company.	
"	20.11.16		Refilling Point for 189 Bde Group changed to Pool E in BERNAVILLE. Refilling Point for 190th.	
" BERNAVILLE	21.11.16		Bde Group was at FERME - LE - QUESNEL. Refilling Point for 190th Bde Group changed to Pool E in BERNAVILLE. No.2 Coy moved to COULONVILLERS. No.3 Coy moved to	
"	24.11.16		troop HQrs moved to MESNIL - DOMQUEUR. + 189	
MESNIL-DOMQUEUR	25.11.16		MESNIL - DOMQUEUR. No. 4 Coy moved to PROUVILLE. Refilling Point for 188 Bde Group was COULONVILLERS. Refilling Point for 189 Bde Group was changed to Pool E in Bernaville Refilling Point for 190 Bde Group was at PROUVILLE.	

Army Form C. 2118.

WAR DIARY
or
INTELLIGENCE SUMMARY.

(Erase heading not required.)

Instructions regarding War Diaries and Intelligence Summaries are contained in F.S. Regs, Part II. and the Staff Manual respectively. Title pages will be prepared in manuscript.

Place	Date	Hour	Summary of Events and Information	Remarks and references to Appendices
Mesnil-Domqueur	22.11.16.		Train H.Qrs. moved to ST. RIQUIER. No 3 Coy moved to Fontaine-sur-Maye. No 3 Coy moved to ST. RIQUIER. No 4 Coy moved to MAISON-PONTHIEU.	
ST. RIQUIER.	23.11.16.		Train H.Qrs. moved to BUIGNY ST. MACLOU. No 3 Coy moved to NOUVION-en-PONTHIEU. No 3 Coy moved to BUIGNY-ST. MACLOU. No 4 Company moved to CANCHY. Refilling Point for 188 Bde Group was at F in FONTAINE. Refilling Point for 189 Bde Group was changed to ST RIQUIER. Refilling Point for 190 Bde Group changed to MAISON PONTHIEU.	
BUIGNY.	24.11.16.		Train H.Qrs moved to RUE. No 3 Coy moved to NOUVELLES-SUR-MER. No 3 Coy moved to LARRONVILLE. No 4 Coy moved to NOUVIONS-en-PONTHIEU. Refilling Point for 188 Bde Group was at NOUVIONS. Refilling Point for 189 Bde Group was at HAUTEVILLERS. Refilling Point was at LAMOTTE BULEUX.	
RUE.	25.11.16.		Refilling Point for 188 Bde Group was changed to NOUVELLES-SUR-MER. Refilling Point for 189 Bde Group changed to LARRONVILLE. Refilling Point for 190 Bde Group was at NOUVIONS-en-PONTHIEU. 2/Lieut V. King RM took over duties of acting S.S.O. vice	
"	26.11.16.		2/Major G.C. Sherman R.S.O on leave. 2/Lt S.H. Middleton RM proceeded on leave to England. 2/Major 2.C. Sherman proceeded to England on leave. 2/Lt. P. Read RM returned from leave.	
"	27.11.16.		2/C. H. Lawrence RM ceased to perform duties of S.O. 188 Brigade and returned to H.Q. Coy.	

Army Form C. 2118.

WAR DIARY
or
INTELLIGENCE SUMMARY.
(Erase heading not required.)

Place	Date	Hour	Summary of Events and Information	Remarks and references to Appendices
RUE	30/11		T/Lt. O. Allard OM No 2 Coy placed on the sick list. T/Lt H. Laurence OM No 4 Coy attached to 2 Coy as supply officer. 188th Bde. H.Q. Coy sent 1 Officer & 25 O.R. to ABBEVILLE by motor lorry to draw remounts which are most urgently needed.	

A. Whitwell
Lieut. Col. ASC.
Comdg. 61st (2nd) Divl. Train

30/11/16.

Vol 8

Confidential
War Diary
of
63rd (RN) Divisional Train

Volume 7

From 1=12=16 to 31=12=16.

A R Liddell
Lieut. Col ASC
Commg 63rd (RN) Div. Train.

Army Form C. 2118.

WAR DIARY
or
INTELLIGENCE SUMMARY.
(Erase heading not required.)

63rd (RN) Divisional Train

Place	Date	Hour	Summary of Events and Information	Remarks and references to Appendices
RUE	4.12.16		190th Bde Group loaded by H.T from Railhead & had their Refilling Point at NOLETTES	
			H.q. Coy arrived from O.1 Central about 5 P.M. & went under Canvas on a field near BONNELLE. Owing to shortage of horses, the Artillery had to use their own horses for the Baggage wagons allotted to them but H.q. Coy received remounts on the	
			H.q. Coy received it was too late.	
			C.O. Train interviewed C.O. ABBEVILLED & arranged for 23 hind wheels to be sent to H.qrs by on 5/12/16.	
	5/12/16		T/Capt J.M. Murdoch RAM placed on sick list	
	6/12/16		T/Capt J.M. Murdoch RAM admitted to 1st Field Ambulance	
	5/12/16		190th Bde Group loaded by H.T. from Railhead	
	7/12/16		T/Major E.C. Shurman ASC returned to duty off leave as SSO.	
	8/12/16		Lt Col A.R. LIDDELL ASC proceeded on leave to England T/Major J. Holmes RM assumed command of the Unit Pr o tem heart to Lt A.R LIDDELL absence on leave.	

Army Form C. 2118.

WAR DIARY 2.

or

INTELLIGENCE SUMMARY.

(Erase heading not required.)

63rd (RN) Divisional Train

Place	Date	Hour	Summary of Events and Information	Remarks and references to Appendices
RUE	10.12.16		T/Lieut P Allard RNR admitted sick to 3rd Field Ambulance. T/Capt LM Murdoch RNR was discharged from 3rd Field Ambulance to 7th (Canadian) General Hospital ETAPLES. T/Lieut RV Muller was interviewed by T/Major F Holmes RM. T/Lieuts Allard & Cook RM were interviewed by O.C. Divn train.	
	11/12/16			
	12/12/16		No 2 Coy moved to billets at CANTEREME. Refilling Point for 188th Inf. Group changed to RUE. T/Lieut P Allard was discharged to 2nd (SA) Hospital ABBEVILLE on 10/12/16. T/Lieut V.C. Numman RNR proceeded on leave to England. Refilling Point 188th Bde changed to CANTEREME.	
	14/12/16 17/12/16 18/12/16		T/Capt LM Murdoch RNR returned to duty from hospital. T/Lieut F Collins RNR proceeded on leave to England. T/Lieut RV Muller RNR temporarily took over duties as OC Wood Issues NOUVION.	
	19/12/16		T/Lieut HE Tooth RNR reported from the Base Depot (MTD) & posted to Hdqr.	

Army Form C. 2118.

WAR DIARY
or
INTELLIGENCE SUMMARY.
(Erase heading not required.)

63rd (RN) Divisional Train

Instructions regarding War Diaries and Intelligence Summaries are contained in F. S. Regs., Part II. and the Staff Manual respectively. Title pages will be prepared in manuscript.

Place	Date	Hour.	Summary of Events and Information	Remarks and references to Appendices
RUE.	20.12.16		Lieut. Col. A.R. Liddell returned from leave. Tmajor T.Holmes ceased to command the Divisional Train. T/Lt. & Adjt. Hon. L.J. Mulholland ASO proceeded on leave.	
"	21.12.16		T/Lieut. V.C. King RM assumed duties of acting Adjutant vice T/Lt. & Adjt. Hon. L.J. Mulholland ASO on leave.	
"	22.12.16		T/Lieut. V.C. Newman RM returned off leave.	
"	24.12.16		T/Lieut. A.E. Stokes RM placed on sick list.	
"	26.12.16		T/Lieut. G.F. Kilwick RM proceeded on leave to England.	
"	27.12.16		T/Lieut. A.E. Stokes RM struck off sick list.	
"	30.12.16		T/Lieut. R.V. Muller RM proceeded to England to report War Office (Auth. A.D.S.T. T.Army H/24/196 dated 24.12.16.)	
"	31.12.16		T/Lt. E.W. Dotes RM, No 2 Coy transferred to HQ5 Coy.	

A R Liddell
Lieut. Col. ASO
Comdg 63rd (RN) Divnl Train.

CONFIDENTIAL.

WAR DIARY

of

63rd (RN) DIVISIONAL TRAIN.

VOLUME 8.

From 1st January, 1917 to 31st January, 1917.

Lieut. Col. A.S.C.
Commdg, 63rd (RN) Divnl. Train.

Army Form C. 2118.

WAR DIARY
or
INTELLIGENCE SUMMARY.

(Erase heading not required.)

63rd (RN) Divisional Train.

Instructions regarding War Diaries and Intelligence Summaries are contained in F.S. Regs., Part II. and the Staff Manual respectively. Title pages will be prepared in manuscript.

Place	Date 1917	Hour	Summary of Events and Information	Remarks and references to Appendices
RUE.	Jan 1	-	T/Lieut. P. Allard, R.M., No.2 Company (sick in hospital) transferred from Supply Officer, 188th Bde to Transport Subaltern No.2 Company. T/Lieut. G.F.Killwick, R.M., No.3 Company transferred to No.4 Company. T/Lieut. A.E.Stocks R.M. No.4 Company transferred to No.3 Company. T/Lieut. H. Lawrence, R.M., No.4 Company transferred from Requisitioning Officer 190th Bde to Transport Subaltern No.4 Company. T/Lieut. J. Maccoun, R.M., returned to duty from Salvage Company.	
"	2nd		T/Lieut.&.Adjt. The Hon.G.J.Mulholland, A.S.C. returned from leave and resumed duties of Adjutant. T/Lieut. V. King, R.M., ceased to perform duties of a/Adjutant. Headquarters Company moved to bivouacs at BUIGNY St. MACLOU. The supply section refilled at BUIGNY St. MACLOU, delivered rations to units in GRAND LAVIERS - CAOURS area, and proceeded to HEIRMONT, where it bivouaced for the night and was joined by Company Baggage and H.Qrs sections.	
	3.		Supply Section refilled at HEIRMONT, delivered to units in BEALCOURT - GUESCART area and bivouaced with H.Qrs of Company for the night at BEALCOURT.	
	4.		Supply Section refilled at FROHEM le GRAND, delivered to units in FROHEM le PETIT - GEZAINCOURT area and bivouaced for the night at AUTHIEULE. Baggage Section and H.Qrs of Company bivouaced the night at SARTON.	
	5.		Supply Section refilled at AUTHIEULE, delivered to units in AUTHIEULE - MARIEUX area, and bivouaced for night near FORCEVILLE. Baggage section and H.Qrs of Company proceeded to VITERMONT - ENGLEBELMER.	

2353 Wt.W3544/1454 700,000 5/15 D.D.&L. A.D.S.S.Forms/C.2118.

Army Form C. 2118.

WAR DIARY
or
INTELLIGENCE SUMMARY.

(Erase heading not required.)

63rd (RN) Divisional Train.

Instructions regarding War Diaries and Intelligence Summaries are contained in F.S. Regs., Part II. and the Staff Manual respectively. Title pages will be prepared in manuscript.

Place	Date 1917	Hour	Summary of Events and Information	Remarks and references to Appendices
RUE.	Jan. 6.		Supply Section refilled at FORCEVILLE, delivered to units in FORCEVILLE – ENGLEBELMER area, and bivouaced for night at FORCEVILLE.	
	7.		Supply Section refilled at FORCEVILLE, delivered to units as before, and joined rest of Company at VITERMONT.	
	9.		The Company vacated the camp at VITERMONT, and proceeded to P.23.a (Sheet 57D). 2nd Corps Commander inspected transport of Nos.2, 3, and 4 Companies.	
"	10		Train H.Qrs moved to billets at BUIGNY St. MACLOU. No.2 Company moved to billets at FOREST L'ABBAYE. No.3 Company moved to billets at BUIGNY St. MACLOU. No.4 Company moved to billets at CANCHY. 188th Bde refilling point was at NOUVION. Refilling point for 189th Bde. group was at 1 mile S.E MOYELLES-sur-MER on main road to PORT le GRAND. Refilling point for 190th Bde group was at NOUVION.	
"	13.		T/Lieut. J. Macoun, R.N., No.2 Company admitted to 1st Field Ambulance, sick. Train H.Qrs moved to billets in MOYELLE en CHAUSSEE. No.2 Company moved to billets in FROYELLES. No.3 Coy moved to billets in MOYELLES-en-CHAUSSEE. No.4 Company moved to billets in BERMATRE. Refilling point for 188th Bde group was N.E. of CANCHY S. of cross roads. Refilling point for 189th Bde group was Main Road N.E. of WILLENCOURT S. of cross roads. Refilling point for 190th Bde group was N.E. of CANCHY S. of cross roads.	
BUIGNY St. MACLOU.	14.			

2353 Wt. W2544/1454 700,000 5/15 D.D. & L. A.D.S.S.Forms/C.2118.

Army Form C. 2118.

WAR DIARY
or
INTELLIGENCE SUMMARY.
(Erase heading not required.)

63rd (RN) Divisional Train.

Instructions regarding War Diaries and Intelligence Summaries are contained in F.S. Regs., Part II and the Staff Manual respectively. Title pages will be prepared in manuscript.

Place	Date 1917.	Hour	Summary of Events and Information	Remarks and references to Appendices
MOYELLE en CHAUSSEE.	Jan. 15.		Train H. Qrs moved to billets in FEINVILLERS. No.3 Company moved to billets in AUTHEUX. No.3 Company moved to billets in FEINVILLERS. No.4 Company moved to billets in LONGUEVILLETTE. Refilling point for 188th Bde group was main road S. of cross roads S. of HEIRMONT. Refilling point for 189th Bde group was S. of main cross roads W. of COMTEVILLE. Refilling point for 190th Bde group was 2 miles E. of WAVAM on main road.	
Feinvillers.	16		Refilling point for 188th Bde group was main road AUTHEUX – Le QUESNEL Farm, near Le QUESNEL Farm. Refilling point for 189th Bde group was main road BERMAVILLE – FEINVILLERS just outside FEINVILLERS. Refilling point for 190th Bde Group was GEZAINCOURT, opposite hospital.	
	17.		Train H. Qrs moved to billets in VAL DE MAISON. No.2 Company moved to billets in BEAUQUESNE. No.3 Coy moved to billets in VAL DE MAISON. No.4 Company moved to billets in PUCHEVILLERS. Refilling point for 188th Bde group was Main road DOULLENS–BEAUVAL at H in HAMENCOURT. Refilling point for 189th Bde group was main road CAMAPLES – HAVERMAS, half way between two towns. Refilling point for 190th Bde group was GEZAINCOURT opposite hospital.	
Val de Maison.	18		Refilling point for 188th Bde was at BEAUQUESNE. Refilling point for 189th Bde was at VAL de MAISON. Refilling point for 190th Bde was at PUCHEVILLERS.	
"	19		No.2 Company moved to billets at Q.25.c. (map Ref. sheet 57.d. No.3 Company moved to FORCEVILLE. Refilling points for 188th and 189th Bdes were at Q.13.d. Refilling point 190th Bde group was at PUCHEVILLERS.	

Army Form C. 2118.

WAR DIARY
or
INTELLIGENCE SUMMARY.

63rd (RN) Divisional Train.

(Erase heading not required.)

Instructions regarding War Diaries and Intelligence Summaries are contained in F.S. Regs., Part II. and the Staff Manual respectively. Title pages will be prepared in manuscript.

Place	Date 1917	Hour	Summary of Events and Information	Remarks and references to Appendices
Val de Maison.	Jan. 20		Train H.Qrs. moved to billets in ENGLEBELMER. No.3 Company moved to bivouacs at Q.25.c (map Ref. Sheet 57D) No.4 Company moved to billets in FORCEVILLE. Refilling point for 188th Bde group was Q.13.d. Refilling point for 189th Bde group was Q.13.d.. Refilling point for 190th Bde group was FORCEVILLE. T/Lieut. P. Allard, R.M., No.3 Company report for duty from hospital. T/Lieut. A.E.Stocks, R.M., No.3 Company transferred to No.2 Company.	
	22.		T/Lieut. P. Allard, R.M., took over command of No.2 Company, vice T/Capt. A.E.Balfour, R.M. sick.	
	23.		T/Lieut. F.G.McPherson, R.M., H.Qrs Company granted leave to England. T/Capt. A.E.Balfour R.M., admitted to 2nd Field Ambulance, sick. T/Lt. J. Macoun, R.M., returned to duty from 1st Field Ambulance. T/Surgeon W.R.E.Unthank, R.M., posted as M.O. i/c 1st R.M.Battalion. T/Capt. F.G. McNaughton, R.A.M.C. (S.R) posted as M.O. i/c 63rd (RN) Divisional Train. T/Lieut. A.E. Stocks, R.M., No.2 Company transferred to No.3 Company.	
	24.			
	25.		T/Lieut. H. Lawrence, R.M., No.4 Company transferred to Headquarters Company as S.O. Divisional Troops, vice T/Capt. L.M.Murdoch, R.M., on leave.	
	27.		T/Lieut. J. Macoun, R.M., No.2 Company admitted to 2nd Field Ambulance, sick. T/Lieut A.E. Stocks, R.M., No.3 Company transferred to No.2 Company.	
	30.		Owing to all leave being stopped, T/Lt. H. Lawrence, R.M., returned to duty with No.4 Coy.	

Lieut Col A.S.C
Commdg 63rd (RN) Divnl Train France

Vol X10

Confidential

War Diary

of

63rd (RN) Divisional Train

Volume 9

From 1st Feb 1917 to 28th Feb 1917

John Mulholland
Lieut & Adjt for.
Major A.S.C.
Comdg 63rd (RN) Divnl Train

Army Form C. 2118.

WAR DIARY
or
INTELLIGENCE SUMMARY.
(Erase heading not required.)

63rd (RN) Divisional Train

Place	Date	Hour	Summary of Events and Information	Remarks and references to Appendices
Englebelmer	1.2.17		Lieut H. Lawrence RM No 4 Coy transferred from Transport Esstb. to Repository Officer after 196th Bergade	
"	2.2.17		T/Lt N Lawrence RM attached to H.Qs Coy as S.O.	
"	3.3.17		T/Capt L.M. Murdock RM Detail Troops vice Capt L.M. Murdock proceeding on leave	
			H.Qs Coy proceeded on leave to England. D.D.S.+T. I Army inspected	
			No 4 Company Transport at Puchvillers. T/Lt V. King R.M. H.Qs Coy attached to 2nd Corps for	
"	4.2.17		Agricultural duties.	
"	6.2.17		T/Lieut J. Magennis R.M. No 2 Coy struck off strength on transfer to England	
"	8.2.17		D.D.S+T. I Army inspected H.Qs 2 and 4 Companies. T/Capt A.E Balfour R.M. returned from Hospital	
			T/Major J Holmes R.M. H.Qs Coy proceeded on leave to England. T/Lt S.J Philcock R.M. granted	
			Sick leave for 1 month. T/Lieut C.E Stocks R.M. No 2 Coy transferred to No 4 Coy	
"	9.2.17		G.O.C. 63rd (RN) Division inspected No 4 Company. T/Major A.E Balfour RM resumed command	
			of No 2 Coy.	
"	11.2.17		T/Lieut E.M Potter RM 319th Coy admitted to 2nd Camb. Esstb. and transferred to 47th C.O.S.	
"	14.2.17		Refilling Pount for 188th Brigade was changed to Englebelmer. T/Capt L.M Murdock RM returned from light	
"	18.2.17		Duty. Presentation Same with force. T/Capt J. Stevenson RM inspected by 190 Bde. to Receipent DR No 2 Coy	
"	19.2.17		No 3 Coy moved to HEDAUVILLE. Only fresh rations drawn from Railhead. Major. Gen. C.E Laurie	
			took over command of 63rd (RN) Division vice Major. Gen. C.D Shute, C.B, C.M.G to	
			32nd Division. T/Lieut E.M. Potter RM struck off strength of Divl Train on transfer to England	
"	23.2.17		T/Lt A.H Bryer RM to perform duties of RO Division temporarily in addition to his duties as S.O. No 2 Coy	

Army Form C. 2118.

WAR DIARY
or
INTELLIGENCE SUMMARY.

(Erase heading not required.)

Instructions regarding War Diaries and Intelligence Summaries are contained in F. S. Regs., Part II. and the Staff Manual respectively. Title pages will be prepared in manuscript.

Place	Date	Hour	Summary of Events and Information	Remarks and references to Appendices
ENGLEBELMER	26.2.19		Thaw Recommenced.	
"	24.2.19		2nd Lt Whittle ASC proceeded on 3 days leave to Paris. T/Major B.C Sherman MSC assumed command of Div Train. vice. A Col Whittle on leave.	

John Mulholland
Major A.S.C.
Commg 63rd (RN) Div'l Train

Vol XI

63rd
(ROYAL NAVAL)
DIVISIONAL TRAIN.
No........
Date........

War Diary

March 1917.

Volume 10.

A.R.Liddell
Lt. Col. A.S.C.
Commdg. 63rd (RN) Div. Train.

Army Form C. 2118.

WAR DIARY
or
INTELLIGENCE SUMMARY.
(Erase heading not required.)

63rd (RN) Divisional Train

Place	Date	Hour	Summary of Events and Information	Remarks and references to Appendices
ENGLEBELMER	1/3/17		Lieut Col A.K. Liddell A.S.C. returned from leave and assumed command of Train.	
"	2.3.17		Train HQs moved to BOUZINCOURT. No 1 Coy moved to V.5.c.6.9. (Sheet 57D). No 2 Coy moved to V.11.a.5.5. No 4 Coy moved to NORTHUMBERLAND AVENUE. Divisional Troops Groups Refilling point changed to V.11.a.9.5. 188th Bde Group Refilling point changed to W.3.a.9.1. 189th Bde Group Refilling point renewed to MARTINSART. 190th Bde Group Refilling point moved to W.3.a.6.6. Major J. Holmes R.M. granted extension of leave to 24.2.17 on Medical Certificate by War Office. Third V. King R.M. No 1 Company struck off strength of Red Coy and brought on strength of Train HQs. T/Cl. W.J. Balfour R.M. No. 3 Coy struck off strength of that Company and brought on strength of Train HQs. Third R.V. Muller R.M. No. 4 Coy transferred to No. 3 Company. No. 1 Coy moved to billets in BOUZINCOURT. No. 2 Coy moved to billets in BOUZINCOURT. No. 3 Coy moved to billets in MARTINSART.	
BOUZINCOURT.	6.3.17.			
"	9/3/17		Divl. Troops Refilling Point changed to NORTHUMBERLAND Avenue.	
"	11/3/17		A.S.v.S. instructed with two of No. 1 Coy 2 detachment gun ball to be evacuated.	

Army Form C. 2118.

63rd (2nd) Divisional Train

WAR DIARY
or
INTELLIGENCE SUMMARY.
(Erase heading not required.)

Instructions regarding War Diaries and Intelligence Summaries are contained in F.S. Regs., Part II. and the Staff Manual respectively. Title pages will be prepared in manuscript.

Place	Date	Hour	Summary of Events and Information	Remarks and references to Appendices
Bouzincourt	12.3.17		T. Reno S.S. the Princess Pats 1st Coy. struck off also Reno	
"	13.3.17		T. Reno of Ammunition Pm 1st Coy. transferred to No 2 Coy. T. Reno S.S. Millwork Pm, No 4 Coy. attached from Reno transferred to No 3 Coy. T. Reno Supernum Pm, No 2 Coy attached not any transferred to No 4 Coy but remain attached to No 1 Coy.	
"	14.3.17		I.O. Train sent D.D.S.+S.	
"	18.3.17		T/Major E.C. Thurman A.S.C. granted leave to England. 18 reinforcements arrived from A.H.T.D. Div Train moved in accordance with Appendix A. The supply column received its normal duties this day.	A
Harponville	19/3/17		Train received that T/Major F. Holmes Dm is struck off strength of Divl Train.	
Beauval	20/3/17		5 & 6 remounts received during the march.	
"	25/3/17		Sent to 1st Field Ambulance 6 & 2 horses to enable them to move.	
Perines			No 1 Coy attached to 7th Canadian Divl Train.	

Army Form C. 2118.

WAR DIARY
or
INTELLIGENCE SUMMARY.
(Erase heading not required.)

Place	Date	Hour	Summary of Events and Information	Remarks and references to Appendices
BUSNES	28/3/17		C.O. Train inspected Transport of Divl Hdqrs.	
BUSNES	29/3/17		No 2 Coy attached to 6th Divl Train	
"	29/3/17		T/Major E.C. Atwumen HC returned off leave.	
"	30/3/17		C.O. Train inspected 1st line Transport of 7th Royal Fusiliers	

A. Russell
Lieut Colonel ASC
Comdg 63rd (RN) Divl Train

Appendix A

MOVES & RE-FILLING POINTS.

The following moves have taken place since 19.3.17 inclusive:-

Date.	Company.	From.	To.
19.3.17.	No 1.	-	-
"	No 2.	BOUSINCOURT.	HERISSART.
"	No 3.	MARTINSART.	WARLOY.
"	No 4.	BOUSINCOURT.	HARPONVILLE.
20.3.17.	No 1.	BOUSINCOURT.	RUEBEMPRE.
"	No 2.	HERISSART.	GEZAINCOURT.
"	No 3.	WARLOY.	PUCHEVILLIERS.
"	No 4.	HARPONVILLE.	BEAUVAL.
21.3.17.	No 1.	RUEBEMPRE.	FROHEN LE GRANDE.
"	No 2.	GEZAINCOURT.	LIGNY.
"	No 3.	PUCHEVILLERS.	OCCOCHES.
"	No 4.	BEAUVAL.	BONNIERES.
22.3.17.	No 1.	FROHEN LE GRANDE.	CONCHY.
"	No 2.	LIGNY.	GAUCHEN.
"	No 3.	OCCOCHES.	SIBIVILLE.
"	No 4.	BONNIERES.	HERLIN LE SEC.
23.3.17.	No 1.	CONCHY.	SIRACOURT.
24.3.17.	No 1.	SIRACOURT.	BRYAS.
"	No 2.	GAUCHEN.	CAUCHY A LA TOUR.
"	No 3.	SIBIVILLE.	MAREST.
"	No 4.	HERLIN LE SEC.	PERNES.
25.3.17.	No 1.	BRYAS.	3rd CANADIAN DIV AREA (FOSSE 7, Nr BARLIN)
"	No 2.	CAUCHY A LA TOUR.	EQUEDECQUES.
"	No 3.	MAREST.	AUCHY AU BOIS.
"	No 4.	PERNES.	ESTREE BLANCHE.
26.3.17.	No 2.	EQUEDECQUES.	LES AMUSOIRES.
"	No 3.	AUCH AU BOIS.	CHOCQUES.
"	No 4.	ESTREE BLANCHE.	BUSNES.
27.3.17.	No 2.	LES AMUSOIRES.	VERQUEGNEUL.

Train Hqrs were billeted with No 4 Coy on the march.

Re-Filling points have been as under since 20.3.17:-

Date.	Brigade Group.	Location.
20.3.17.	Divnl Troops.	Northumberland Avenue.
"	188th Bde.	BOUZINCOURT.
"	189th Bde.	PUCHEVILLERS.
"	190th Bde.	VERT GALAND.
21.3.17.	Divnl Troops.	HEM.
"	188th Bde.	HEM.
"	189th Bde.	GEZAINCOURT.
22.2	190th Bde.	HEM.
22.3.17.	Divnl Troops.	Q IN VACQUERIE LE BOURQ.
"	188th Bde.	HERLIN LE SEC.
"	189th Bde.	1st Road junction from FREVANT on FREVANT - NUNC road.
"	190th Bde.	1st Road junction from FREVANT on FREVANT - NUNC road.
23.3.17.	Divnl Troops.	Y in CONCHY.
"	188th Bde.	ST POL - CROIX road. ½ mile west of railway crossing.
"	189th Bde.	MONCHEAUX - SIBIVILLE road at 1st road junction from SIBIVILLE.
"	190th Bde.	NUNC - ST POL road. 500 yards South of HERLIN LE SEC

MOVES & RE FILLING POINTS

(2)

RE - FILLING POINTS.

Date.	Brigade Group.	Location.
24.3.17.	Divnl Troops.	ST POL - ANVIN road. At 2nd N in ANVIN.
"	188th Bde.	ST POL - PERNES road, ½ mile south of VALHUON.
"	189th Bde.	ST POL - PERNES road at X of TROISVAUX.
"	190th Bde.	ST POL - PERNES road. ½ mile south of VALHUON.
25.3.17.	Divnl Troops.	ORTON BRUAY road. South of the N of DEVION.
"	188th Bde.	LILLERS - ST HILAIRE road, at Q in Bourecq.
"	189th Bde.	PERNES - LILLERS road, at the U in CAUCHY.
"	190th Bde.	PERNES - LILLERS road, at the U in CAUCHY.
26.3.17.	188th Bde.	BURNES - ST VENANT road. ½ mile south of ST VENANT.
"	189th Bde.	LILLERS , CHOCQUES road, at T in PONT.
"	190th Bde.	LILLERS - ST HILAIRE road, at Q in BOURECQ.
27.3.17.	188th Bde.	BETHUNE - HESDIGNEUL road, ¼ mile south of railway crossing
"	189th Bde.	CHOCQUES.
"	190th Bde	BUSNES.

Vol 12

(ROYAL NAVAL)
DIVISIONAL TRAIN.

War Diary

April 1917.

Volume 11.

A.R.Liddell
Lt.Col. A.S.C.
Commdg. 63rd (R.N.) Div. Train.

Volume 11

WAR DIARY
or
INTELLIGENCE SUMMARY

Army Form C. 2118.

ROYAL NAVAL DIVISIONAL TRAM.

Place	Date	Hour	Summary of Events and Information	Remarks and references to Appendices
BUSNES	1/4/17		T/Lieut W R Johnston granted leave to England to 11/4/17	
"	2/4/17		C.O. Train attended conference on probable future active Operations at Divl Hqs. C.O. Train attended demonstration of P'sch scaling at BARLIN under the auspices of the 2 D. Isl Army C.O. Train visited No 1 Coy at town ? & No 2 Coy at MOEUX LES MINES T/Lieut V Ling RE reports the Divl Tram trams ceased to be employed on Engineer's urgent work to the II Corps. T/Lieut W R Lohnston RM was appointed in O.C.	
"	3/4/17		24th Batt'n full by RE attached to Canadian Corps into will feed them on consumption 8/4/17 & onwards	
"	6/4/17		24 Drivers & 2 Lemurs refumes from Base.	
"	7/4/17		T/Major F Holmes reported his arrival from England, Lieut V Ling RM & 20 OR proceeded to CA HS to draw remounts	

WAR DIARY or INTELLIGENCE SUMMARY.

Army Form C. 2118.

Place	Date	Hour	Summary of Events and Information	Remarks and references to Appendices
BRUAY	8/4/17		Train H.Qs & No 4 Coy moved to BRUAY. No 3 Coy moved to FOSSE 7 BARLIN	
	9/4/17		No 2 Coy ceased to be attached to 6th Divn Train	
	10/4/17		247th Field Coy & 14th Worcesters moved to near ARRAS, supply wagons went loaded & will remain with them	
	11/4/17		Train H.Qs moved to OURTON. No 2 Coy to DIEVAL. No 3 Coy to FREVILLERS. No 4 Coy to LA COMTE. 28 Remounts were received for the Train & distributed, No 106 & Coy 6 & 2 Coy 6 to 3 Coy 6 to 4 Coy.	
	12/4/17		t/Capt W.R. Lidington RAVC returned off leave. No 3 Coy moved to ECOIVRES	
	14/4/17		No 2 & 4 Coy moved to X hutments at ECOIVRES. Refilling point for 187th 189th 190th Bdes changed to near ARRAS, St Pol Road 1 mile East of HAUTE AVESNES. Train Hqs moved to camp E 29 sheet 51 C. Also No 4 Coy.	
E29	15/4/17			

WAR DIARY or INTELLIGENCE SUMMARY

Army Form C. 2118.

Place	Date	Hour	Summary of Events and Information	Remarks and references to Appendices
E.29.6 sheet 57c	16/4/17		No 1 Coy supply section camped at E.29.6 sheet 57c. Railhead changed to MAROEUIL.	
"	17/4/17		No 1 Coy refilled at VILLERS au BOIS. No 1 Coy moved to camp at the CEMETERY MAROEUIL.	
"	18/4/17		No 3 & 4 Coy moved to camp near CEMETERY MAROEUIL.	
"	19/4/17		No 1 Coy refilled at E.22.c sheet 57c. No 2 Coy moved to camp at the Cemetery MAROEUIL. All Coys refilled at F.2.c sheet 57c. C.O. & adjutant inspected road from ARRAS to BAILLEUL with a view to future refilling points etc. Railhead MONT ST ELOY	
MAROEUIL	20/4/17		No 2 Coy drew by Horse Transport from Railhead. Baggage wagons sent to all Bn'ns no horses & harness from H.Q.'s moved to camp opposite Cemetery at MAROEUIL.	
"	21/4/17		No 3 & 4 Coy drew by Horse Transport from Railhead.	
	22/4/17		No 1 Coy drew by Horse Transport from Railhead. 7/Lieut N. Dugan RM proceeded on leave to England.	

Army Form C. 2118.

WAR DIARY
or
INTELLIGENCE SUMMARY.
(Erase heading not required.)

Place	Date	Hour	Summary of Events and Information	Remarks and references to Appendices
MAROEUIL	23/4/17		Lorries received drawing from Roadhead for Divnl Troops. 19th Bde Group refilling point moved to MRU SOUCHEZ road. map reference S.9.a.6.3. about S.L.	
"	24/4/17		Refilling point for 189th Bde Group changed to near Cemetery MAROEUIL.	
"	25/4/17			
"	28/4/17		No 3 Coy moved to FREVILLERS No 3 Coy moved to LA COMTE Refilling point being on LA COMTE MAGNICOURT Road.	
"	29/4/17			
"	30/4/17		Train tipa moved to MINGOVAL Refilling point for 188th Bde Group changed to near Cemetery MAROEUIL	

A. Rhodell
Lieut Colonel A.S.C.
Commdg 63rd (RN) Divnl Train

Vol 13

War Diary,
May 1917.
Volume 12.

A.R.Liddell
Lt Col A.S.C.
Commdg. 63rd (RN) Div. Train

WAR DIARY or INTELLIGENCE SUMMARY

Army Form C. 2118.

Place	Date	Hour	Summary of Events and Information	Remarks and references to Appendices
MINGOVAL	1/5/17		No 2 Coy moved to Eau du BOIS HAUT near FREVILLERS. Refilling point for 188th Bde changed to MINGOVAL.	
"	3/5/17		T/Capt F Foley RM & T/Capt L B Jenkins RM reported than arrived from A.S.C. Base Depot # 798 the former was posted to 1 coy the latter to 2 coy. T/Lieut V King RM transferred to 2 coy T/Lieut H Lavarack RM ceased to be attached to No. 1 coy. T/Major L B Jenkins RM attached to 3 coy. No 3 coy moved to MAROEUIL supply section to ST CATHERINE. Refilling point for 189th Bde MINGOVAL. T/Lieut H Duggan RM returned off leave. Lieut G L McDowell ASC granted from 6/5/17 to 16/5/17. Capt F.G. McNaughton RAMC (SR) granted leave to England from 6/5/17 to 16/5/17. Trumpeter arrived from the Base. 1 O.R. No 4 coy wounded.	
"	4/5/17			
"	5/5/17			

Army Form C. 2118.

WAR DIARY
or
INTELLIGENCE SUMMARY.
(Erase heading not required.)

Place	Date	Hour	Summary of Events and Information	Remarks and references to Appendices
MINGOVAL	7/5/17		Refilling point for 189th Bde changed to MAROEUIL. 1 S.O.R. under Lieut McPherson sent to ECOIVRES to draw Remounts	
"	8/5/17		No 2 Coy moved to ECOIVRES. Owing to the move of the 190th Bde to the 19th Div. not moving back until 9/5/17 Supplies for the Details left behind such as D. Hq Signal Coy CRE for conveyance 10th inst had to be dumped at MINGOVAL & the supply wagons were a 2nd time this day to their camp. Three supply wagons will remain with units night 8/9 to join toMorrow 10/5/17. No 2 Coy moved to CAMBLIGNEUL	
"	9/5/17		A No 4 Coy moved to CAMBLIGNEUL Refilling point for 185th Bde being ST CATHERINE to MAROEUIL. Refilling point for 190 Litered No 2 Coy drew by HORSE TRANSPORT from AMMLITERED (MONT ST ELOI)	
"	10/5/17		Refilling point for '9' 6th Bde CAMBLIGNEUL	

WAR DIARY
or
INTELLIGENCE SUMMARY.

Army Form C. 2118.

Place	Date	Hour	Summary of Events and Information	Remarks and references to Appendices
MINGOVAL	19/5/17		Lieut Colonel A.R. Liddell ASC returned off leave. Supply wagons allotted to 5th Royal Fusiliers detached from 4 Coy & to No 3 Coy.	
"	20/5/17		No 2 & 3 Coy commenced drawing by Mown Transport from FREVIN CAPELLE	
MAROEUIL	21/5/17		No 4 Coy moved to MAROEUIL	
"	22/5/17		Train HQs moved to MAROEUIL	
"			No 4 Coy commenced drawing from Railhead by Mown Transport. Refilling Points for the 5 Guy Bde Groups are now on ST CATHARINE – SOUCHEZ Rd near ST CATHERINE.	
"	25/5/17		XIII Corps Commander instructed the Divnl Train at 10/am Railhead changed to ECURIE.	
Near ECURIE	26/5/17		Train HQ & No 1 Coy moved to G3 & S.S. No 2 Coy to A26c9.3. No 3 Coy to A26d S.S. No 4 Coy to G3C5.5. Divnl troops Refilling point to G36.7.9. W.T.	
"	27/5/17		No 1 Coy commenced drawing from Railhead by M.T.	

WAR DIARY
or
INTELLIGENCE SUMMARY

Army Form C. 2118.

Place	Date	Hour	Summary of Events and Information	Remarks and references to Appendices
Near ECURIE	29/5/14		Corpl S. Harrington RAMC (T.R.) returned off leave	
"	31/5/14		C.O. Train inspected transport & '169'th Labour Coy	

A.R. Riddell
Lieut Colonel ASC
Commdg 63rd (RN) Divnl Train

Ya 14

War Diary.
Volume 13.
June 1917

A R Liddell
Lt Col. ASC
Commg 63rd (RN) Divisional Train

1.7.17.

Army Form C. 2118.

63rd Divisional ?

WAR DIARY or INTELLIGENCE SUMMARY.
(Erase heading not required.)

Instructions regarding War Diaries and Intelligence Summaries are contained in F. S. Regs., Part II. and the Staff Manual respectively. Title pages will be prepared in manuscript.

Place	Date	Hour	Summary of Events and Information	Remarks and references to Appendices
Mar. St Catherine	2/6/17		T/Lieut V.C. Newman on Leave.	
"	3/6/17		T/Lieut & A/M. Maj. J. Mulholland Leave 3/6/17 to 13/6/17. T/Lieut R. E. Cook returned from leave.	
"	4/6/17		T/Captain & Tr Tisley RM took over the duties of Adjutant 4/6/17 to 14/6/17.	
"	5/6/17		T/Lieut G. F. Kilvert Bn. placed on the Sick List.	
"	6/6/17		T/Captain E. L. Chapman Bn. T/Lieut A. L. Stocks returned from leave.	
"	9/6/17		T/Lieut G. F. Kilvert Bn. taken off the Sick List.	
"	10/6/17		No 2 Coy moved to ECOIVRES	
"	11/6/17		No 3 Coy moved to MAROEUIL Billets	
"	12/6/17		No 4 Coy moved to MAROEUIL Camp T/Lieut J Ellison T/Lieut V King Leave 12/6/17 to 22/6/17. Repelling Bomb Changed to Indian.	Date — Strength 11.6.17 — 158 Bde 189 – " — 190 — " — Location Z 20. b. 5. 8. Sheet 51.C. MAROEUIL – ST CATHERINE Rd. L. 6. a. 3. 4. Sheet 51. C. MAROEUIL – ST CATHERINE Rd. L. 6. a. 2. 6. Sheet 51. C.

WAR DIARY
or
INTELLIGENCE SUMMARY
(Erase heading not required.)

Army Form C. 2118.

63rd (RN) Divisional Train

Place	Date	Hour	Summary of Events and Information	Remarks and references to Appendices
Near GEOURIE	14/6/17	-	T/Lieut V.C. Newman returned from Leave. Didn't Horse show held	
"	15/6/17	-	T/Capt S.J. Mulholland ASC returned off leave	
"	19/6/17	-	T/Capt S.J. Mulholland ASC resumed duties of adjutant. T/Lieut F.W. Tinley RN returned to duty with No 1 Coy. C.O. Train inspected at his Transport by Drake Relvin Hawke & Hood Battns.	
"	17/6/17		T/Capt I.m. Murdoch RM o T/Lieut F.P. Mulholland RM proceeded on leave; Draft of 20 Ptes RM reported C.O. Train judged at 31st Divn Horse Show. Sent 2 ASC & RM recruits C.O. Train judged at Canadian Corps Horse Show.	
"	18/6/17 19/6/17		Sent 4 ASC as trophy to Base Sent 44 RM Ptes who were warriors to Base for transfer to England.	
"	20/6/17		XIIIth Corps Horse Show Took place. No 4 Coy won Best HD Horse Stripped	
"	21/6/17		Sent 3 RM Ptes who were warriors to Base for Transfer to England	

63rd (R.N.) Divisional Train

WAR DIARY
or
INTELLIGENCE SUMMARY.
(Erase heading not required.)

Army Form C. 2118.

Instructions regarding War Diaries and Intelligence Summaries are contained in F. S. Regs., Part II. and the Staff Manual respectively. Title pages will be prepared in manuscript.

Place	Date	Hour	Summary of Events and Information	Remarks and references to Appendices
ECURIE	22/6/19		Refilling point for 188th Bde Group moved to ANZAC	
"	23/6/19		" " " 189th " " " " "	
"	25/6/19		T/Capt HE Balfour RN proceeded on leave	
"	26/6/19		Routine Army Horse Show took place	
"	27/6/19		Railhead changed to ECURIE 188 Refilling Point moved to 63 B.g. & that of 189 B. 189th to ANZIN. Co train inspected, & no Transport of Horse Battn	
"	28/6/19		ADVS inspected horses of the Divl Train.	
"	29/6/19		C.O. Town inspected 1st line Transport of 2nd Bn. Battn.	
			T/Capt JM Murdoch RM & T/Lieut FJ McPherson returned etc leave	

A. R. Russell
Lieut Colonel ASC
Commdg 63rd (RN) Divnl Train

63 Div Train Vol 15

War Diary.
Volume 14

July 1917

July 31st 1917

A.R. Liddell
Lieut Col. A.S.C.
Commdg.
63rd (RN) Divisional Train

Volume No 14   63rd (RN) Divisional Train

WAR DIARY
or
INTELLIGENCE SUMMARY

Army Form C. 2118.

Instructions regarding War Diaries and Intelligence Summaries are contained in F.S. Regs., Part II. and the Staff Manual respectively. Title pages will be prepared in manuscript.

Place	Date	Hour	Summary of Events and Information	Remarks and references to Appendices
Near BEAUMONT	2/7/17		1/ Major E.C. Thomson ASC proceeded on leave.	
"	5/7/17		No 4 Coy. drew 2 horses as remounts. XIII Corps Commander inspected the Divisional Train today. 3 ASC Supply Details reported from the Base. 2 Pam. 2 Coy A/Supply Details Staff Sergeant also reported. Notification received that Thos Hurst Lawrence was transferred to 30th CCS on 27/6/17 & Lawrence Wm 2 Coy returned off leave.	
"	8/7/17		1/Capt C.E. Balfour RN on tour own command of No. 4 Coy from T/Capt A.R. Fielding RN who was brought on the strength from the Base.	
"	11/7/17		His Majesty the King visited this area. T/Capt A.B.R. Fielding RM took over command of No. 4 Coy from T/Capt A.R. Fielding RM who purchasing a requisitioning debtor for 3 Coy.	
"	12/7/17		T/Capt E.W. Tuohy RM returned on attch to Staff & R. Islington. RM attached to Staff in Hd.qrs. to take over transport to Nelson Batt.	

WAR DIARY
or
INTELLIGENCE SUMMARY.

(Erase heading not required.)

Army Form C. 2118.

(3rd (Res) Divisional Train

Place	Date	Hour	Summary of Events and Information	Remarks and references to Appendices
Nunn Ecurie	12/7/17		1 NCO & 3 Ptes from each of the Coltns of the 189th Bde reported for course of Instruction in Transport duties. Capt F.W. Risby RM Junior in charge of instruction for NCO & men of Infantry in this them-short- commenced.	
	13/7/17		Capt F.W. Risby RM admitted to 2nd Field Ambulance sick	
	14/7/17		Lt J Macpherson RM returned from Bourges with 15 HD 2 Picton Renounts. Renounts issued to Companies	
	15/7/17		C.O. Train inspected Transport of 1st Field Ambulance Capt F. Macnaughton RAMC (M) admitted to & at Field Ambulance sick	
	16/7/17		C.O. Train inspected 1st line Transport of 2nd Field Ambulance C.O. Train inspected 1st line Transport of 1st Artist Rifle RM & 1 Band played at Train H.Q.S.	
	18/7/17			

63(RD) Divisional Train
Army Form C. 2118.

WAR DIARY
or
INTELLIGENCE SUMMARY.

Place	Date	Hour	Summary of Events and Information	Remarks and references to Appendices
Nr ECURIE	20/4/17		C.O. Train inspected Transport detached to 7/Mil Corps Training centre at PETRES & 4 Butty 223rd Bd RFA at AIRE. T/Major R.C. Thorman DSO ASC returned off leave. T/Lieut S.A. Marketham proceeded on leave.	
	24/4/17		C.O. Train inspected pairs Transport of 189th Wiercaster Pioneer Battn. Baggage section horses sent to A Arlt 317 & Bd [?] [?] [?] Rep. rejoined his arrival from the Base & is posted to A Coy	
	24/4/17		C.O. Train inspected 150th Field Ambulance, Transport T/Lieut P A Donel RM No 2 Coy returned off leave	
	29/4/17		C.O. Train inspected 1st train transport of 188th M.G. Coy	
	28/4/17		7 Remounts arrived from Base.	

A R Russell
Lieut Colonel ASC
Commdg 63rd (RN) Divnl Train

63 Div Train
Vol 16

War Diary.

Volume No 15

A R Liddell
Lt Col ASC
Commdg
63rd (RN) Divisional Train

63rd (RN) Divisional Train
Army Form C. 2118.

WAR DIARY
or
INTELLIGENCE SUMMARY.
(Erase heading not required.)

Place	Date	Hour	Summary of Events and Information	Remarks and references to Appendices
Near Ecurie	1/5/17		C.O Train attended lecture at ECURIE on the Yukon Pack to the Tank from T/Lieut S.A Middleton. RN returned off Leave	
	2/5/17		The instructional class for Infantry 1st line Transport ended Personnel of Instructional class returned to their units	
	3/5/17		T/Lieut J.A Middleton RN detached to Rhine Battn at Transport Officer T/Capt W.R Edgington RN remained detached to 189th Bde as Bde Transport Officer	
	5/5/17		5 Officers & 20 OR attended Parade Service for commemoration of 3rd year of war held by 1st Army at RANCHICOURT. C.O Train inspected wagons detached with Divnl Foundry & PERNES & Labour Coy at BEUGIN.	
	6/5/17		Visit to Tillwich & 17 OR left for BOULOGNE to draw remounts	
	7/5/17		Ride & Drive class commenced for a Junior NCO of the Divnl Train & for 1 NCO from each Field Ambulance.	

63rd (RN) Divisional Train

WAR DIARY
or
INTELLIGENCE SUMMARY.

Army Form C. 2118.

Place	Date	Hour	Summary of Events and Information	Remarks and references to Appendices
Near ECURIE	10/4/17		T/4/Lt 1469 2nd Lieut Cartmur. E. acc. wounded.	
"	11/4/17		11 Remounts arrived from BOULOGNE. CO. Train inspected transport of 190th M.G. Coy. Train HQ's moved from J.21.c.5.2. to G.32.b.3.7. Sheet 51.C	
"	13/4/17		ARRAS – SOUCHEZ Rd. Owing to the new instructional class for Junior NCO's was discontinued. T/Capt W.R. Aclington R.A.M. the latter officer took over command from 13/4/17 2 lt 88 Jutsum R.M. purchasing & regimenting officer. 2 lt Myc Further R.M. took over command of No. 1 Coy on	
"	14/4/17		1 Coy. 4 2/Lieut W6 Coote Dsm Train Transport of Shropshire Bath arrived Cotyven completed. Transport of 189th M.J. Coy	

63rd (RN) Divisional Train
Army Form C. 2118.

WAR DIARY
or
INTELLIGENCE SUMMARY.
(Erase heading not required.)

Place	Date	Hour	Summary of Events and Information	Remarks and references to Appendices
Mt Eerie	25/8/17		10 Royal Marine Reinforcements arrived. 8 NISSEN huts drawn. Two for each Coy.	
	28/8/17		3 NISSEN huts drawn for Train H.Qrs. Fire reinforcements arrived from BOULOGNE	
	29/8/17		That #F Coltier R.M. accidentally injured. Went to 149th Fd Ambulance & on to 21 C.C.S. Each Coy drew one NISSEN hut	
	31/8/17		T/Lieut V. King R.M. took over our command of 3 Coy vice T/Capt C.J. Chapman R.M. on return Courier. T/Capt C.J. Chapman R.M. & our Lorries conveyed from each Coy proceeded to ABBEVILLE to go through a return course	

A.P. Riddell
Lieut Colonel A.P.C.
Comdg 63rd (RN) Divn Train

63D Train Vol 17

Volume 16

N R Liddell
Lt. Col. A.S.C.
Commanding
63rd (RN) Divisional Train

Sept 30 - 1917.

Army Form C. 2118.

63rd (RN) Divisional Train

WAR DIARY
or
INTELLIGENCE SUMMARY.
(Erase heading not required.)

Place	Date	Hour	Summary of Events and Information	Remarks and references to Appendices
Nr ECURIE	2/9/17		T/Major T Holmes RM assumed command of No 1 Coy vice Lt Hunt Colonel to detail ASC who proceeded on leave to England. Two Junior NCO's sent to XIII Corps Training School. Parties for Instruction. They left by train on 1/9/13.	
	3/9/17 4/9/17		Coy drill. T/Lieut V Turing RM, MSSEN Hut having been accepted on probation as an observer in the Flying Corps proceeded to HQ1 RFC to go through strength of Divn Train. T/Lieut F Kellwell took over Command of No 2 Coy. Sgt Cornish ASC reported his arrival from the Base Loading at Railhead commenced 8.30am	
	6/9/17		No 1 Coy drew 2 MSSEN Huts, each Brigade Coy drew one MSSEN Hut	

WAR DIARY or INTELLIGENCE SUMMARY

Army Form C. 2118.

63rd (RN) Divisional Train

Place	Date	Hour	Summary of Events and Information	Remarks and references to Appendices
Near ECURIE	7/9		A Battery 317 Bde RFA returned to the Divn. The 223rd Bund Machine Gun Coy arrived & will be administered to by No 3 Coy.	
	8/9		T/Lieut A.H.H. Jayes RNR took over duties of Q.M. 188th Bde temporarily vice T/Lieut A.L Dugdale RNR on leave to England.	
	9/9		T/Capt W.R Irving-Levy RM took over command of No 4 Coy from T/Lieut AS Stark RM on his return from leave. No 1 Coy was in the company workshop on hours back competition & No 3 Coy was second. T/Capt L.B.G. Andrew proceeded to 1st Army Rest Camp.	
	14/9		Three Remounts received	
	15/9		T/Capt L.B.G. Andrew returned from 1st Army Rest Camp	
	16/9		T/Capt L.M. Murdoch RM proceeded on six months leave	

Army Form C. 2118.

63rd (RN) Divisional Train

WAR DIARY
or
INTELLIGENCE SUMMARY.
(Erase heading not required.)

Place	Date	Hour	Summary of Events and Information	Remarks and references to Appendices
ECURIE	18/9		T/Capt L.B.B. Sutton RM attached to No 3 Coy. T/Lieut JA Middleton RM took over duties of SO 188th Bde. T/Lieut HH Sayer RM " " " " " " 189th Bde. affiliating point moved to G 2 c 7.8 shut S.16. T/Capt LM Mumford RM proceeded on one month's special leave. Lieut B Allard RM took over his duties of S.O. Divn' Troops.	
	19/9		Lieut Colonel AR Dolbell having returned from leave resumed command of the Divn Train. T/Lieut JA D'Ugan resumed duties of SO 188th Bde. T/Lieut JA Middleton resumed duties of T/Capt F Collins struck off strength of Divn Train from 10/9/17. Transport returned SMV when working C.O. Train motored SMV when looking for suitable billets for Coys.	
	20/9			

Army Form C. 2118.

63rd (C.N.) Divisional Train

WAR DIARY
or
INTELLIGENCE SUMMARY.
(Erase heading not required.)

Instructions regarding War Diaries and Intelligence Summaries are contained in F. S. Regs., Part II and the Staff Manual respectively. Title pages will be prepared in manuscript.

Place	Date	Hour	Summary of Events and Information	Remarks and references to Appendices
Near ECURIE	21/9/17		No 2 Coy Less Baggage Section moved to TINQUES. Baggage wagons sent to units.	
	22/9/17		No 2 Coy refilled on TINQUES - CHELERS road & moved to ROCOURT.	
	23/9/17		Refilling Point 188th Bde changed to ROCOURT. No 4 Coy moved to LA COMTE on Baggage Section. Lieut. E.M. Potter RM reported from HQ Base Depot & posted to 1 Coy.	
	24/9/17		No 3 Coy moved to VANDELICOURT (environs) 190th Bde refilled at windmill FREVILLER. Train HQ's moved to SAVY. 189th Bde refilled at LA COMTE.	
	25/9/17		at VANDELICOURT. 190th Bde refilled at BETHENCOURT. 189th Bde refilled at BETHENCOURT.	
	27/9/17		Major C.S. Fatzgerson RM reported to the train for 2 days for instruction to be attached for instruction.	

Army Form C. 2118.

63rd (RN) Divisional Train

WAR DIARY
or
INTELLIGENCE SUMMARY
(Erase heading not required.)

Place	Date	Hour	Summary of Events and Information	Remarks and references to Appendices
SAVY	29/9/17		Clothing commenced. Major C.S. Farquharson DSO ceased to be attached to the Divl Train. T/Lieut E.M. Potter RN transferred from 1 Coy to 4 Coy to HQ.	
	29/9/17		150 Bch. Soyer Camp Kettles No perfect no serviceable, from 9th Divisne Park & distributed as follows, 1 Coy to HQ 2 Coy to HQ & Coy to HQ 2/HD	

ARidwell
Lieut Colonel ASC
Commandg 63rd (RN) Divnl Train

63D Train
J 1 15

War Diary

Volume No. 17

October 1917.

A R Liddell
Lt. Col. A.S.C.
Commanding
63rd (RN) Divisional Train.

WAR DIARY
or
INTELLIGENCE SUMMARY.

Army Form C. 2118.

63rd (RN) Divisional Train

Place	Date	Hour	Summary of Events and Information	Remarks and references to Appendices
SAVY	1/10/17		2/Lieut W Robotti MC RM reported for duty with Divnl Train from 189th Inf Bde. Dvn notified to mobilise. CO Train motored ahead to WORMHUDT to settle Refilling Points & get acquainted with forward areas.	
WORMHUDT	2/10/17		The Dvn commenced entraining for Vth Army. Following system of supplies was adopted:- Rations for consumption 2/10/17 & 3/10/17 were delivered to all units on 1/10/17. Rations for consumption 4/10/17 were loaded on supply wagons early on 2/10/17 loaded then supply wagons to entrain with their unit. As MT section of D.A.C. do not entrain till late 3/10/17 they were rationed for consumption	

Army Form C. 2118.

63rd (R.N.) Divisional Train

WAR DIARY
or
INTELLIGENCE SUMMARY.
(Erase heading not required.)

Instructions regarding War Diaries and Intelligence Summaries are contained in F. S. Regs., Part II. and the Staff Manual respectively. Title pages will be prepared in manuscript.

Place	Date	Hour	Summary of Events and Information	Remarks and references to Appendices
WORMHOUDT	5/9/14		Some Sqn arrive WORMHOUDT. 2 Coy FAROL2H except Sgt g.n.c.s.s. + 1 1 m War ZEGNEZEELE. Going to Brook track maintained (a) 5 Coy moves to wrong camp & was wrongly informed entering refuting into Wagt. 2 Rifleman short of Rum & took over amount for 1 n.c.o. + 24 ls. [?] for unaided ridge	
	6/9/14		Coy arrived at F.O.h. 6 m.2. at appendix comm... from the Division and...	
	8/9/14			
	10/9/14		No. 4 Coy moved to EISCSR Sheet 29 No. 1 Coy arrived in POPERINGHE Debounces at PESELMOEK & moved to 23 a 58. Sheet 27.	
	11/9/14			
	21/9/14		2 Sgts + 4 Opls + 2 orderlies arrived from K.R. Base Depot H.T.T.S.	

Army Form C. 2118.

WAR DIARY
or
INTELLIGENCE SUMMARY.
(Erase heading not required.)

63rd M.G. Divisional Train

Instructions regarding War Diaries and Intelligence Summaries are contained in F.S. Regs., Part II. and the Staff Manual respectively. Title pages will be prepared in manuscript.

Place	Date	Hour	Summary of Events and Information	Remarks and references to Appendices
WORMHOUDT	13/10/17		8 Plts MM arrived from ASC Base Depot H'te	
"	16/10/17		1 Fam G/L MM arrived from ASC Base Depot. No 1 Coy moved to new BRIELEN	
	17/10/17		No 1 Coy drew 9th Dunl Park at	
	19/10/17		REIGERS BURG" & dumps) at Q 28 d 5.5. sheet 28.	
"	21/10/17		No 3 Coy moved T/heat S M Potter arm No 9 Coy transferred to No 1 Coy & meet Officer i/c of taking water to St JULIEN T/heat Gallant M2h transferred to No 4 Coy as J.O. 19.0th by God T/heat WL Bob 4th MM No 1 Coy transferred to No 2 Coy No 2 Coy moved to H 3 cd 7.7 sheet 27 moon	
"	22/10/17		VLAMERT IN GHE taking over from 16S Coy ASC 9th Dunl Train	
"	23/10/17		No 2 Coy delivered two extra days rations less forage to most units of 58th Divn Group.	

Army Form C. 2118.

WAR DIARY
or
INTELLIGENCE SUMMARY.
(Erase heading not required.)

63 U.K./M.T./Divisional Train

Instructions regarding War Diaries and Intelligence Summaries are contained in F.S. Regs., Part II. and the Staff Manual respectively. Title pages will be prepared in manuscript.

Place	Date	Hour	Summary of Events and Information	Remarks and references to Appendices
WORMHOUDT	23/10		No 4 Coy moved to H.Q. of 7.7. shut 28 taking over from 107 Coy A.S.C. 9th Divl Train. No 3 Coy myself & return moved to Bivouacs on QRIEJEN – VLAMERTINGHE M at B 29 c shut 25. Refilling point for 188th Bde group moved to B 29 c shut 28. Two days rations delivered to Food Battn.	
"	24/10		No 2.3.4 Coy drew from Railhead by Ham Transport. Refilling point for 189th Bde group moved to B29C shut 28 & for 190th Bde group to H3Q99 shut 28. Two days rations were delivered to Food Battn.	
"	25/10		Train H.Qs & No 3 Coy moved to H3d 77 shut 28 Delivered two days rations to Food Battn.	
"	26/10		Delivered to 188th Bde for consumption 26/10/17 B.C.I not usual rations but undecreen	
nr VLAMERTINGHE	27/10		Delivered action days rations to Hawke Battn & 19th Bde Delivered action days rations to NELSON Battn.	

2353 Wt. W2544/1454 700,000 5/15 D. D. & L. A.D.S.S. Forms/C 2118.

Army Form C. 2118.

WAR DIARY
or
INTELLIGENCE SUMMARY.
(Erase heading not required.)

63rd (RN) Divisional Train

Place	Date	Hour	Summary of Events and Information	Remarks and references to Appendices
near VLAMERTINGHE	29/10 31/10		One O.R. Wounded. The following large formations are now being thrown in addition to units of 63rd (RN) Divn. 1st Divnl Artillery 2nd Divnl Artillery 58th Divnl Artillery 64th Bde A.F.A. 155th Bde A.F.A. Making a total strength of approximately 28,000 all ranks 13,500 animals. For the last four nights Divnl Train have been bombed at night during the day a few shells have dropped in or about the camps. A.R.Knapp Lieut Colonel A.S.C. Commdg 63rd (RN) Divnl Train	

63ᴅ Train Vol 19

War Diary.

Volumn. 18.

November. 1917.

A.P.Russell
Lt. Col. A.S.C.
Commanding
63ʳᵈ R.N. Divisional Train.

WAR DIARY
or
INTELLIGENCE SUMMARY.
(Erase heading not required.)

Army Form C. 2118.

63rd (RN) Divisional Train

Place	Date	Hour	Summary of Events and Information	Remarks and references to Appendices
near VLAMERTINGHE	2/11/17		T/Capt C.L. Chapman temporarily attached Train Hqs. T/Capt W.E. Cook was temporarily assumed command of No 3 Coy	
	3/11/17		No 4 Coy moved to F.27 & 29 sheet 28 190th Bde group drew by lorry from Railhead	
L 46 5.55 sheet 27	5/11/17		Train Hqs moved to L.46 3.55 sheet 27 No 3 Coy moved to L 23 a 5.5 sheet 27 Refilling point for 190th Bde group moved F.27 & 29	
POPERINGHE	7/11/17		Refilling Point for 189th Bde group moved to F.21 c 6.5 sheet 27 T/Capt J.T. Greig RN arrived from A.S.C. Base Depot with St 9th & 6th Nos 1 & 4 T/Lt J Young RN attached to No 4 Coy No 2 Coy moved to L 23 a 5.5 sheet 27 Coy drew from Railhead PROVEN A.T.	
	9/11/17		189th Bde group refilling point moved to L 23 a 5.5 sheet 27 190th Bde group refilling point moved to F.21 c 6.8 sheet 27	

Army Form C. 2118.

63rd (W.R) Divisional Train

WAR DIARY
or
INTELLIGENCE SUMMARY.
(Erase heading not required.)

Place	Date	Hour	Summary of Events and Information	Remarks and references to Appendices
Near POPERINGHE	10/10/17			
near LEDERZEELE	11/10/17		No 3 Coy moved to WINNEZEELE area. Train H.Qrs moved to near LEDERZEELE. No 3 Coy moved to near RUBROUCK	
	12/10/17		No 2 Coy moved to WINNEZEELE area. No 4 Coy moved to D 13 a 3, 5. Tpr/Cpl Balfour R'rn admitted to 63rd CCS	
	13/10/17		No 3 Coy drawn by H.T. from Railhead. 1st line transport obtaining from Refilling Point. Tpr/Cpl C. Chapman over duties over duties of adjudant Capt 40/17 Millward of AHC on leave	
	14/10/17		No 2 Moved to H 23 a 7.9	
	17/10/17		No 2 & 4 Coy drawn by H.T. from Railhead. No 2 Coy delivers supplies 190 Bde, drawn from Refilling Point by 1st line Transport. Trans-A.E Shorter R'rn Sick. T/Sub Lieut-W Watson RNVR Hawke Ball attached to No 4 Coy for Transport course	
	18/10/17		T/Capt W. Tisley R'rn Shrick M/S establishment of Train from 17/10/17	

2353 Wt. W2544/1454 700,000 5/15 D. D. & L. A.D.S.S. Forms/C. 2118.

WAR DIARY or INTELLIGENCE SUMMARY

Army Form C. 2118.

(3rd (M) Stationary Train

Place	Date	Hour	Summary of Events and Information	Remarks and references to Appendices
LEDERZEELE	18/11/17		T/Lieut HE Skolfield RMO No 4 Coy admitted to No 13 CCS.	
	20/11/17		S/1718 Pte (A/Sergt) G.H. Crank R.H. (2nd Ing Sucd Amt-) awarded Military Medal. T/Lieut G F Killweek placed on Sick List (16/11/17) T/Lieut. G.F. Killweek taken off Sick List 20/11/17 No 2 Coy horses from H.23.a.7.9 (Sht. 3) to A.16.a.7.4 (Sht. 28) 188 Bde Refilling Point to A.16.a.7.4 (Sht. 28)	
	22/11/17		No 2 Coy drew by H.T. from PESELHOEK. Rations.	
	23/11/17		No 2 Coy drew rations to make up Baggage wagon. T/Capt V.C. Newman RAMC assumes duties of Major of 187 Bde, having returned off leave. T/Capt L.B.B. Guttim RAMC ceases to perform duties of S.O. 187 Bde.	
	24/11/17		No 3 Coy horses from H.5.a.15 (Sht-2.7) to H.23.a.7.9 (Sht 27)	
	26/11/17		T/Capt LBB Guttim RAMC are Lieutenant of No 2 Coy fm T/Lieut ST. Mirabelle RH	
	28/11/17		G.O.C. inspected transport of No. 3 u Coy. No 3 Coy moved to NOUVEAU MONDE and May toy to HOUTKERQUE.	
Near to PERINGHE	29/11/17		Capt Hon in S.J. Mullholland A.S.C. resumed duties of Adjutant. Train HQ moved to near PERINGHE on PROVEN-POPERINGHE Rd F.27 b.2.9 Sht. 27 No 1 Coy moved to F.27 b.2.9 Sht. 27	

Army Form C. 2118.

63rd (N.W.) Divisional Train

WAR DIARY
or
INTELLIGENCE SUMMARY.
(Erase heading not required.)

Place	Date	Hour	Summary of Events and Information	Remarks and references to Appendices
POPERINGHE	30/11		No 4 Coy moved to L4 & 57 about 2p T/Capt L. Jowing RM No 4 Coy took over duties of D.A.D.M.S. vice 2/Lieut L. M. Murdoch from attached Train Hqs	

A. Riddell
Lieut Colonel ASC
Commdg
63rd (N.W.) Divnl Train

63 D Train
Vol 20

December War Diary
　　Volumn No. 19.

Jan 1/1918

John MacMichael
Capt & Adjt.
for Major. A.S.C.
Commanding
63rd (RN) Divisional Train

Army Form C. 2118.

WAR DIARY
or
INTELLIGENCE SUMMARY.
(Erase heading not required.)

63rd (N.) Divisional Train

Place	Date	Hour	Summary of Events and Information	Remarks and references to Appendices
Root	1/12/17		T/Capt C.L Chipman OM resumed command of No 3 Coy	
POPERINGHE	2/12/17		T/Capt W.E Cook OM returned to duty with No 1 Coy.	
"	3/12/17		Co. SSO selected refilling points for their Divisions in	
			School Camp Hotel Camp, & HOUTKERQUE.	
			T/Major E.C Sherman ASC proceeded on leave. T/Lieut M.	
			Murdoch OM took over duties of SSO.	
"	6/12/17		No 4 Coy Train moved to GODEWAERSVELDE area	
	7/12/17		188th Bde Group drew from 63rd Divn'l Pack	
			The Bdes are now in their correct Bde groups	
			ready for entrainment at 11 hours notice.	
	8/12/17		C.O. Train motored to new area. 13 Reinforcements	
			arrived. Instructions No. 107 issued to 3rd Army	
			The Division moved by No 2 Coy to BEAULENCOURT	
	9/12/17		V th Corps. BAPAUME area. No 4 Coy to ROCQUIGNY	
			No 3 Coy to BARASTRE No 4 Coy to ACHIET LE PETIT	
	10/12/17		Train HQ to ACHIET LE PETIT	

Army Form C. 2118.

WAR DIARY
or
INTELLIGENCE SUMMARY.
(Erase heading not required.)

63rd (R.N.) Divisional Train

Place	Date	Hour	Summary of Events and Information	Remarks and references to Appendices
ACHIET LE PETIT	11/12/17		The Divnl Train drew by H.T. from Railhead ROCQUIGNY. No.3 Coy moved to ETRICOURT area, lorries drew from Railhead for 189th Bde group	
	12/12/17		No. 3 & 4 Coy moved to LE MESNIL area lorries 188th & 190th Bde Groups drew from Railhead	
	13/12/17		Train HQ & No 2 Coy moved to LE MESNIL area 188th & 190th Bde Groups drew by lorry from Railhead T/Lieut Sgt. Middleton R.Am. No 2 Coy was placed on sick list 12/12/17 & struck off str 17/12/17 T/Capt F Collins R.A.M reported from A.C. Rouen Depot & posted to No 4 Coy on S.O. 190th Bde 10/12/17 T/Lieut O Attwood R.Am No 2 Coy transferred to No 2 Coy as Transport Subaltern 13/12/17. T/Lieut D.L. Notcutt R.Am transferred from HQ to 4 Coy	
LE MESNIL 0.35.d Sheet 57 C	14/12/17			

Army Form C. 2118.

WAR DIARY
or
INTELLIGENCE SUMMARY.
(Erase heading not required.)

by ? R/? Divisional Train

Place	Date	Hour	Summary of Events and Information	Remarks and references to Appendices
LE MESNIL	16/14/?		All Bde Group Refilling Points are situated at LE MESNIL located N.W. of the Quartermaster Stores and of F/W	
	17/19		Co Train & T/Lieut C.L. Chapman are sent as members of a G.C.M.	
	19/14/?		Railhead changed to YPRES T/Major E.C. Thurman ASC returned off leave	
	20/19		T/Major E.C. Thurman ASC resumed duties of SSO vice T/Capt L.M. Murdoch who was owing to the change in refilling points railhead refilling points have been moved more forward in the ETRICOURT area 189th & 190th Bde Group Refilling Points were bombed one OR- J & Coy Supply Detail wounded at duty & one OR 3 Coys Supply Detail wounded - died of wounds on admittance to CCS. A small quantity of supplies were damaged clarification has been made to home supplies replaced Coast to home supplies replaced	

2353 Wt. W2544/1454 700,000 5/15. D.E.& L. A.D.S.S. Forms/C. 2118.

Army Form C. 2118.

WAR DIARY
or
INTELLIGENCE SUMMARY.
(Erase heading not required.)

Instructions regarding War Diaries and Intelligence Summaries are contained in F. S. Regs., Part II. and the Staff Manual respectively. Title pages will be prepared in manuscript.

63 (2/N) Divisional Train

Place	Date	Hour	Summary of Events and Information	Remarks and references to Appendices
LE MESNIL	23/12		179 Bde AFA Train section attached to No 4 Coy C.O. Train visited DDST re system of AFA Bdes Train Section	
	24/12		[illegible]	
	25/12		No 1 Coy arrived. Then precautions put into force but ceased to be attaken to for Div worthily to 61 Divn for rations the I by Ash troops drew by light railway from Audruiu a deriver upon EWS No 1 Coy drew by M.T. from Rietteur	
	26/12		Co train proceed on line to Esquerd A Major C.C. Transport ASC assumed command of Divnl Train	
	27/12			

John Mulholland
Captain & Major
Comm'd 63 (2/N) Divn Train

WAR DIARY
or
INTELLIGENCE SUMMARY

Army Form C. 2118.

63rd CRA Summer Camp

Place	Date	Hour	Summary of Events and Information	Remarks and references to Appendices
A Division Hythe	7/7/13		7th A.F.A. moved at 1 MESNIL causing articulation ASC Base Depot to 6 A.F.A. 6 OR 8pm assumed command of the last wear a Posture ASC train to southern 7 A.F.A. to R ASC to APA Beds Army & 7th Corps inspected Durst Train Camp H.Q. Shops inspected Screw Train by self no Shop needed that compts between 1 & 2 tops Flagstaff Beechmann RM Branch off to lookout	
	8/7/13		1am Col. Mitchell All returned off train maneuver command of Durst Train 7/8 & A.F.A. together The Sum for Brigham train to cars at last 6–2/16 Bels inspected by the Long am 31/7/13 returning to Barrow for cab fires cer 11 Jones the detail of wagons for the days has been about 45 J.S mules 25	

WAR DIARY
or
INTELLIGENCE SUMMARY.
(Erase heading not required.)

Army Form C. 2118.

Place	Date	Hour	Summary of Events and Information	Remarks and references to Appendices
Le MESNIL	16/4/18		A considerable amount is running through. A certain amount of Ghahama Biscuit Train also a D.H.V.S. inspection Farm of Meurgy on No 1 & No 3 Coys attached to No 1 Coy. Allotted to 77th MT Bde stables have now been erected by all Coys. Wood is being drawn from MANANCOURT Forest daily when wagons are available. 3rd complete turnout returned to No 2 Coy Party from being attached with Corps Fred Party	by 5th Cav Divisional Train
	17/4/18		No 4 Coy drew by H.T. from Rainhiel & dumped at BEAUENCOURT. No 2 Coy delivered to 19th Bde front today to No 2 & No 3 Coys	
	21/4/18			
	24/4/18		In HQ moved to BARCOURT Nos 2 & 3 BARASTRE No 1 & 4 BEAULENCOURT. No 3 & 4 drew by H.T. from Rainhiel 9 dumps of No rations deliv to 19 & 18 Bde this day	

Army Form C. 2118.

WAR DIARY
or
INTELLIGENCE SUMMARY.
(Erase heading not required.)

63rd (RN Division) Train

Place	Date	Hour	Summary of Events and Information	Remarks and references to Appendices
BANCOURT	23/1/18		Nos 2.3.4. Coy all drew by M.T. from Railhead FREMICOURT. The Div. Train is feeding the 2nd Div. Artillery which the 2nd Div. Train is feeding the 63rd (RN) Div. Artillery	
	25/1/18		2/Lieut. & Adjt. Hon H.J. Mulholland HSL proceeded on 4 days official leave to Le Treport. Count has sent 2/Lt. J.M. Murdoch RM to carry over acting Adjutant during his absence.	
	29/1/18	8 AM	11 Remounts (10 H.D. and 1 Rider) arrived at BAPAUME for Div. Train.	
		11 AM	C.O. inspected 1st Line Transport of 223 M.G. Coy	
	30/1/18	2:30 AM	C.O. inspected 1st Line Transport of 1/4 K.S.L.I. 2/Lieut & Adjt. Hon H.J. Mulholland HSC returned off official leave to Le TREPORT. C.O. inspected 1st Line Transport of 6th Bed. Regt & 7th Royal Fusiliers	
	31/1/18			

A.R. Liddell
Lieut Colonel ASC
Commdg. 63rd (RN) Divn'l Train

War Diary.

63rd (RN) Divisional Train.

February Volumn 21.

1/3/18

John N Mulholland
Capt & A/Adjt for
Lt. Col. A.S.C.
Commanding
63rd (RN) Divisional Train.

Army Form C. 2118.

WAR DIARY
or
INTELLIGENCE SUMMARY.
(Erase heading not required.)

63rd (N) Divisional Train

Place	Date	Hour	Summary of Events and Information	Remarks and references to Appendices
BANCOURT	1/2/18		Capt J.M. Buchanan RM took over duties of Supply officer. 188th Inf Bde visit T/Sgt A.L. Dugan RM to try an Transport mutation	
	2/2/18		C.O. Train sat on Court of Enquiry as President on loss of Sim boots at H.Q. 188th Inf Bde	
	3/2/18		C.O. Train inspected Train Transport allotted to 1/4 & 5/1 Myself section completed turnouts allotted to this unit transferred to 1/9 M D vis Train.	
	4/2/18		C.O. Train inspected 1st Line Transport of 1st cordist Rifle & 190th M.G. Coy.	
	5/2/18		C.O. Train inspected 1st line Transport 1st RM Batn & Hown Baton. 90R reported from Bde including 1 Foord Serg	
	6/2/18		C.O. Train inspected 1st Line Transport of Anson Batn	
	7/2/18		C.O. Train inspected 1st Line Transport of 2nd RM Baton 188th M.G. Coy. T/Lieut HStocks RM & QR proceed to ROSEVILLE to train remounts T/Capt JW Buchanan on detail for 14 days to V Corps Troops Supply Column T/Capt RM Murdoch RM took over duties of S.O. 188 Bde.	

WAR DIARY or INTELLIGENCE SUMMARY

Army Form C. 2118.

63rd (RN) Divisional Train

Place	Date	Hour	Summary of Events and Information	Remarks and references to Appendices
BMCOURT	8/7/15		C.O. Train inspected 1st line Transport of DRAKE Battn, NELSON Battn, HAWKE Battn, HOOD Battn.	
	9/7/15		C.O. Train inspected 1st line Transport of 189 M.G. Coy	
	11/7/15		C.O. Train inspected 1st line Transport of 148th (OM) Field Ambulance 12 H.D. & 1 Riden Remount arrived and stayed with No 4 Coy Train the night 4 gd wagons complete turnout Transferred from 189 2nd line Train	
	12/7/15		Two Pts RM reported as reinforcements — One sent to 189 Bde H.Q. & one sent to 149 Field Ambulance. Remounts were distributed as under. 3 HD to 1 Coy 3 HD to 2 Coy 4 HD to 3 Coy 4 HD to 4 Coy 1 Rdn to 4 Coy	
	13/7/15		190th Bde Group moved to Brickfield near YPRES. Drew rations Map 2 3/8 Coy sheet 57.C. also dumped at NEUVILLE-YPRES Road. drew by lorry No 3 Coy also dumped on NEUVILLE-YPRES Road.	

Army Form C. 2118.

WAR DIARY
or
INTELLIGENCE SUMMARY.
(Erase heading not required.)

63rd (N) Divisional Train

Place	Date	Hour	Summary of Events and Information	Remarks and references to Appendices
NEUVILLE	19/7/16		Train H.Qrs moved to NEUVILLE. Railhead changed to YTRES. 189 & 190th Coy Groups drawn by Light Railway. No 2 Coy drawn by M.T.	
"	17/7/16		T/Lt F. Collin RM took over command of No 2 Coy from this date inclusive vice T/Lt L. R. Boughton RM transferred to No 4 Coy & No 190 Hy Arm T/Capt W. Cook ARM took over command of No 1 Coy vice T/Major J. Turner RM who left for England to report to estimates.	
	19/7/16		T/Capt V.C. Newman RM took over temporary command of No 1 Coy vice T/Lt L Chapman on duty. Lieut Colonel Michell A&C left to 10 days leave to Paris. T/Major F.C. Newman ASC assumed command of the Divl Train. T/Lt M Buchanan RM returned hospital.	
	21/7/16 24/7/16		No 283 Coy moved to BERTINCOURT No 4 Coy to BUS T/Lieut F.A. McPherson ARM on sick list.	
	23 & 24/7/16 29/7/16			

Army Form C. 2118.

WAR DIARY
or
INTELLIGENCE SUMMARY.
(Erase heading not required)

63rd (ON) Divisional Train

Place	Date	Hour	Summary of Events and Information	Remarks and references to Appendices
NEUVILLE	23/7/15		Railhead changed to ROCQUIGNY all three Brigade Groups drew by light Railway. 153rd Bde Group drew at 9.15 & sheet 57c. 1 A+C Sgt Renfrew went to the Rail of the three Bde Groups drew rations by	
	24/7/15		1st line Transport from Refilling Point. 3 Remounts (Riding horses) arrived Transport detail now consist of 28 pairs of horses & 16 G.S. wagons complete turnouts on coys work	
	25/7/15		Drew two H.O. horses from 1/4th Batn. Worcester Regt. & issued them to No 2 Coy	
	27/7/15		Lieut Colonel M. Liddell A/C returned off leave from PARIS & resumed command of Divis Train F/Lieut F.S. McMahon R.M to 149th (om) Field Amb to on to 48th CCS sick	

A.R. Liddell
Lieut Colonel A/C
Commdg 63 (ON) Divis Train

War Diary.
63rd (RN) Divisional Train

March 1918.

Volume 22

A.R. Liddell
Lt Col. A.S.C.
Commanding
63rd (RN) Divisional Train

Apl 3/1918

WAR DIARY
or
INTELLIGENCE SUMMARY.
(Erase heading not required.)

Army Form C. 2118.

63rd (RN) Divisional Train

Place	Date	Hour	Summary of Events and Information	Remarks and references to Appendices
NEUVILLE	4/3/18		The Qr. M. & 2 Pts RM reported from Base. T/Major Holmes RM allowed to terminate his commission from 27/2/18 to take up a civil appointment.	
	9/3/18 10/3/18		2 Reprounts received from 5th Reserve Park. T/Capt Howd S/f 9/3/18 T/Capt L Chapman 11/3/18 - 25/3/18 ASC granted leave (father's) over duties of acting adjutant.	
	11.3.18		Lieut Z. G. MacPherson RM. Struck off Strength of 63 (RN) Bat from Authorit. D.R.O. No 3817 dated 10/3/18.	
	15.3.18		T/Capt Murdock RM having returned off leave 13/3/18 resumes duties of Requisitioning Purchasing Officer. Gunner N.C.O. arrived from A.S.C. Base Depot (H.T.S.) 13/3/18 and are posted to Corps as follows 7/630 Corpe Hutton W.Rn. to No 3 Coy. 2/1772 L/Corpe Riley E.P. Rn. No 1 Coy.	

Army Form C. 2118.

WAR DIARY
or
INTELLIGENCE SUMMARY.
(Erase heading not required.)

63M(RN) Divisional Train

Place	Date	Hour	Summary of Events and Information	Remarks and references to Appendices
NEVILLE	18/3/18		T/Lieut S.H. Booth RM & T/Lieut S.A. Webb RM reported from ASC Base Depot (HTS) and were posted as follows T/Lieut S.H. Booth to No 3 Coy, T/Lieut Barwell to No 4 Coy, T/Lieut Killowicks RM No 3 Coy. 63 (RN) Divl Train is still at N strength from 16/3/18. Heavy bombardment started about 4:30 am & continued all day. A few shells dropped in village occupied by No 2 & 3 Coys. (BERTINCOURT) Am drivers attached to Divisional HQ with Batn Transport were killed by shell fire. Two Cherriers ? Follows were brought down at Flers. Infantry Division. The Enemy dropped a few bombs in NEVILLE	
At —	21/3/18		Still very heavy bombardment again, a number of shells dropping in the village occupied by 2 & 3 at BERTINCOURT. No 4 Coy at BUS. No 2 & 4 Coy Spending most of the day in the open because of the Camps. No 3 Coy had one horse wounded by shell fire. S/Lieut Pk Foster RM SRMs about 11 PM were again turned to BARASTRÉ in afternoon. Train HQ moved to camp MESNIL (035A) about No 2 & 3 Coy moved to BARASTRÉ. Le TRANSLOY Spending the night on the side of the Le TRANSLOY-LESBOEUFS Road. Roads very congested. Enemy dropped some bombs near ROEQUIGNY. No 4 Coy were instructed to park up ambulance of 189 Bde at BOS & proceed to BARASTRÉ and camp near No 2 & 3 Coy. No 1 Coy were instructed to proceed to LE TRANSLOY about 12:30 AM. No 2 3 & 4 Coy were instructed to proceed to Le TRANSLOY then being very slow owing to	

2353 Wt. W2544/1451 700,000 5/15 D.D.&L. A.D.S.S. Forms/C.2118.

Army Form C. 2118.

WAR DIARY
or
INTELLIGENCE SUMMARY.
(Erase heading not required.)

63rd (NN) Divisional Train

Place	Date	Hour	Summary of Events and Information	Remarks and references to Appendices
NEUVILLE	22/3/18		Congestion of Traffic.	
LE TRANSLOY	23/3/18		Railhead LES ROCQUIGNY. All coys of the Div. Train turned in a LE TRANSLOY - Rethier	
			BAPAUME filled from Railed by Stran Transport after the supply wagons had un-loaded. Amm'n dumped. The first line transport had to draw from Rafilly point's after drawing from Railhead. No 12.3.4 Coys proceeded to BAZENTIN-LE-GRAND also THQ. moved to TRANSLOY - LE BOEUFS - GINCHY - LONGUEVAL. T/Capt T. Gorring Rm. returned. H. Leave and took over duties of	
BAZENTIN-LE-GRAND	24/3/18		Supply Offr. Asst. Prov. Troop from T/Lieut W.L. Robott Rm. to transport duties No1 Coy. Apm from Railhead ALBERT 4 horry and dumped. In the DERNANCOURT - ALBERT Road. Supply wagons refilled after delivering supplies. Said Troops have a lot of difficulty in finding the location of Brit ARTY. Brans nature to the RFA. stores dumped. No1 Coy lost 2 wagons destroyed by bomb. 5 H.D. Horses killed. 1 horse miss wounded (S/2420 Pte Spindell Pan Rh. N°183 Gun Cameron B.I.A. Batt. DIV. Rdm. RFA. 915815 Gm. Finigg. BEDDALL.317 Brig RFA. These hur m wounded in the night 24/25). The army horses carps when have found the roads the Div. Train spent the night at DERANCOURT (horses of N°24 Cay E30A 80. T.H.Q. N°182 Corps E30A 80)	
DERANCOURT	25/3/18		Apm from Railhead CORBIE 4 loop. and dumped at LEALVILLERS (O23c4). St. Div. Tram moved to BOUZINCOURT, 11AM then to LEALVILLERS at 6:30 PM.	

Army Form C. 2118.

WAR DIARY
or
INTELLIGENCE SUMMARY.
(Erase heading not required.)

63rd (R.N.) Divisional Train

Place	Date	Hour	Summary of Events and Information	Remarks and references to Appendices
LEALVILLERS	26/3/18	4 p.m.	Drew from Railhead PUCHVILLERS, and dumped at LEALVILLERS (023066) Very little water for horses, had three wells & drink ponds	
LEALVILLERS	27/3/18	4 p.m.	Drew from Railhead PUCHVILLERS and dumped at PUCHVILLERS (N256) The dump dumped in location (N256). No movement in the water supply.	
PUCHVILLERS	29/3/18		Drew from Railhead ROSEL 4 horses and dumped at PUCHVILLERS (N256) from 28/3/18 onwards. Water supply for horses still bad.	
	30/3/18		No 1 Coy moved to locations le Soudet - Rations per(?) to Nel Troops 29/3/18 onwards le Soudet. T/Capts Adjt Hon Mr G.J. Mulholland ASC returned off leave	

A. Rhodes
Lieut-Colonel ASC
Comondg 63rd (RN) Divnl Train

Vol 24

War Diary.

63rd (RN) Divisional Train.

April. 1918   Volumn 23

May 1 - 1918.

V R Liddell
Lt Col A.S.C.
Commanding
63rd (RN) Divisional Train.

Army Form C. 2118.

WAR DIARY
or
INTELLIGENCE SUMMARY.
(Erase heading not required.)

(3)(M) Divisional Train

Place	Date	Hour	Summary of Events and Information	Remarks and references to Appendices
near PUCHEVILLERS	1/9/18		Majt Hon'ble G.J. Mulholland ASC resumed duties of Adjutant	
"	2/9/18		Tt/Capt C L Chapman RM resumed duties of O.C. 3 Coy	
"	3/9/18		Tt/Capt V C Newman RM resumed duties of S.O. 189th Inf Bde	
			No 1 Coy moved from PERNOIS to billets near PUCHEVILLERS	
PUCHEVILLERS	4/9/18		HQ moved into PUCHEVILLERS Nos 2 & 3 Coy moved to near RAINCHEVAL	
	5/9/15		Nos 2 & 3 Coy drew from Railhead BELLE EGLISE by A.T.	
near TOUTENCOURT	6/9/18		HQ moved to near TOUTENCOURT No 1 Coy to near ARQUEVES Present system of supplies for 3 Inf Bdes proofs is one echelon composed of some supply section wagons & 20 Reserve Park wagons which ordinarily go to the Daily Train drawn from Railway & dump at Refilling Point. The other echelon which delivers to units is composed of some supply section wagons some other transport & some baggage section wagons which ordinarily 6 units.	

Army Form C. 2118.

WAR DIARY
or
INTELLIGENCE SUMMARY.
(Erase heading not required.)

63rd (N.M.) Divisional Train

Place	Date	Hour	Summary of Events and Information	Remarks and references to Appendices
near TOUTENCOURT	9/9/15		Despatched 12 (GTD) wagons for despatch to AHTD AUBEVILLE. There were surplus turnouts owing to 1 Battn Fm Rcde being disbanded. CO Train inspected the Horse transport of these Battns.	
"	11/9/15		No 1 Coy commenced drawing from Railhead by H.T. Baggage wagons sent out to Batteries RFA who were deficient of Baggage wagons. Refilling Points for the 3 Infy Bdl Groups changed to TOUTENCOURT - LEALVILLERS not 026 Sheet 57d Railhead was shelled & transport had to scatter. Time of loading at Railhead 6 a.m.	
	13/4/15		13 Remounts HD arrived	
	14/4/15			
	15/9/15		No 2 Coy moved to ARQUEVES for Divnl Train	
	17/9/15		attached were returned to 46th Labor Group. All reserve pack wagons	
	18/9/15		Railhead moved to ROSEL. Drew from Railhead by Lorry. T/Lieut SM Potter R.M. awarded M.C. for bravery in the field.	

2353 Wt W2544/1454 700,000 5/15 D.D.&L. A.D.S.S. Forms/C 2118.

Army Form C. 2118.

WAR DIARY
or
INTELLIGENCE SUMMARY.
(Erase heading not required.)

4th (M) Divisional Train

Place	Date	Hour	Summary of Events and Information	Remarks and references to Appendices
Near TOUTENCOURT	22/4/15		T/Lieut. G.F. Killick RM reported from England & posted to No 2 Coy. T/Lieut. P Allard RM transferred to No 1 Coy as 2nd in command. No 4 Coy moved to LA VICOGNE. 1 Wo RM & 7 Pts RM arrived as reinforcements. Board of officers held at Nov 253 Coys & 600n S. Smiths. A detachment of 1/1 Artists Rifles went to near	
"	24/4/15		ACHEUX for work thus necessitating No 4 Coy detaching one Supply Section wagon to No 2 Coy. No 4 Coy Officers was held at No 2 & 4 Coy to test shoeing smiths of 190 by HQ role	
"	25/4/15		R ADVS went & inspected all Coys	
"	26/4/15		Co Trans conducted 1st train transport of C&D Coys Divn Baton MC Corps. No 4 Coy moved from LA VICOGNE to old camp near route de court & shell H.V. small calibre fell in TOUTEN court but no jet.	

Army Form C. 2118.

63rd (N) Divisional Train

WAR DIARY
or
INTELLIGENCE SUMMARY.
(Erase heading not required.)

Instructions regarding War Diaries and Intelligence Summaries are contained in F. S. Regs., Part II. and the Staff Manual respectively. Title pages will be prepared in manuscript.

Place	Date	Hour	Summary of Events and Information	Remarks and references to Appendices
WAR TOOTENCOURT	27.4.15		C.O. Train inspected 1st line Transport of A & B Coys Divnl Battn M.G. Corps. 17 Otes Category B of Divnl Empl Coy reported last night to be attached also suitable a.v. leaders	
"	30.4.15		C.O. Train inspected 1st line Transport of X-2nd a.m. Battn prior to its departure to the Base	

A. Russell
Lieut Colonel ASC
Commdg
63rd (N) Divnl Train

Vol 25

War Diary.
      May 1918
         Volumn No 24.

                    A.R.Liddell
                    Lt Col. ASC
                      Commanding
                   63rd (RN) Divisional Train.

June 2nd/1918

ROYAL NAVAL
DIVISIONAL TRAIN.
No.
Date.

WAR DIARY
or
INTELLIGENCE SUMMARY.
(Erase heading not required.)

Army Form C. 2118.

63rd (N) Divisional Train

Place	Date	Hour	Summary of Events and Information	Remarks and references to Appendices
new TOUTENCOURT	2/5/18		Sent T/Lieut W L Roberts R.M & 9 O.R. to ABBEVILLE to draw remounts. C.O. Train motored to ABBEVILLE re remounts etc. T/Lieut A E Balfour R.M & T/Lieut M.T. Curnow R.M. reported their arrival from England.	
	4/5/18		Baggage Section horses sent to 223 Bde RFA for move returned same day.	
	5/5/18		10 HD Remounts arrived for Train.	
	7/5/18		Baggage Section horses sent to 317 Bde RFA for move No 4 Coy moved to ARG-VE VES Railway chang'd to ELUSE EPUSE – Div Train are No 4 Coy drew by H.T. Time of loading 2 a.m.	
	8/5/18		No 4 Coy drew from Railhead by H.T. Time of loading) 4 a.m. Train not in position until 5.20 am. From American Supply furly reported for instruc Dr Time of loading 4 a.m. at Railhead.	
	9/5/18			
	10/5/18		Time of loading Railhead 4 a.m. Train not in position until 7 a.m.	

T2134. Wt. W708—776. 500000. 4/15. Sir J. C. & S.

Army Form C. 2118.

WAR DIARY
or
INTELLIGENCE SUMMARY.
(Erase heading not required.)

63rd (RN) Divisional Train

Instructions regarding War Diaries and Intelligence Summaries are contained in F. S. Regs., Part II. and the Staff Manual respectively. Title pages will be prepared in manuscript.

Place	Date	Hour	Summary of Events and Information	Remarks and references to Appendices
Near TOOTENCOURT	11/5/16		Train of Coaches at Railhead 4 a.m. TOOTENCOURT was shelled from 6.20 am to 6.45 am. T/Capt A.E. Ralfour RM took over S.O. 155 & of RdR	
"	12/5/16		Train of Coaches at Railhead 2 a.m. T/Capt JM Richardson RM took over command of No 2 Coy from T/Capt Farlie RM who is transferred as 2nd in command. T/Lieut D Aitcock RM transferred from No 1 Coy to No 2 Coy.	
	13/5/16		Train of Coaches at Railhead 2 a.m. Four American Sergt attached to No 2 Coy returned to Depot H.Q.	
	14/5/16		Train of Coaches Railhead 2 a.m T/Lieut JF Killick RM No 2 Coy attached 63rd (RN) Divnl Baton M.G. Co/s under instruction.	
	15/5/16		Train of Coaches Railhead 2 a.m 190 & Inf Bde Rifling point bombed about	

Army Form C. 2118.

63(RN)Divisional Train

WAR DIARY
or
INTELLIGENCE SUMMARY.
(Erase heading not required.)

Place	Date	Hour	Summary of Events and Information	Remarks and references to Appendices
PONT TOUTENCOURT	15/9/17	3.30 a.m.	1 Bomb dropped about 100 yards from dump & 1 Bomb about 15 yards from dump. 1 OR 63rd D.E.C. att. No 4 Coy loader to 14th Wounded. 2 ORs killed, 1 OR supply Detail No 4 Coy severely wounded. 1 OR 249 Fld Coy R.E. att 4 Coy severely wounded. 1 OR supply Detail No 4 Coy slightly wounded "at duty". 1 OR D.E.C. att No 4 Coy loader to 14th Worcesters Battn slightly wounded "at duty". 1 HD horse wounded by Machine Gun fire from enemy aircraft.	
	16/9/17		Loading at Railhead Achonvellers been 5 a.m. Train did not arrive until 4 pm	
	17/9/17		Train of loading at Mailly 4 pm	
	18/9/17		Train of loading at Mailly 5 am	
	19/9/17		Train of London Railhd 5 am Voluntary Parade Divine Service 2 pm 11 Officers & 160 OR attended Rifle competition in afternoon	

Army Form C. 2118.

WAR DIARY
or
INTELLIGENCE SUMMARY.
(Erase heading not required.)

63rd (RN) Divisional Train

Place	Date	Hour	Summary of Events and Information	Remarks and references to Appendices
2nd or TOUTENCOURT	20/9/18		Train of Railhead 6 am - Loading commenced 9 a.m. 1 O.R. accidently gassed	
	21/9/18		Train of Railhead 4 am	
	22/9/18		Train of Railhead 7 a.m. T/Lieut JF Killwich returned to No 2 Coy from M.D. Ratts	
	23/9/18		Train of Railhead 4 am - commenced 5 am	
	24/9/18		Train of Railhead 4 a.m. T/Lieut JF Killwich proceeded to DOULLENS to be interviewed by officer of RAF C.O. Train set on court of enquiry at BERGUETTE	
	25/9/18		Train of Railhead 3 a.m.	
	26/9/18		Train of loading Railhead 3 am.	
	27/9/18		Train of loading Railhead 6am C.O Train went to ABBEVILLE to see A.H.T.D	
	28/9/18		Train of loading Railway 4 a.m. Railhead & Northern end of ARQUEVES shelled intermittly from 7.30 am to 12.30 pm. No casualties to Divl Train though one shell landed about 20 yards from coal dump.	

Army Form C. 2118.

63rd (R.N.) Divisional Train

WAR DIARY
or
INTELLIGENCE SUMMARY.
(Erase heading not required.)

Instructions regarding War Diaries and Intelligence Summaries are contained in F. S. Regs., Part II. and the Staff Manual respectively. Title pages will be prepared in manuscript.

Place	Date	Hour	Summary of Events and Information	Remarks and references to Appendices
Near TOUTENCOURT	29/5/18		1 O R wounded at duty loading at Railhead 1 a.m. No shelling at that hour.	
"	30/5/18		BELLE EGLISE Railhead closed down owing to shelling. Railhead changed to RAINCHEVAL - Time of loading midnight 29th/20th.	
"	31/5/18		Railhead changed to ROSEL - drew by lorry. 1 O R wounded at duty.	

A. Riddell
Lieut Colonel HC
Commdg
63rd (RN) Divnl Train

63 D Train Vol 26

War Diary.
63rd (RN) Divisional Train
June 1918
Volumn 25.

A R Liddell
Lt Col A.S.C.
commanding
63rd (RN) Divisional Train.

July 2/1918.

Army Form C. 2118.

WAR DIARY
or
INTELLIGENCE SUMMARY.
(Erase heading not required.)

[(Signed) W.M Divisional ??]

Place	Date	Hour	Summary of Events and Information	Remarks and references to Appendices
NR TOUTENCOURT	2/4/18		1 O.R. DAC attacked wounded	
	4/4/18		7/Lt L Killurich RM took over duties of Supply Officer. 189 Bde in T/Capt VC Newman proceeded on leave to England. No 3 Coy moved to VAL DE MAISON. No 4 Coy took over No 3 Coys old coy, on LEALVILLERS — TOUTENCOURT Road. 1 O.R. wounded by bomb from enemy aircraft.	
HERISSART	5/4/18		Tn Hq moved to HERISSART — No 2 Coy & VAL DE MAISON	
	6/4/18		No 1, 2 & 3 Coy drew by M.T. from Railhead ROSEL	
	7/6/18		Co Train inspected by Div Transport O. Anson Battn & 2/1 RIR	
	8/4/18		Co Train inspected at hrs Transport O R.M. Battn & arrival	
			14th Worcester Battn. 5 Reinforcement O.R. arrived	
	9/4/18		Co Train inspected at 14:5 (Pm) Field Ambulance	
	10/4/18		Co Train inspected 1st her Transport of Hawke & Hood Battns	

Army Form C. 2118.

WAR DIARY
or
INTELLIGENCE SUMMARY.
(Erase heading not required.)

63rd (N) Divisional Train

Place	Date	Hour	Summary of Events and Information	Remarks and references to Appendices
HERISSART	12/8/15		T/Major E C Sherrin BSO ASC proceeded on one months special leave to England. T/Capt D M Murdoch RW took over duties of acting SSO.	
	13/8/15		No 1 Coy held Coy Sports this day.	
	14/8/15		Nos 2 & 3 Coy held Coy Sports	
			3 HD horse Remounts arrived. C.O. Train proceeded	
	16/8/15		at 189 Inf Bde Sports	
			CO Train inspected Mn Transport of Divn	
			Scottish. CO Train & OC 226 Coy were introduced	
			to Coy's Commands 188th 1st Corps	
	17/8/15		CO Train inspected Transport of 149 Field Ambulance	
	19/8/15		4 Mules came up 2 for 1 Coy & 2 for 4 Coy	
	20/8/15		C.O. Train inspected 1st Lin Transport of 7th R.F. & 4th Beds	
	21/8/15		SOC Divn inspected Transport of the 3 Inf Bde Groups	
			CO Train accompanied GOC, SOC v Corps also present	
	22/8/15		No 4 Coy moved to O 4 d 22 sheet 57d	

Army Form C. 2118.

WAR DIARY
or
INTELLIGENCE SUMMARY.
(Erase heading not required.)

63rd (RN) Divisional Train

Place	Date	Hour	Summary of Events and Information	Remarks and references to Appendices
near RAINCHEVAL	23/9/15		Train HQ moved to near RAINCHEVAL No 2 & 3 Coy to ST HYPPOUNTE, ARQUEVES - LOUVENCOURT Road	
	24/9/15		T/Capt R.C. Newman RN having returned off leave resumed duties of S.O. 1 & 9 Role T/Lieut JP Tillurch RN Temporarily doing duties of R.O.	
	29/9/15		The Divnl Train is being severely handicapped by an epidemic of P.U.O. Being devoid of S.O. 1 O.R. with O.i/c O.R. in hospital & numerous men excused duty	

A. P. Wall
Lieut. Colonel A.S.C.
Commdg. 63rd (RN) Divisional Train.

Vol 27

War Diary
63rd (RN) Divisional Train

July 1918.   Volumn. No. 26

Aug. 1918

E. Chaman   Major A.S.C.
Commanding
63rd (RN) Divisional Train.

Army Form C. 2118.

WAR DIARY
or
INTELLIGENCE SUMMARY.
(Erase heading not required.)

63rd (RN) Divisional Train

Instructions regarding War Diaries and Intelligence Summaries are contained in F. S. Regs., Part II. and the Staff Manual respectively. Title pages will be prepared in manuscript.

Place	Date	Hour	Summary of Events and Information	Remarks and references to Appendices
RAINCHEVAL	6/7/15		C.O. Train inspected "Horse Transport of 150th (RN) Field Ambulance	
"	7/7/15		DADVS reported "very good" on Horse management of the Divnl Train	
"	9/7/15		CO Train inspected 1st Divnl Transport of 1/1. Artist Rifles	
"	4/7/15		T/Lt A L Dugan RM proceeded to LE TOUQUET for MP Course	
"	6/7/15		T/Lt S+ Middleton RM took over Temporary command of No 3 Coy vice T/Capt C Chapman RM to 3rd Army Ry Camp.	
	13/7/15		T/Major SC Sherman DSO ASC returned off leave & resumed duties of SSO	
	14/7/15			
	19/7/15		DDST 3rd Army inspected the Companies of the Divnl Train	
	24/7/15		CO Train inspected Rich & Divn class.	

Army Form C. 2118.

WAR DIARY
or
INTELLIGENCE SUMMARY.
(Erase heading not required.)

63rd (M) Divisional Train

Place	Date	Hour	Summary of Events and Information	Remarks and references to Appendices
RAINCHEVAL	27/7/15		T/Major E.C. Sherman DSO ASC assumed command of Divn'l Train. Lt Col A.A. Holdoll DSO ASC having proceeded on leave. E/Lt Col Chafiman RM assumed command of No 3 Coy having returned from 3rd Army Rest Camp	
"	25/7/15		No 2 Coy moved to BEAUQUESNE, No 3 Coy moved to PUCHEVILLERS.	
"	29/7/15		Nos 2 & 3 Coy drew by Horse Transport from railhead.	
"	29/7/15		188 & 189 Inf Bde Groups drew from Railhead by MT. Nos 2 & 3 Coys moved to AUTHIE T.H. of No 1 Coy	
PAS	31/7/15		Hotchkiss Gun Class for officers & NCOs in Divn Train commenced at Nos 3 & 2 Coys respectively	

E.C. Sherman Major ASC
Comnd'g 63 (RM) Divn'l Train

War Diary.

63rd (RN) Divisional Train
Aug 1918

Volumn. 27.

A R Liddell
Lt Col a.S.C.
Commdg
63rd (RN) Divisional Train

Aug 31/1918.

WAR DIARY
INTELLIGENCE SUMMARY.

(63rd(?) Divisional Train)

Place	Date	Hour	Summary of Events and Information	Remarks and references to Appendices
PAS	2/8/18		Hotchkiss Gun Class temporarily suspended owing to 5 clerks R.M. reported for A.S.C. Rein Depot HQ.	
RAINCHEVAL	4/8/18		T.H.Q. moved to near RAINCHEVAL. No.2 Coy to VAUCHELLES - ARGUEVE Rd. Nos 3 & 4 Coy to BEAUQUESNE. Supply sections entrained late in the afternoon as the troops move on night of 4/5th	
"	7/8/18		63rd Divnl Troops transferred from 21st Divnl Pack. 63rd Divnl Pack	
"	8/8/18		No 3rd Corps drew from RAILHEAD by HT. T.H.Q. moved to EBART FARM. No 1 Coy to PONTAY - TOUTENCOURT Rd. No 2 Coy to PONTAY - HERISSART Rd. near PONTAY. No.3 Coy to BEHENCOURT - BEAUCOURT near PONTAY. No 4 Coy to BEAUCOURT	
EBART FARM	8/8/18		Owing to the short notice of the move, rations had already been delivered in the morning of 8th to all units for consumption on the morning of 8th. Supply lorries had to return to units to pick up tonight's rations delivering to units in new area. Lorries were able to carry their rations	

Army Form C. 2118.

WAR DIARY
or
INTELLIGENCE SUMMARY.
(Erase heading not required.)

63rd (RN) Divisional Train

Place	Date	Hour	Summary of Events and Information	Remarks and references to Appendices
EBART FARM	night 8/9/18 9/9/18		It was only necessary in the Divisional Train to meet the foregt. Lorries drew from Rutland for all the Division. They dump at 6am. Wagons are loaded up but do not deliver until the evening in the Division. G.H.Q. Rations liable to not at our hour notice. D.H.Q. Groups however have their rations delivered to the moment as is the front of a sort they are able to carry their lorries. During the night several bombs were dropped in the proximity of T.H.Q. Owing to uncertainty of moving at short notice return on being different between 6 & 7.30 pm.	
	13/9/15 night 13/9/15 14/9/15		Nos 2,3,4 Coys moved to PAS & PANECOTE as usual respectively.	
	15 night 15/9/16		They moved to Camp nur PAS No 1 Coy moved to SARTON area	
PAS	16		No 1 Coy moved to COVIN.	
	17 245 9/18/9		No 3 Coy moved to AUTHIE	

Army Form C. 2118.

WAR DIARY
or
INTELLIGENCE SUMMARY.
(Erase heading not required.)

63rd (M) Divisional Train

Place	Date	Hour	Summary of Events and Information	Remarks and references to Appendices
PAS	night 19th/20th		Nos 3 & 4 Coys moved to PAS area.	
	20th		Delivered to fighting units iron rations covered from rations for consumption 21st in addition to rations for consumption 21st.	
	21st		HQrs & Nos 2 & 4 Coys moved to HENU Supply Sections of all Coys to SOUASTRE – COUIN Rd. Baggage wagons are being utilised for moving ammunition & carrying units necessitating baggage & supply wagons being dumped at Corps camps and being loaded up into Echelon on completion of delivery as not being loaded up into Echelon for consumption the following day, horses some days on rations not drawn from Railhead.	
	22nd		Nos 1 & 3 Coys delivered rations in the vicinity of BUCQUOY, all rations for the other Rds Coys being delivered in the vicinity of SOUASTRE	
	24th		Supply Sections moved to FONQUEVILLERS – SAILLY Rd.	

Army Form C. 2118.

WAR DIARY
or
INTELLIGENCE SUMMARY.
(Erase heading not required.)

(13th (M) Divisional Train)

Instructions regarding War Diaries and Intelligence Summaries are contained in F. S. Regs., Part II. and the Staff Manual respectively. Title pages will be prepared in manuscript.

Place	Date	Hour	Summary of Events and Information	Remarks and references to Appendices
PAS.	24 April		Lieut Col A.R. Idell D.S.O. A.S.C. returned off leave & assumed command of the Special Train.	
R. BUCQUOY	25th		Train H.Q. moved to between BUCQUOY & ACHIET-LE-PETIT. HQ No 1 Coy & Nos. 2.3 & 4 Coys (less Supply Sections) formed their Supply Sections on the FONQUEVILLERS - AILLY Road. All Coys moved to PIGEON WOOD. near ESSARTS.	
MIRAUMONT	29th		Nos 2.3 & 4 Coys moved to MIRAUMONT - ACHIET-LE-PETIT Rd. THQ moved to MIRAUMONT	
MIRAUMONT	30th		Drew from RAILHEAD MIRAUMONT by H.T. Railhead was shelled. No 2 Coy had 13 OR (including 7 Sgt party) wounded by a big shell dropping in their camp, 1 horse was killed & 6 horses ??? HD wounded & unfit to be worked.	
DOUCHY	night 30/31st		THQ moved to DOUCHY LES AYETTE. Nos 2.3 & 4 Coys to near BOIRY St RICTRUDE	

2353 Wt W2544/1454 700,000 5/15 D.D. & L. A.D.S.S. Forms/C 2118.

Army Form C. 2118.

WAR DIARY
or
INTELLIGENCE SUMMARY.
(Erase heading not required.)

63rd (RN) Divisional Train

Place	Date	Hour	Summary of Events and Information	Remarks and references to Appendices
BLAIREVILLE			Down from Railweil by M.T. T Hq moved to war BLAIREVILLE	

ARussell
Lieut Colonel ASC
Commdg
63rd (RN) Div'nl Train

63rd (RN) Divisional Train.

War Diary
September 1918.   Volumn no 28

A R Liddell
Lt Col A.S.C.
Commdg
63rd (RN) Divisional Train

Sept 30/1918.

Army Form C. 2118.

WAR DIARY
or
INTELLIGENCE SUMMARY.
(Erase heading not required.)

63rd (RN) Divisional Train

Place	Date	Hour	Summary of Events and Information	Remarks and references to Appendices
BLAIRVILLE	3/9/18		No 4 Coy had 3 horses killed 1 horse fall & wounded by bombs from G.A. also 1 G.S. wagon destroyed	
	3/9/18		Nos 2,3,4 Coy moved to near HENIN AUX COJEUL	
CROISILLES	4/9/18		THQ & 2,3,4 moved to near CROISILLES. 3 HQ came up for 2 Coy & HQ for 4 Coy.	
			THQ moved to BAVINCOURT. No 2 Coy to BEAUMETZ	
BAVINCOURT	7/9/18		No 4 Coy to BAILLEULVAL. No 3 Coy to BARLY	
"	9/9/18		10 O.Rs Reinforcement reported from Base	
"	10/9/18		No 4 Coy drew from Railhead	
"	11/9/18		No 2 Coy drew from Railhead by M.T. On motor car detached T.S.O. Div T/Lt/Lieut T/Major E.C. Stickman D.S.O. A.S.C. On Divisional RM & E Cook RSM proceeded on leave. T/Capt J.M Divisional RM took over duties of T/S.S.O. & T/Capt. P Attwell RTM took over duties of T/O.C. 1 Coy.	
"	12/9/18		C.O. Train inspected 1st line Transport of ANSON Battn.	
"	13/9/18		10 HQ horses received	
"	14/9/18		1 G.S. wagon received by DADOS from 4 Coy	
"	15/9/18		19.0.15 Adv Group drew from Railhead G Lorry	
"	16/9/18		No 4 Coy moved to near ST LEGER	

Army Form C. 2118.

63rd (RN) Divisional Train

WAR DIARY
or
INTELLIGENCE SUMMARY.
(Erase heading not required.)

Place	Date	Hour	Summary of Events and Information	Remarks and references to Appendices
ST LEGER	17/9/18		Train HQ moved to near ST LEGER. No 2 Coy & same place. 185 Bde Group drew by lorry. Railhead moved to BOISLEUX AU MONT. No 3 Coy moved to BELLACOURT.	
"	18/9/18		No 3 Coy moved to near ST LEGER.	
"	19/9/18		CO Train attended conference of Staff Captains at HQ's 63rd Divn. Nos 2, 3, 4 Coy drew by #7 from Railhead. delivered to Battns & Battns & Batty by Baggage section. Remaining units drew by their own Transport.	
"	20/9/18		Capt How Martin inspected horses of No 2 Coy. 2 Ctos arrived from AHTD for No 2 Coy.	
"	26/9/18		Drew by lorry from Railhead. No 2 Coy moved to soon 1 mile west of ECOUST-ST-MEIN. THQ No 2, 3 & 4 Coys moved & delivered two days rations & forage 1/2 r ST LEGER Rd to Fr. Transport on DOIGNIES-QUEANT Rd. consumption 27 & 28 Ensuing to two days delivered supplies for midway between two trains. No 2 Coy on authority of QDEANT. consumption 27 & 9 rations for consumption 28 & 9th	
nr ECOUST				

Army Form C. 2118.

63rd (RN) Divisional Train

WAR DIARY
or
INTELLIGENCE SUMMARY.
(Erase heading not required.)

Place	Date	Hour	Summary of Events and Information	Remarks and references to Appendices
ECOUST	26/9/18		Lorries dumping supplies for consumption 28th by the Companies on 26th up the Railhead	
"	27/9/18		6 baggage wagons were sent to Advanced D H Q on muck S.E. of PRONVILLE to move them across the CANAL DU NORD. 1 Baggage wagon was left with each unit – one Baggage wagon for each WT Station to Train lines for detail by D H Q. No 2 coy delivered supplies for consumption 28th to Signal Coy M.P. 1 Smile S.E of PRONVILLE. They did not deliver to units as they had already been delivered to their units on 26th. No 3 Coy delivered supplies for consumption 28th midway between MOREUIL & QUEANT. No 4 Coy delivered forage for consumption 28th to units midway between MOREUIL & QUEANT. Lorries dumped supplies for consumption 29th in afternoon at Corps Refilling Point near ECOUSTE. Forward Coal Dump was situated at DOIGNIES. T/Major E.C. Sherwood D.S.O A.S.C. returned off leave & Co adjutant visited Advanced D H Q 10 a.m.	

WAR DIARY or INTELLIGENCE SUMMARY

Army Form C. 2118.

63rd RN Divisional Train

Place	Date	Hour	Summary of Events and Information	Remarks and references to Appendices
near MOEUVRES	29/1/?		Railhead changed to VAULX VRAUCOURT. Try Hqrs & 3 Sqy Coys moved to ½ mile South of MOEUVRES. Adjutant & Lindsell arrived. 2 Fd. Amb. East of HAVRINCOURT & am & 2 unit TPD & Coys at GRAINCOURT at BOURLON lightening train when to move on. No 2 Coy delivered supplies Rations & their group Hqrs. No 2 field ambulance & SUCRERIE, 1 mile unit to ## units of GRAINCOURT. No 3 Coy delivered supplies to ## units of 189 Inf Bde. To 1 mile East of ANNEUX, supplies for East coy to SUCRERIE & supplies for and Bde to mile Eof. MOEUVRES. No 4 Coy delivered supplies to units of 190 Inf Bde to ½ miles East of MOEUVRES to the Fd Coy ½ mile Sof MOEUVRES. All Field ambulances had myth believed near LOUVERVAL. A cart horse was found about ½ mile South of MOEUVRES. A rein rgtd supply of cabbages is being sent up for troops the Army apparently not realizing that cabbages cannot be obtained by Infantry stranded present conditions. No 3 Coy had 1 O.R. very slightly wounded at duty.	

Army Form C. 2118.

WAR DIARY
or
INTELLIGENCE SUMMARY.
(Erase heading not required.)

63rd (RN Divisional Train)

Place	Date	Hour	Summary of Events and Information	Remarks and references to Appendices
near MOEUVRES	29/9/18		Div Train did not move. No 2 had 1 OR killed & 1 OR wounded by bomb when detached with Royal Irish Regt. No 3 Coy 1 OR wounded. No 2 Coy delivered supplies to 188Bde ½ a mile W. of FONTAINE-NOTRE-DAME in CAMBRAI Road. No 3 Coy DHQ group had supplies delivered to a mile East of GRAINCOURT. Royal Marine Battn only had forage delivered as they undoubled owing to casualties.	
	30/9/18		No 3 Coy delivered 189 Bde ½ a mile East of ANNEUX. No 4 Coy delivered 190 Bde a mile East of GRAINCOURT. Coys delivered to almost the same locations as yesterday. M.G. Battn a little E. of GRAINCOURT. DHQ group in CANTAING	

A. Rhodwell
Lieut Colonel A/C
Commdg
63 t (RN) Divnl Train

War Diary
63rd (RN) Divisional Train
October 1918   Volumn 29.

A.R.Riddell   Lt Col. A.S.C.
Commanding
63rd (RN) Divisional Train

Nov 2nd 1918.

Army Form C. 2118.

WAR DIARY
or
INTELLIGENCE SUMMARY.
(Erase heading not required.)

639th(M) Divisional Train

Place	Date	Hour	Summary of Events and Information	Remarks and references to Appendices
New MOEUVRES	1/10/18		Supplements sent up by baggage wagons to transport lines. Sun coln into reserve Infantry returning to their Transport lines.	
"	2/10/18		As much fresh meat as possible was sent to units.	
"	5/10/18		The CTO detached with Div HQ was returned to No 4 by. The Sun was to have moved to 1st Army Area but now has been cancelled.	
"	6/10/18		Winter time came into force. 1 CTO destroyed by bombs when attached to Drake Battn.	
"	7.10.18		New CTO wired for to replace casualty	
"	8.10.18		Railhead moved to VELU	
"	9.10.18		THQ moved to quit ECOUST. Sun 2.3 by to VAULX VRAUCOURT	
"	11.10.18		Sun moved by Tactical Train - 75 Sr Pet ann - Transport moved by road - BAILLEULMONT own	
ECOUST			moving by road to a staging camp at STATION Ration for convoy from 12th when allowed and THQ moved to RIVIERE	
			frost being delivered at staging camp. THQ to ST MICHEL - No 2 by to	
			Railhead moved to TINQUES + THQ to ST MICHEL - No 4 by to	
			RAMECOURT - No 3 by to PETIT HOUVIN - No 4 by to	
			BOSSURT ST LAURENT	
ST MICHEL	14.10.18		T/Panks E+C Sons & EC McGuidham own reinforcements arriving as reinforcements	

Army Form C. 2118.

WAR DIARY
or
INTELLIGENCE SUMMARY.
(Erase heading not required.)

63rd (R.N.) Divisional Train

Place	Date	Hour	Summary of Events and Information	Remarks and references to Appendices
ST MICHEL	15/10/18		Major B. Islington RM. OC Div Train returned from 15 days special leave to the Div Train. No 4 Coy drew from Railhead.	
BERLINCOURT	22.10.18		T.H.Q. moved to BERLINCOURT – No 2 Coy to AMBRINES – No 3 G.DENIER – No 4 to DOEUVRE FARM. 190th Bde front drew from Railhead by M.T.	
	24.10.18		No 2 & 3 & 4 coys drew by H.T. from Railhead	
	25.10.18		T/Major E.J. Chapman RM. took over duties as Adj. in Vent of Capt Shelton G.S. instead of Capt. A.S.C. on leave	
	26/10/18		Capt H. Moore RM took over duties as A.S.C. officer from Capt B.F. Shelton Ren. on leave	
			No 3 Coy went to K7 a 4.2 Sheet 57b on 23.10.18	
	30/10/18		T/Capt W.S. Bulpen Murphy Rn. assumed the extra duties of Supervisor Remain enlisted & proceeded to No 3 Coy on orders from No 5 Group Supple	
ST REMY	31/10/18		Enlistment have taken place. T.H.Q. GARGNON No Coy LOUTE. (N⁰S.L.O. RnB.I.N) No Coy ABLIN ST NAZAIRE No 3 Coy K CAGNEY No 4 & ABLIN ST NAZAIRE. Reping points are on the road on Div Train to S.E.Z. (N⁰S.P. 40 B.I.N)	

A. Ridwell
Lee R.S.C.
Commdt
63rd (R.N.) Divisional Train

War Diary
63rd (RN) Divnl Train

Volume XXX

A.R. Liddell
Lieut-Colonel ASC
Commdg
63rd (RN) Divnl Train

3/12/18

Army Form C. 2118.

WAR DIARY
or
INTELLIGENCE SUMMARY.
(Erase heading not required.)

Instructions regarding War Diaries and Intelligence Summaries are contained in F. S. Regs., Part II. and the Staff Manual respectively. Title pages will be prepared in manuscript.

Place	Date	Hour	Summary of Events and Information	Remarks and references to Appendices
LE FOREST	1/11/18		TWR moved ELH FOREST HOL marched to EVIN MALMAISON & AIBY NOYELLE IN FOREST. Rifle Coys Bns, 188 Train 188 Arty 190 Infantry	
QUINCY	2/11/18		TWR 23rd Inf Coy marched to QUINCY. 188 189 190 Bns Rifle Bns to AUBY-COURCELLES Rd	
	4/11/18		North moved to DOIGNY. No 4 Coy moved to MASTAING	
MONCHAUX	5/11/18		No 2 Coy moved to HARLEPIN No 4 Coy moved to MASTAING	
	6/11/18		Rifle Coys moved to 188 190 Bns to MASTAING. 189 Bn DOUCHY. No 2 & 3 T of Coy moved to JOLIMETZ. 189 Bn ATULCHIN 189 Old ARLNOY. Divisional HQ moved to THIANT. Train HQ & coy moved to THIANT	
PRULTAIN	7/11/18		Train HQ & Bn Companies moved to PRULTAIN. Train HQ moved to ANGRE. 3 Bn Companies to AUDREGNIES Infantry though on BHQ 2 of great difficulty owing to Rd destruction & large cratering kept onto 4 THA. Click. See attached.	
ANGRE	9/11/18		Coy moved to T H.A. 2 & 3 Bn moved to BEAUMES. No 4 Coy to 1 Coy Artillery T No. 2 & 3 Eh moved to Blue Line Train HQ to SSWN 9.0	
BLAUGIES	10/11/18		Train Hdqrs to No. 1 Eh to AIRVILLIES SERI LA BRUYERE to HARVENG. No 2 & 3 Eh Train Hdqrs moved East & England carried out also	
	11/11/18		Saw little off this day	

D. D. & L., London, E.C.

Army Form C. 2118.

WAR DIARY
or
INTELLIGENCE SUMMARY.
(Erase heading not required.)

Place	Date	Hour	Summary of Events and Information	Remarks and references to Appendices
HARVENG	19/10/15		Cl. Tram inspected 1st line Transport of 7th Royal Fusiliers & 1/1 Artists	
HARVENG	28/10/15		9a & log Train moved to FAYT LE FRANC.	
"	29/10/15		No 2 Coy moved to SARS LA BRUYERE & No 3 Coy to AULNOIS.	
FAYT LE FRANC	29/10/15		Train HQ moved to FAYT LE FRANC.	

A R Ridsdell
Lieut Colonel ASC
Commdg 63(ᵃᵐ) Divnl Train

Vol 32

War Diary.

December 1918   Volumn No. 31
63rd (R.N.) Divisional Train.

A R Liddell
Lt Col R.A.S.C.
Commdg
63rd (R.N.) Divisional Train

1st Jan 1919.

Army Form C. 2118.

WAR DIARY
or
INTELLIGENCE SUMMARY.
(Erase heading not required.)

Place	Date	Hour	Summary of Events and Information	Remarks and references to Appendices
AUDREGNIES			THQ moved to AUDREGNIES. No 3 Coy to DOUR	
"	24/10/18		No 1 Coy moved to BAISIEUX	
"	7/11/18		73 A.S.C. Drivers arrived as reinforcements	
"	13/11/18		Co Train on journey of a board completed for training purposes	
"			MANS of artillery	
"	14/11/18		30 A.S.C Drivers arrived as reinforcements	
"	26/11/18		Co Train on purchase of a band supplied men of 109 Bde for Brigade Infantry transferred to 74th Battn Royal Inniskilling Fusiliers	
"	31/12/18		T/Capt AE Balfour RM transferred to 79th Battn. In addition Total number of cad moved despatched during month 51.	
"			1 pivotal man was despatched	
"			The D unit Train was defeated in the 3rd round of the Divisional competition by Ambce Battn, or have reached the 2nd round of the football competition. Education scheme has not yet taken up as for many lack of facilities.	

A R. Dodwell
Lt. Col. RASC
Comm. 63rd (RNA) Div Train

War Diary

January 1919
Volumn 32

63rd (RN) Divisional Train

Feb 2nd 1919.

A R Liddell
Lt Col R.A.S.C.
Commdg
63rd (RN) Divisional Train

WAR DIARY
or
INTELLIGENCE SUMMARY.
(Erase heading not required.)

Army Form C. 2118.

Remarks and references to Appendices: (a) M. Swimming Team

Place	Date	Hour	Summary of Events and Information
AUDRESELLES	2.1.19		Small draft of reinforcements arrived from Base
	3.1.19		Nos. 3 & 4 Coys. arrived to DESVRAIN 26/1/19 driven from Railhead by MT.
	21.1.19		Nos. 1 & 2 Coys. arrived from Railhead by MT.
	6.1.19		Major O.C. Thornton D.S.O. made took over command of Divil. Train and was met by Lt. Col. F.R. Iredell D.S.O. on leave. The Major O.C. Chapman from took over duties of D.S.O.
	10.1.19		No. 2 Coys horses Veterinary Board classified.
	14.1.19		82 O.R. Royal Marine Reinforcements arrived from Base.
	19.1.19		Motor car & 1 clerk returned to duty from C.P.B.
	23.1.19		Lieut Colonel A.R. Iredell D.S.O. R.A.S.C. returned & resumed command of the Divil. Train having returned from leave
	25.1.19		All horses of the Coys Train have now been classified by Remount & Veterinary Board with exception of a few attached horses

Army Form C. 2118.

WAR DIARY
or
INTELLIGENCE SUMMARY.

63rd (RN) Divisional Train

(Erase heading not required.)

Place	Date	Hour	Summary of Events and Information	Remarks and references to Appendices
AUBREQ(MES)	31.1.19		T/Capt. F. Allen RM proceeded to RM Corps Concentration Camp for demobilization as a "Pivotal Man" Total number of OR demobilized up to date is:- Div Train personnel 51 Attached personnel 27	

A. Rhodell
Lieut Colonel RASC
Commdg
63rd (RN) Divnl Train

Vol 34

War. Diary.

63rd (RN) Divisional Train

February 1919. Volume No. 33

1st March/1919

A.R. Liddell
Lt Col. R.A.S.C.
Comnd g
63rd (RN) Divisional Train

WAR DIARY or INTELLIGENCE SUMMARY

Army Form C. 2118.

63rd (R.N.) Divisional Train

Place	Date	Hour	Summary of Events and Information	Remarks and references to Appendices
AUDREHEM	17/4/40		Took precautions came into force as no enemy aircraft from Rocbrune by HT.	
"			Three precautions stood down, normal training from killed by HT.	
"	19/4/40		Total munitions demobilised 2 officers 87 O.R. 66 O.R. Six men burned, landed interned. Total number of horses evacuated in enemy. H2 76 HD 7	

A. R. Russell
Lieut. Colonel R.M.—
Commanding
63rd (R.N.) Divisional Train

Vol 35

War Diary

63rd (RN) Divisional Train

March 1919   Volume No: 34

H. Chapman
Major R.M.
Commanding
63rd (RN) Divisional Train

31 March /1919

Army Form C. 2118.

WAR DIARY
or
INTELLIGENCE SUMMARY.

(Erase heading not required.)

63rd (R.N.) Divisional Train

Instructions regarding War Diaries and Intelligence Summaries are contained in F.S. Regs., Part II. and the Staff Manual respectively. Title pages will be prepared in manuscript.

Place	Date	Hour	Summary of Events and Information	Remarks and references to Appendices
HORNU	12/3/19		The Divisional Train concentrated at HORNU. Lorries drew from Railhead and delivered to one Amalgamated Dump at HORNU for the Division.	
	15/3/19		Lieut Col A.R.M.Liddell, D.S.O, R.A.S.C proceeded to join and command the 62nd Divisional Train. T/Major E.C.Sherman, D.S.O, R.A.S.C took over command of the 63rd (R.N.) Divisional Train.	
	16/3/19		T/Major C.L.Chapman, R.M took over command of the Divisional Train vice T/Major E.C.Sherman D.S.O, R.A.S.C demobilized.	
	26/3/19		Despatched 100 O.Rs to VIII Corps Concentration Camp for demobilization.	
	31/3/19		Total Numbers demobilized since Armistice. Royal Marines and R.A.S.C.: 381. Attached personnel: 95.	
	31/3/19			

Chapman
Major, R.M, Commanding
63rd (RN) Divisional Train.

War Diary
63rd (RN) Divisional Train
April 1919   Volumn 35.

35

30th April 1919.

L Chapman
Major. R.M.
Commdg
63rd (RN) Divisional Train

Army Form C. 2118.

WAR DIARY
or
INTELLIGENCE SUMMARY.
(Erase heading not required.)

63rd (RN) Divisional Train

Instructions regarding War Diaries and Intelligence Summaries are contained in F. S. Regs., Part II. and the Staff Manual respectively. Title pages will be prepared in manuscript.

Place	Date	Hour	Summary of Events and Information	Remarks and references to Appendices
HQRND	1/4/19		Despatched 107 ORs to VIII Corps Concentration Camp for demobilisation	

30/4/19

H. Chipman
Major RA Commanding
63rd (RN) Divisional Train